Red, Black, and Green
Black Nationalism in the United States

Red, Black, and Green
Black Nationalism in the United States

ALPHONSO PINKNEY

Hunter College, The City University of New York

CAMBRIDGE UNIVERSITY PRESS

CAMBRIDGE

LONDON · NEW YORK · MELBOURNE

Published by the Syndics of the Cambridge University Press
The Pitt Building, Trumpington Street, Cambridge CB2 1RP
Bentley House, 200 Euston Road, London NW1 2DB
32 East 57th Street, New York, NY 10022, USA
296 Beaconsfield Parade, Middle Park, Melbourne 3206, Australia

Library of Congress catalogue card number: 75-22550

ISBN 0 521 20887 4 hard covers

First published 1976

Printed in the United States of America

For the liberation of Afro-Americans
and all the oppressed peoples of the world

Contents

Preface

Although I have long maintained an interest in Afro-American nationalism, it never occurred to me to attempt to write a book on the subject. Therefore, it seems appropriate to say a word about the development of this book. In *Black Americans* (Prentice-Hall, 1969), I dealt briefly with the transformation of the civil rights movement into the black power movement. But it was my judgment at the time that contemporary black nationalism had not gained sufficient momentum in the United States to warrant lengthy treatment.

In August 1969, I was invited to present a paper at the annual meeting of the American Sociological Association, as part of a larger panel on ethnic and race relations in the United States. I elected to do a paper entitled "The Case for Pluralism for Black Americans." Researching and writing this paper stimulated my interest in contemporary black nationalist groups in the United States.

Shortly thereafter, I received an invitation to present a paper in a course on black life and culture at Douglass College of Rutgers University to be held in the spring of 1970. It was requested that the paper focus on contemporary developments in the black community; that it should expand on those unfolding events that had been mentioned only briefly in *Black Americans*. There seemed little doubt that nationalism was the dominant ethos of the black movement at that time. This time I chose to do a paper specifically on contemporary black nationalism. All papers presented in this course were later published in a volume edited by Rhoda L. Goldstein, *Black Life and Culture in the United States* (Thomas Y. Crowell, 1971).

By this time I read and clipped all articles on the subject that came to my attention. While teaching at the University of Chicago in 1971, I was asked to offer a seminar, "The Sociology of Black Nationalism." It was while preparing for this course that it became clear to me that it was impossible to discuss contemporary black nationalism without placing the phenomenon in its historical context. The Danforth Fellows (post-doctoral) in history who were members of the seminar reinforced this position, and from them I learned an immense amount about the history of black nationalism in the United States.

Following this course, I was invited to give lectures at the University of Wisconsin–Milwaukee, and Yale University. Both lectures focused on some aspect of black nationalism. Then in 1972, while teaching at Howard University, I again offered a graduate seminar on black nationalism. The students in this seminar, too, were enormously helpful on the subject.

The present work is largely a product of these experiences. Publication was delayed for more than a year for several reasons. Chief among them was what appeared to me to be a state of confusion in the black movement. It was difficult enough to write about groups which were constantly changing ideological positions or shifting strategies, but the changes were often so abrupt that they were impossible to catalog. Some of the changes are reflected in these pages, but others will no doubt have occurred before publication date.

While thinking about making alterations in the material, it was my good fortune to be able to make a study trip to the People's Republic of China in the summer of 1974. This trip afforded an opportunity to observe the minority situation in a socialist society and to evaluate what I had written about black nationalism in the United States. China is a multiethnic society, with 54 groups of people identified and recognized as separate nationalities. These peoples represented approximately 6 percent of the total population, numbering some 38 million in 1957. These national minorities range in size anywhere from several hundred to over one million. Historically, they were oppressed by the dominant Hans. With the liberation of China in 1949, however, national minorities achieved a status equal to that of other Chinese people. In some respects they have been granted preferential treatment as a means of making amends for past injustices. For example, the national government allocates disproportionately large amounts of money for economic development in areas populated by national minorities. The areas where national minorities live are called "autonomous regions," meaning that they exercise autonomy in administering internal affairs. This is a right guaranteed by the Chinese constitution and national laws. Furthermore, national minorities are assured proportionate representation in local government and in the Chinese Communist party.

Unlike Third World minorities in the United States, national minorities in China are assured by the Constitution that their languages, customs, and other aspects of culture will be respected. There is every reason to believe that the People's Republic of China, with its diverse population, has achieved unity. National minorities do not represent an oppressed category of citizens, as is the case in the United States. Although theirs was a bitter past, often as brutal as that of Afro-Americans in the United States, they are now an integral part of Chinese society, and there is no need for nationalist movements so characteristic of the United States.

After observing the Chinese experience with national minorities, I am inclined to agree with Chairman Mao that "In the final analysis, national struggle is a matter of class struggle." The situation in the United States lends support to this statement because capitalism gives rise to and supports various forms of oppression, including racism. Capitalism is the means by which the ruling class maintains its position of dominance in the society. Third World minorities and white workers are deliberately divided from each other as a means of keeping them oppressed. And through the years racism has become so pervasive in the United States that it has achieved a functional autonomy of its own. This situation will continue to preclude alliances between America's oppressed, thereby maintaining the dominance of the ruling class. This is not to imply that the problem would immediately disappear with the elimination of capitalism, but it does appear that capitalist institutions thrive on such oppressive conditions as racism.

Any book that attempts to deal systematically with such a broad subject as black nationalism in the United States, from its inception to the present time, is likely to fall short of its goal. It is not the intent of the present work to be exhaustive. Readers will find many omissions and inadequacies. These include the discussion of Pan-Africanism, for it was felt that a more exhaustive treatment would have required a different type of book; little attention is paid to various forms of economic nationalism, primarily because of the difficulty in approaching a subject which was admittedly found to be too complicated; the prison movement, containing large elements of black nationalism, for the prisons serve as concentration camps for Third World people and the poor, has also been neglected. These are recognized as legitimate criticims of the present work, and there are many others.

It was my hope to prepare a volume that attempted to present a broad, general description and analysis of black nationalism in the United States historically, and to concentrate on the ascendancy of the phenomenon during the peak years of its momentum, roughly the decade of 1963–1973.

Though it is hoped that the book will be of special interest to students, many of whom have not only been concerned with the subject but who have also been involved in the movement, an attempt was made to use lay language throughout in an effort to address the public at large. Finally, through the years many persons read various parts of the manuscript and offered many helpful criticisms and suggestions. They will recognize their contributions, for which I am grateful, in the revisions made in the original text. They are in large part responsible for whatever merits the book possesses; I accept responsibility for its shortcomings.

Alphonso Pinkney

New York City
September 1975

1

Introduction

In any discussion of nationalism among black people in the United States, one must somehow contend with what appears to be a complex of contradictions, for in many respects conventional notions about the concept of nationalism do not apply to America's black population. Yet the ideology of black nationalism is widespread among a significant segment of America's black community, and its influence has been felt among those who do not consider themselves nationalists. Although nationalism in general is a characteristic of modern societies, that is, it was not a significant force in the world prior to the eighteenth century, some of its elements can be traced back into history for many centuries. For example, such beliefs as "the chosen people" or the notion of the "promised land," both nationalist ideas, originated with the ancient Hebrews. Similarly, among black people in the United States, nationalism is often said to have originated in the nineteenth century, but some of its manifestations go as far back as the sixteenth century.

While it is not always possible to specify the precise genesis of nationalist sentiment, in most cases it probably results from a combination of historical factors and social conditions existing at any given time. John Stuart Mill was of the opinion that while many factors give rise to nationalist consciousness among a people, the most important of all is "identity of political antecedents; the possession of a national history, and a consequent community of recollections; collective pride and humiliation, pleasure and regret, connected with the same incidents in the past."[1]

Several writers have addressed themselves to the question of nationalism and have arrived at features characteristic of nationalist movements.[2] The beliefs and circumstances identified with such movements usually include common cultural characteristics such as language and customs; a well-defined geographic territory; belief in a common history or origin; closer ties among

1

fellow nationals than with outsiders; common pride in cultural achievements and common grief in tragedies; mutual hostility toward some outside group; and mutual feelings of hope about the future. It is unlikely that any nationalist group would encompass all of these characteristics, or that any one characteristic can be held to be indispensable to the development of nationalist sentiment. Furthermore, these beliefs and circumstances appear to be narrowly applicable to nationality in the sense of nation-states, rather than to the aspirations and actions of national minorities within already existing states.

Nevertheless, the black community in the United States, in varying degrees, meets many of these characteristics. Its members share certain cultural characteristics which are distinguishable from those of the larger society. This results from a dual set of circumstances in which blacks were prohibited from participating freely in the culture of the larger society, and at the same time denied the right to practice their original cultural patterns. Though Afro-Americans do not own any significant segment of geographic territory in the United States, they are concentrated in sections of cities and rural areas, many of which have been abandoned by whites. As is the case of Jews the world over, blacks in the United States share a common history of oppression, and pride in their common origins is increasingly acknowledged. Since American society responds to blacks collectively, the blacks have been forced to develop closer ties and relations within their community than with other Americans. Common pride in group cultural achievements and common grief in tragedies have always characterized Afro-Americans, but with the increasing spread of nationalist ideology since the end of World War II, these characteristics are perhaps more evident at present than in any previous period. Because of the racism endemic to American society, anti-black prejudice has generated comparable negative attitudes toward whites by American blacks. Finally, mutual feelings of hope about the future have always been expressed in Afro-American music, and again, in recent years these feelings have been on the increase in the black community.

The ultimate objectives of such movements are usually some degree of political, social, cultural, and economic autonomy. Historical circumstances and the specific social conditions of a country determine the form in which nationalism manifests itself. At a given time the group in question might demand complete separation from the dominant group and the right to establish a nation-state of its own, either in a part of the territory of the host society or in a different area. At another time the goal might be some degree of control over the social institutions which are ostensibly responsive to their needs; this usually is referred to as cultural pluralism. Some writers insist that the existence of land, in the form of a nation-state, is fundamental to nationalism. However, a people (e.g., the Jews prior to the establishment of the state of Israel) might focus their efforts on the creation of a nation-state which does not exist at the time.

Depending on the circumstances, diverse groups of people have identified themselves as nationalists. It is impossible to delineate a set of characteristics peculiar to all such groups. Even within a so-called nationalist group one is likely to find divergencies of beliefs and tactics. The black nationalist movement in the United States at the present time, through sharing some common beliefs, is certainly no exception to this general pattern.

According to Hans Kohn, nationalism in the twentieth century has added a social revolutionary dimension, often demanding equality of opportunity for an oppressed minority in all institutions in a society.[3] For example, the oppressed frequently form mass movements in which they demand greater participation in the political, economic, cultural, and social life of the nation. Kohn feels that political self-determination has remained a constant in nationalist movements. Cultural self-determination is equally important, and often it precedes the demand for political self-determination, thereby preparing the groundwork for the latter.

The contemporary black nationalist movement in the United States, with some notable exceptions, appears to focus its major thrust on cultural self-determination, while at the same time emphasizing the importance of political self-determination. The diversity of approaches to black nationalism as a means of achieving black liberation serves to confuse some observers, but it can only be understood within the context of the peculiar status of black people in the United States, both historically and at the present time.

Elements of black nationalist ideology

Historically, black nationalist sentiment in the United States can be traced back to the first slave conspiracy in 1526. Since that time such expressions have taken a variety of forms, depending upon conditions prevailing at the time. As a movement black nationalism has evolved through several stages, including colonization, emigration, internal statism, and cultural pluralism. These are the means blacks in the United States have advocated to achieve self-determination and ultimate liberation. The movement has never been able to attract a majority of blacks to its ranks, yet it has persisted through the centuries. And after a marked decline between 1930 and the mid-1960s, the black nationalist movement is currently experiencing a revival, during which its influence in the black community is greater than in any previous period. In addition to individual expressions of nationalist sentiment, numerous formal organizations operate on the international, national, state, and local levels.

Many of the participants in this movement, as well as those who remain neutral or who oppose it, maintain somewhat different views about the methods and even the goals of the movement. Indeed, the divergence of position between black nationalists is often as great as that between nationalists and those convinced that assimilation into the larger society is the only means through which black liberation can be achieved. Nevertheless, the ideology of black nationalism has always contained a core of widely shared beliefs.

In recent years a number of works have appeared on the resurgence of black nationalism in America, and several of these authors have attempted to explicate the concept. For example, E. U. Essien-Udom, in his study of the Nation of Islam, sees black nationalism as "the belief of a group that it possesses, or ought to possess, a country; that is shares, or ought to share, a common heritage of language, culture, and religion; and that its heritage, way of life, and ethnic identity are distinct from those of other groups."[4]

James Turner has put forth a definition of black nationalism that includes (1) the desire by blacks to control their own destiny through control of their own organizations and institutions; (2) group unity in a common community; (3) resistance to oppression; (4) ethnic self-interest and race pride; and (5) revaluation of self.[5]

Eric Foner sees black nationalism not only as a rejection by blacks of a society which has rejected them, but also as "an affirmation of the unique traditions, values, and cultural heritage of black Americans."[6] Bracey, Meier, and Rudwick distinguish several forms that black nationalism in the United States has assumed and conclude that "the simplest expression of racial feeling that can be called a form of black nationalism is *racial solidarity*. It generally has no ideological or programmatic implications beyond the desire that black people organize themselves on the basis of their common color and oppressed condition to move in some way to alleviate their situation. The concept of racial solidarity is essential to all forms of black nationalism."[7]

George Breitman defines black nationalism as "the tendency for black people in the United States to unite as a group, as a people, into a movement of their own to fight for freedom, justice and equality.... This tendency holds that black people must control their own movement and the political, economic, and social institutions of the black community." He concludes that race pride, group consciousness, hatred of white supremacy and independence from white control, and identification with the Third World, are the central attributes of black nationalism.[8]

Edwin S. Redkey sees "the bitter protest against American hypocrisy and white nationalism" as the core of black nationalism. "This has been accompanied by a call for blacks, who in an individualistic society are oppressed as a group, to face this collective aspect of their situation and to increase their solidarity and power as a group."[9]

In establishing the Organization of Afro-American Unity, Malcolm X, one of the most influential black nationalist thinkers of the twentieth century, declared, "Our political philosophy will be Black Nationalism. Our economic and social philosophy will be Black Nationalism. Our cultural emphasis will be Black Nationalism." He later elaborated by saying, "The political philosophy of black nationalism is that which is designed to encourage our people, the black people, to gain complete control over the politics and the politicians of our own community.... Our economic philosophy is that we should gain economic control over the economy of our own community.... Our social philosophy means that we feel that it is time to get together among our own kind and eliminate the evils that are destroying the moral fiber of our society"[10] Although his views changed during the last years of his life, mainly as a result of discussions with Third World leaders, Malcolm X maintained that the philosophy of black nationalism "had the ability to instill within black men the racial dignity, the incentive, and the confidence that the black race needs today to get up off its knees, and to get on its feet, and get rid of its scars, and to take a stand for itself."[11]

Imamu Amiri Baraka (LeRoi Jones) sees black nationalism as black unity through which blacks will achieve "power, black power, for black people to control our own lives, to build our own cities, and re-create the glorious civilizations of our history."[12]

Stokely Carmichael feels that black nationalism and African nationalism are synonymous, and that "African nationalism finds its highest aspiration in Pan-Africanism." His program for the black community at the present time is three-fold: the unification of the community; the control of all political institutions in the community, including law enforcement, education, and welfare; and the development of independent economic bases in the community so that its institutions will be more responsive to the needs of the people.[13]

Finally, Harold Cruse distinguishes between those blacks who advocate integration into American society and the exponents of what he calls "Afro-American ethnic group consciousness." The latter represent a persistent strain in Afro-American thought "that encompasses all the ingredients of 'nationality,'" although they have been overshadowed historically by the assimilationists.[14]

As can be seen from the foregoing, both scholars and leaders agree on certain central features of black nationalist ideology. This is not to imply that blacks who advocate assimilation through integration are not in agreement with the nationalists in some respects; the crucial distinguishing feature between the nationalists and the integrationists is that the nationalists view integration as neither desirable nor likely as a means of achieving black liberation in the United States at the present time.

Perhaps the most essential and elementary component of contemporary black nationalist ideology is the notion of unity or solidarity. This is, of course, true of all nationalist movements, and it receives a place of prominence in the utterances by all who consider themselves black nationalists. Historically there has been a tendency among blacks in the United States, with notable exceptions, to somehow view the United States as an individualistic society, when in fact it has always been a nation in which groups (racial, ethnic, class, etc.) have utilized cohesion as a means of advancement for their members. The notion of the melting pot held that members of diverse groups in the society would shed whatever characteristics of their social heritage that were at odds with those of the host society and would come to share the same body of sentiments, loyalties, and traditions, thereby becoming incorporated into the cultural life of the society. While this process held, to a degree, for many of the earliest immigrants to what is now the United States, especially those from northern and western Europe, it was by no means the situation for most immigrant groups.[15] Black people were not only denied the right to participate freely in the culture of the larger society, but in addition, the brutal institution of slavery virtually precluded the retention of their original cultural characteristics. These circumstances, combined with the American practice of responding to blacks collectively rather than individually, might have served to unify people of African descent, but for a variety of reasons (to be discussed later) this was not the case. Indeed the black community has been maintained in an oppressed state, in part because of its lack of unity.

A second major element in black nationalist ideology is pride in cultural heritage and its component, black consciousness. These elements take on added significance for Afro-Americans because of the widespread American practice of deprecating African cultural elements. Generations of Americans, both black and white, have perpetuated the myth of Africa as a savage continent, lacking cultural achievements. Consequently, the Europeans who colonized Africa were seen as altruistic in that they brought "civilization" to the "barbarians." The result has been that all vestiges of African culture were suppressed. Black nationalism attempts to instill in Afro-Americans pride in and consciousness of their cultural heritage. These two are linked, because without awareness of the cultural past, it is impossible to educate a people to value their heritage. Throughout much of the time that blacks have spent in America the very notion of blackness has been an anathema to Afro-Americans and whites alike.

Finally, black nationalism maintains that in order for Afro-Americans to liberate themselves from oppression some degree of autonomy is essential. While differences of opinion exist as to the extent to which autonomy from the larger society is necessary (ranging from local community control to the formation of a separate nation-state), there is general agreement that given the nature of American society, some degree of autonomy is necessary for self-determination. Furthermore, disagreement exists among nationalists on the amount of time achieving such autonomy should entail. That is, some maintain that temporary autonomy is sufficient, while others advocate permanent separation from the United States.

These three elements—unity, pride in cultural heritage, and autonomy—form the basis of contemporary black nationalist ideology. They are not only linked to each other, but to some degree they are interdependent. Whether they can be achieved by Afro-Americans at the present time is one of the questions explored in this work. And should they be accomplished, the question remains whether they will result in black liberation.

Conditions giving rise to black nationalism

Before proceeding to a discussion of the black nationalist tradition in America, it is necessary to examine briefly some of the conditions which have led to and sustained black nationalist ideology through the centuries. It is quite conceivable that if the Africans who were brought to America had initially been responded to simply as people, nationalist sentiment would not have developed among them. But given the circumstances of their importation to America, it is unlikely that their encounters with whites could have resulted in anything other than friction. It is even possible that at the end of the Civil War, if the society had moved forthrightly to make amends for past injustices, the nationalist movement might not have persisted. But given the nature of black–white relations in the United States, accommodation and assimilation were destined to be overshadowed by conflict and competition. The purpose here is not to delineate the history of black oppression, for this has been accomplished in hundreds of volumes. The essential point here is that Afro-Americans have always been responded to as a colonized people, not unlike the overseas victims of European colonialism, and relegated to a system of birth-ascribed stratification, similar to that of India's untouchable caste. And this colonial-caste status has generated and sustained black nationalist ideology through the generations.

Both the colonial and the caste statuses of Afro-Americans have been denied by black and white scholars and laymen alike. However, in recent years there has been greater acceptance in the black community of the formulation put forth by Harold Cruse:

From the beginning, the American Negro has existed as a colonial being. His enslavement coincided with the colonial expansion of European powers and was nothing more or less than a condition of domestic colonialism. Instead of the United States establishing a colonial empire in Africa, it brought the colonial system home and installed it in the Southern states. When the Civil War broke up the slave system and the Negro was emancipated, he gained only partial freedom. Emancipation elevated him only to the position of a semidependent man, not to that of an equal or independent being.[16]

Cruse was not the first writer to characterize the relations between blacks and whites in the United States as essentially that of colonized and colonizer. As early as 1852, Martin Delany compared blacks in the United States to the Poles in Russia; the Hungarians in Austria; the Irish, Welsh, and Scotch under British domination. Of blacks in the United States he wrote: "We are a nation within a nation."[17] In recent years many other scholars and writers have viewed the status of blacks in the United States as one of internal colonialism.

There are obvious differences between the internal colonialism of blacks in the United States and classical colonialism of European powers in Africa, Asia, and Latin America. However, if colonialism is defined broadly as the subordination of a people, nation, or country by another, with power for the administration of life chances of the subordinate group vested in the hands of the dominant group for purposes of exploitation, the concept is applicable to both internal and external colonialism.

Colonialism may be seen as a system of relations with the following characteristics:

1 *The system operates out of force; that is, it is involuntary. The involuntary subjection of people may result either from military force or forced servitude.*

2 *The colonial power systematically executes a policy which constrains, transforms, or destroys the culture of the colonized. Such was the policy of the British in Nigeria, for example, and of the United States during the period of ante-bellum slavery.*

3 *The colonized are administered by representatives of the dominant power. Internally, teachers, police, social welfare workers, etc., in the black community are responsible to the white power structure in much the same way as officials of the Home Office represented the interests of the mother country.*

4 *Racism is usually used as the means for maintaining social dominance over the colonized. Virtually everywhere colonialism (internal or external) has existed, it has resulted in the domination by Europeans of the Third World peoples of Africa, Asia, and Latin America.*

5 *The colonizing power profits economically from the arrangement. Just as cheap colonial labor led to the wealth of the British Empire, black slave labor during the ante-bellum period and cheap labor since are in part responsible for the economic development of the United States.*[18]

In the classical colonial situation of pre-World War II, dominance was maintained over a geographically external political unit, but the question of geography need not be the defining characteristic of such a relationship. If one looks at the structure of the colonial system and the relationships between the parties involved, it is clear that the concept can be applied cross-culturally and can describe both classical colonialism and internal colonialism. That is, the structure of colonialism and the relations between the colonizer and the colonized, rather than geography or time, give the concept its broad applicability for all parties concerned.

Colonialism can be defined so narrowly as to exclude those situations in which the colonizer establishes the system at home. But there is no reason that the concept should be so constricted; in order to make comparisons and derive valid generalizations, the concept must be broadly defined. This is not to ignore obvious differences, for twentieth-century America is different from nineteenth-century Africa or India, but the similarities overshadow the differences. Furthermore, from the point of view of the colonized, the consequences of the system are similar. Indeed, in many ways internal colonialism is more destructive of human beings than external colonialism. In the former, the colonized come into direct contact with the colonizer, thereby leading to greater psychic damage in the form of self-hatred, which leads to confused identities. In external colonialism few of the colonized are forced into situations of interaction with the colonizers. Hence, except for lower-level bureaucrats and service workers, most of the indigenous people are spared the destructive effects that result from close personal interaction with those who consider themselves superior.

As a system colonialism is characterized above all by the political domination and economic exploitation of one group by another, and it is increasingly recognized that black–white relations in the United States have been so characterized since the appearance of black people in what is now the United States.[19] In classical colonialism the colonizing power exploited the raw materials of the colonial possession, often shipping them to the mother country for manufacture and returning the finished product to the native population at exorbitant prices. Thus, the colonial power could create its market for these goods. In the system of internal colonialism in the United States, the black community has historically served as a source of cheap labor for the mother country. Black people export their labor to the white community for salaries that do not permit them to share equitably in the goods and services they produce. Furthermore, when white merchants maintain business enterprises in the black community, they characteristically remove the profits from the community, refusing to reinvest them there.

As has been observed by I. F. Stone, black people in the United States, in addition to their colonial status, are "an underdeveloped people in our midst."[20] According to the United Nations, the so-called developing (Third World) nations differ from the industrialized countries on a number of characteristics. If one compares the black community with Third World nations on these characteristics, one is able to see that their plights are similar. The black community is distinct from the industrialized white nation which surrounds and controls it. Black people are experiencing a high birth rate and a declining death rate, which result in a rapid growth rate. The infant and maternal mortality rates are especially high; the former is about double the rate for whites, while the latter is approximately six times the white rate.

The life expectancy is significantly lower for blacks than for whites. Furthermore, black people continue to die at dispropor-tionately high rates from diseases that are easily controlled by modern medical techniques. For example, tuberculosis is no longer a major cause of death in the United States, but the rate for blacks is about three times that for whites. A high proportion of black people falls within the dependent-children and dependent-aged categories, thereby rendering them too young or too old for the labor force. Finally, like underdeveloped people the world over, blacks are migrating from rural to urban areas at rapid rates. As they enter cities, they are crowded into the most dilapidated housing, in much the same way that Latin American rural peasants are forced into shantytowns.

Robert Allen, in *Black Awakening in Capitalist America*, sees the black community attempting to liberate itself, that is, to become decolonized. In an effort to stem the tide, the white power structure is seeking to substitute neocolonialism for direct col-onialism, in much the same way that European colonial powers effectively maintain control over their former colonial territories. The black rebellions of the 1960s and black demands for control over institutions in the black community may be seen as attempts at decolonization. That is, as Blauner has written, they may be seen as claims by blacks to territoriality. At the same time, the concessions made to blacks in the last few years serve as a means of effecting the transition to neocolonialism. To cite but one example: black enrollment in colleges and universities doubled between 1965 and 1970. This does not mean that twice as may black students were eligible for college in 1970 as was the case in 1960. Rather, it means that the more youth in college classrooms, the fewer who are available for rebellions and the more pacific the black community becomes. In other words, it is an attempt by those in positions of power to postpone as long as possible the process of decolonization. The same might be said about such programs as nominal public school decentralization, black capitalism, and the federally funded community action programs.

While the analogy between external and internal colonialism does not hold in precise detail, the similarities are sufficient to justify the comparison. The essence of colonialism is the powerlessness of the colonized. Black people in the United States are powerless in economics, politics, and cultural affairs. This is as true in the 1970s as it was in the 1670s. Recognition of this colonial status is essential for any understanding of the persistence of the phenomenon of black nationalism through the centuries. And the increasing recognition by black people of their colonial status in recent years has led to the spread of the ideology of black nationalism on a wider scale than in any previous period of history.

Regardless of the rationalizations offered by the oppressor group, the oppressed are conscious of their degradation, resent it, and devise various methods of coping with their status. Above all, the oppressed continually attempt to alter their status, utilizing whatever means are available to them. Black nationalism has historically been viewed by Afro-Americans as one means of escaping the stigma attached to their subordination.

In *The Colonizer and the Colonized*, Albert Memmi maintains that the colonized may become liberated either through assimilation or revolt. Assimilation means the rejection of self and traditions and the emulation of the colonizers. Afro-Americans have long attempted to assimilate into the larger society as a means of liberating themselves from oppression, but they have continually been rebuffed by the colonizers. The very nature of the colonizer–colonized relationship is such that assimilation is impossible, because the price is too high and the results too uncertain. Assimilation is ultimately an individual solution and does not necessarily lead to collective liberation. In the meantime, the colonial relationship continues, and "assimilation and colonization are contradictory." Given this situation, Memmi asks, "What is there left for the colonized to do?" His answer: "Being unable to change his condition in harmony and communion with the colonizer, he tries to become free despite him . . . and will revolt."

Although Memmi's analysis grows out of his experience with colonization in North Africa, its applicability to the internal colonial status of blacks in the United States explains the current emphasis on black nationalism among Afro-Americans. That so many people fail to understand the mood of the black community indicates an unwillingness to apply the model of colonialism to the experience of black people in the United States.

Varieties of contemporary black nationalism

Because of the complexities of black life in the United States, it is to be expected that while the goal of the black nationalist movement is the ultimate liberation of black people from oppression, the means for achieving this goal vary widely. Probably the earliest expressions of black nationalism manifested themselves in revolts against slavery, and throughout the period of slavery up to the present time, repatriation to Africa has been one of the major thrusts of black nationalism. With the advent of the 1960s, however, the back-to-Africa movement gave way to other forms of nationalist sentiment.

In addition to manifestations of black nationalism on the individual and collective levels, recent years have witnessed a proliferation of formal black nationalist organizations on the local, state, national, and international levels. Though it is not possible to neatly categorize these organizations, for many of them overlap, four major groupings appear to have emerged: cultural nationalism, educational nationalism, religious nationalism, and revolutionary nationalism.

Cultural nationalism holds that black people throughout the world possess a distinct culture and that before black liberation can be achieved in the United States, blacks must reassert their cultural heritage, which is fundamentally different from that of the larger society. Cultural nationalists maintain that a cultural revolution in the black community is essential before Afro-Americans can command the unity necessary to revolt effectively against their oppressors. On the national level cultural nationalism is best represented by the Congress of African Peoples. Two additional organizations which are locally based, but which are national in their impact, are the Committee for a Unified NewArk in Newark, New Jersey, and the US Organization in Los Angeles.

It is difficult to distinguish between educational nationalism and cultural nationalism, for the cultural component of educational nationalism is essentially the same as that of cultural nationalism. However, educational nationalism tends to operate within the framework of educational institutions, both conventional and unorthodox. The proponents of educational nationalism see conventional American education as destructive of Afro-Americans in that the schools miseducate the youth and thereby do not prepare them for liberation. This category of nationalism includes the many black studies programs in high schools, colleges, and universities throughout the country; the Center for Black Education in Washington; The Institute of the Black World in Atlanta; Malcolm X College in Chicago, and Nairobi College in California.

The importance of religion in black life in the United States gives religious nationalism special significance. At present religious nationalism takes roughly three forms: the rejection of Christianity by blacks, black unity within traditional Christianity, and the separate black church in which God is viewed as a black man. These manifestations of religious nationalism are represented by the Nation of Islam, the National Committee of Black Churchmen, and the Shrine of the Black Madonna.

Finally, one of the most controversial types of black nationalism is revolutionary nationalism. There are differences in the programs of groups that define themselves as revolutionary and nationalist, but most maintain that Afro-Americans cannot achieve liberation in the United States within the existing political and economic system. Therefore, they call for revolution to rid the society of capitalism, imperialism, racism, and sexism. Most base their ideological position on a combination of black nationalism and Marxism-Leninism and envison some form of socialism to replace capitalism. The major revolutionary nationalist groups at present are the Black Panther Party, the League of Revolutionary Black Workers, and the Republic of New Africa.

The foregoing classification will no doubt be criticized by many, and some will maintain that the categorization of groups in such a manner contributes to the continuing splintering of the black nationalist movement. In most cases, however, the leaders of the various groups identify with the positions set forth and usually label their organizations as such. The divisions within black nationalism are often as real as those between the integrationists and the nationalists. And while all groups support black unity, the concept remains an elusive ideal. When the leaders of the various groups succeed in bridging differences in programs and concentrate on emphasizing the common goal of black liberation, a true nationalist movement will result.

Whether a strong, unified black nationalist movement can liberate Afro-Americans from their caste-colonial status remains to be seen. Complete assimilation into the society seems unlikely; racism is endemic in the United States and the capitalist system nurtures and thrives on its ideology. At the same time, the complete separation of blacks into an autonomous nation–state within the United States seems unrealistic. Black nationalism as an ideology has been around for centuries, but it has never been manifested on a scale comparable to the present time. Given this situation, it is not difficult to become so engrossed with the phenomenon that one fails to recognize the enormous complexities of American society and the extraordinary problems black people face.

The present generation of black nationalists is continuing in the heroic tradition of their forefathers, for nationalist sentiment is not new. What is new, however, is its pervasiveness in the black community and the widespread political consciousness of Afro-Americans. Given these circumstances, the likelihood is that nationalist sentiment will grow rather than decline.

2

The black nationalist tradition

One of the fundamental components of nationalist ideology is the
expression of unity by a people in their struggle for self-
determination. Obviously such expressions assume different
forms, depending upon a variety of circumstances. In the case of
people of African descent in the United States these expressions
have varied widely over a period of more than four centuries.
Perhaps the first collective expressions of black unity in what is
now the United States took the form of slave conspiracies and
revolts in the early years of European colonization. Herbert Aptheker traces the first slave revolt back to 1526 in what is now
South Carolina, and the first serious slave conspiracy is said to
date back to the Virginia colony in 1663.[1] Later in the colonial era
two blacks were burned alive and an additional 29 were executed
in New York City in 1741 for their part in a slave conspiracy that
left many buildings destroyed by fire. Such conspiracies and
revolts continued throughout the period of legal slavery.

In addition, black solidarity manifested itself in the early years
through petitions by slaves for freedom, especially immediately
prior to and during the Revolutionary War. In 1773, for example,
the slaves of Massachusetts petitioned the colonial governing officials to grant them the freedom to work in order to earn money for
transportation to, as they put it, "some part of the Coast of *Africa*,
where we propose a settlement."[2] After the Revolutionary War,
Afro-American solidarity was expressed through the formation of
black organizations, established for a variety of purposes, such as
the Philadelphia Free African Society, founded in 1787 "in order
to support one another in sickness, and for the benefit of their
widows and fatherless children."[3] In 1787 a group of 80 blacks
from Boston again petitioned the state legislature for money and
other assistance to settle in Africa. They were anxious to leave
America because they found themselves "in very disagreeable and
disadvantageous circumstances."[4] These "free" Afro-Americans

16

were interested in colonizing territory on the west coast of Africa. The African Society, founded in Boston in 1796, contained the following article in its charter: "The basis of the society, and ulterior objects in encouraging emigration, shall be Self-Reliance and Self-Government on the principle of an African Nationality, the African race being the ruling element of the nation, controlling and directing their own affairs."[5] Furthermore, Afro-Americans were among the first to organize antislavery activities during the ante-bellum period. Several organizations were formed for the express purpose of protesting the enslavement of Africans. Such activity mushroomed at the turn of the nineteenth century.

Among the earliest petitions to Congress by Afro-Americans was that of 1797, in which several "free" blacks from Philadelphia requested redress of their grievances. They had fled from North Carolina where a law had been passed forbidding the manumission of slaves; North Carolina offered 20 percent of the sale price of each captured slave to the person who informed on the slave, thereby causing a reign of terror among the "free" blacks of the state. The petition was returned to the petitioners without action. Three years later, in 1800, a petition directed against the fugitive slave act of 1793, the slave trade, and slavery itself was presented to Congress by "free" blacks of Philadelphia, headed by Absalom Jones, a minister. Though this petition was debated in Congress, it ultimately died in committee.[6]

Religion has always played an important role in the black community, as it is one of the most cohesive and well-organized institutions. During the ante-bellum period, when blacks were allowed to worship at all, they frequently did so at white Christian churches, most often occupying a segregated section of the church. In 1786, responding to the practice of segregation in white churches, a former slave, Richard Allen, and his fellow black worshippers founded the African Methodist Episcopal Church in Philadelphia. This signaled the beginning of autonomous black Christian churches in the United States. They were soon to mushroom throughout the country, and as Essien-Udom has noted, they served a four-fold relationship to black nationalism: they were the best-organized institution in the Afro-American cummunity; they provided for greater participation among blacks than any other organization; the leadership of the church was largely independent of white control; and the church provided an important center of social life for its members.[7] Though the black church can hardly be considered nationalist in its general orientation, it did serve to foster the drive for autonomy in the black community. For example, some 70 years after its founding, one of its bishops, Daniel A. Payne, said: "We were dependent upon them [the Methodist Episcopal Church] for government. Not only were the presiding elders and preachers in charge all white men, but in a multitude of instances the very classes were also white." He continued, "The separation of our Church from the M.E. Church...has been beneficial to the man of color by giving him an independence of character which he could neither hope for nor attain unto, if he had remained as the ecclesiastical vassal of his white bretheren."[8] While it was, and still is, patterned after its white counterpart, the black church nevertheless maintains some black nationalist characteristics.

The same might be said of the early black fraternal, mutual aid, and cooperative organizations. Although not nationalist in the strict sense of the term, they promoted black solidarity and unity and played crucial roles in black survival in the United States. The first such organization, the Masons, was chartered in 1787, and was followed in the same year by the African Lodge No. 459. Similar organizations soon followed. And like the black church, they resulted from discrimination by parallel white organizations. In practice, however, they may be considered among the first black nationalist-type formal organizations in North America.

During the period of slavery and the years between the Civil War and the 1930s, much of black nationalist expression was dominated by individual leaders. This is not to say that these individuals were unable to build mass movements, for they frequently did; rather, the movements tended to center around the personalities of the leaders. In most cases black nationalism manifested itself in emigration movements. This is especially true of the earliest organized expressions, for many of the leaders were convinced that Afro-Americans could never achieve equality with their white counterparts. Most of these movements centered on repatriation of blacks to Africa, but others advocated resettlement to other areas. The brutality of slavery and the failure of Reconstruction meant that many blacks, leaders and rank and file, had lost all hope of peaceful coexistence between black and white Americans. Like their black counterparts, many white leaders, including Thomas Jefferson and Abraham Lincoln, felt that Afro-Americans should be separated from white Americans, preferably in some territory outside the United States. When the American Colonization Society was founded in the House of Representatives in 1817, for the purpose of repatriating blacks to Africa, it attracted such supporters as Henry Clay, Andrew Jackson, James Madison,

James Monroe, Daniel Webster, and a nephew of George Washington, Justice Bushrod Washington.[9] Inasmuch as the American Colonization Society was white America's approach to dealing with the problems confronting Afro-Americans in the United States, it was clearly not a black nationalist organization.

Paul Cuffee and the African institution

Emigration was the major thrust of the black nationalist movement at the beginning of the eighteenth century, and although it was not new, such programs had usually been proposed and organized by whites. One of the first blacks to become involved in the back-to-Africa movement was Paul Cuffee, a prosperous sea captain born on an island off the coast of Massachusetts in 1759.[10] It would be stretching the point, as some have done, to call Cuffee the "father of black nationalism," for although he was a black man who championed the cause of repatriation of blacks to Africa, his philosophy was hardly black nationalist.

Cuffee became a member of the Society of Friends and became deeply interested in the welfare of Afro-Americans. His interest in black emigration to Africa was many-faceted: the opening of trade with Africa, the cessation of the slave trade, spreading Christianity to Africans, and relocating those "free" American blacks who wanted to settle there. On balance he appeared to be more concerned about equality for American blacks than relocating them in Africa. Cuffee's father was born in Africa and brought to the Massachusetts colony as a slave. He ultimately purchased his freedom and married an Indian woman. The father died when Paul Cuffee was 14, leaving 10 children and extensive land holdings. Along with his brother John, Paul Cuffee refused to pay taxes in Massachusetts during the Revolutionary War on the grounds that "taxation and the whole rights of citizenship were united." When he presented his petition on taxation to the Massachusetts legislature, a law was passed declaring that free blacks had the same rights and privileges as whites. In this act Cuffee became the first Afro-American to win a civil rights case on behalf of his fellow blacks.

In addition to his taxation case, Cuffee demonstrated his interest in equality by building a school on his property in 1797. Although the school was open to the public, it was mainly for the education of black and Indian children in New Bedford. It was Cuffee's view that self-help and mutual aid would improve the condition of Afro-Americans and Africans. Consequently, he traveled extensively in connection with these efforts, organizing mutual benefit societies in New York, Philadelphia, and ultimately in Sierra Leone.

At the age of 16, Cuffee went on a whaling voyage which took him to Mexico and the West Indies. He was to take several such voyages, and on the third trip he was captured by the crew of a British ship and detained for three months in New York City. When he was 20 years old, he built a boat, the first of several he was to own. His interest in Africa was generated by the British experiment in Sierra Leone, where some 332 blacks were settled after being rounded up on the streets of London. Many of these blacks were American slaves who had fought with the British in the War for Independence. When the British soldiers were repatriated, the slaves went to England with them. Cuffee was invited to visit Sierra Leone and made his first trip there in 1811. While there he held meetings with the governor and other officials about conditions in Sierra Leone and about the possibility of repatriating some Afro-Americans there. From Sierra Leone he went to England, where he met with officials of the African Institution, a private organization established to assist the British government in managing the colonial affairs.

Upon his return to the United States, Cuffee made a public report on conditions in Sierra Leone, which was largely favorable.[11] He also enlisted the aid of other "free" blacks in the formation of a parallel African Institution in the United States. Although the African Institution managed to establish branches in such large cities as Baltimore, New York, and Philadelphia, it met militant opposition from large segments of black leadership, many of whom were opposed to the notion of colonization.

During the short life of the African Institution, which was primarily the official organ of Paul Cuffee, its accomplishments were limited. In 1814, Cuffee petitioned the President, Senate, and House of Representatives for assistance with his colonization scheme. This petition, among other things, "solicits your aid so far as to grant permission that a vessel may be employed...between this country and Sierra Leona, to transport such persons and families as may be inclined to go, as also, some articles of provision, together with instruments of husbandry, and machinery for some mechanic arts and to bring back such of the native productions of that country as may be wanted." He concluded with the plea, "Your petitioner therefore craves the attention of Congress to a concern which appears to him very important to a portion of his fellow creatures who have been long excluded from the common advantages of civilized life, and prays that they will afford him and his friends such aid as they in their wisdom may think best." Another important part of the petition was a plea to prohibit the slave trade.

Although he received no official support, Cuffee, at his own expense, made a second trip to Sierra Leone in 1815. On this trip he transported 38 Afro-Americans to their ancestral land. These 38 passengers were from nine families, and they ranged in age from eight months to 60 years. In addition to providing transportation, Cuffee maintained his passengers for two months in Africa in order to ensure that they were properly settled. The expenses involved in the trip were such that Cuffee realized that although he had owned several sea-going vessels, it was impossible for him to continue without support from the government. Thousands of Afro-Americans had expressed interest in repatriation to Africa, but before another voyage could be arranged, Paul Cuffee died in 1817. With his death the African Institution ceased to function.

Months before his death, however, the American Colonization Society was founded by a group of white people, with financial support from philanthropists and federal and state sources. The founders of the American Colonization Society, impressed with Cuffee's accomplishments, turned to him for advice. However, Cuffee, and most free blacks opposed the society, because they felt that the federal support the organization received would ultimately lead to the deportation of all Afro-Americans, including those who were determined to remain in the United States to fight for civil rights. In other words, they saw the society as an instrument designed to exile Afro-Americans from the United States. Nevertheless, because of his success in transporting blacks to West Africa, Cuffee is largely responsible for the establishment of the American Colonization Society, which soon grew into a massive colonization movement.[13]

The American Colonization Society, because it was well-financed (it had received a Congressional appropriation of $100,000 in 1819), was able to purchase a strip of land 3 miles wide and 36 miles long on the west coast of Africa.[14] This land was called "Liberia" for freeman, and its capital was named "Monrovia," in honor of President Monroe. Gradually more land was acquired and the Republic of Liberia was formed in 1847, ostensibly for former slaves, but in reality it was seen by whites as the answer to the American race problem. These Afro-Americans became the ruling class of Liberia, exploiting the native population in much the same way they had been exploited by whites in the United States. In spite of widespread opposition by blacks to its activities, the American Colonization Society is estimated to have transported some 13,000 Afro-Americans to Liberia by the outbreak of the Civil War. Emigration activity tapered off during the Civil War, but the society continued to exist until 1964. Throughout its many years of existence, however, it was operated and controlled by whites, and opposed by most black leaders, including the officials of the Negro Convention Movement, and the influential Martin R. Delany.

The Negro Convention Movement, organized in Philadelphia in 1817, was perhaps the best-organized group to oppose the American Colonization Society. The members of this movement protested the activities of the society on the grounds that its purpose was the deportation of all "free" blacks from the United States in order to make the institution of slavery more secure. The Convention Movement met annually between 1830 and the beginning of the Civil War.[15] In addition to opposing the activities of the American Colonization Society, the Convention Movement sought ways to improve the status of Afro-Americans and supported the emigration of American blacks to Canada. At its first national meeting in 1830, the Convention Movement recommended the purchase of land in Canada, and in 1831 it was able to report that "wonders have been performed far exceeding our most sanguine expectations; already have our brethren purchased eight hundred acres of land–and two thousand of them have left the soil of their birth, crossed the lines, and laid the foundation for a structure which promises to prove an asylum for the coloured population of these United States."[16] This meeting closed with an appeal to the American Colonization Society to cease its colonization program in Africa.

In 1832 the Convention Movement met in Philadelphia and resolved to raise funds to support the Afro-American immigrants in Canada, to boycott slave-made products, and to petition Congress and state legislatures against both slavery and discrimination. While the Convention Movement championed the cause of black unity, as well as emigration to Canada, its members were bitterly opposed to repatriation of Afro-Americans to Africa. Their opposition was so strong that they rejected the use of the term "African" to apply to Afro-American institutions and organizations. At its 1835 meeting, the membership resolved "That we recommend as far as possible, to our people to abandon the use of the word colored,' when either speaking or writing concerning themselves;

and especially to remove the title of African from their institutions, the marbles of churches, and etc."[17] The Convention Movement's main activities centered around the abolition of slavery, civil rights for "free" blacks and emigration of Afro-Americans to Canada. Throughout its existence, opposition to repatriation to Africa was intense. According to Essien-Udom, "They were ashamed of their African origins. They, too, had come to accept uncritically the white man's caricature of Africa as populated by comic-opera savages."[18] But documents emanating from the Convention Movement indicate that its members were not so much opposed to Africa as to the notion of the colonization of the continent as proposed by the American Colonization Society. A dissident faction within the Convention Movement convened a meeting in 1854 to consider emigration to other areas, including Africa, the Caribbean, and Central America.

Martin R. Delany: "Africa for the Africans"

Because of its success in settling Afro-Americans in Liberia, some black leaders ultimately supported the work of the American Colonization Society. Notable among them was Alexander Crummell, a Cambridge University-trained Episcopal clergyman, who later went to Africa as a missionary under the auspices of the American Colonization Society. The most formidable opponent of the society was Martin R. Delany, a Harvard-trained physician. Delany was unquestionably the leading advocate of black nationalism in the two decades preceding the Civil War. He continued his activities after the failure of Reconstruction. Although little has been written about him, Delany has been called the "father of black nationalism."[19]

Martin R. Delany was born in Charleston, Virginia, in 1812, the grandson of slaves. He was proud of his heritage, a descendant of African chiefs and princes. At an early age his family moved to Chambersburg, Pennsylvania, and at the age of 19 he went to Pittsburgh to attend school. By the age of 31, in 1843, he published a weekly newspaper, the *Mystery*, and in 1846 he co-edited the *North Star* with Frederick Douglass. After working with Douglass for a few months, he left to attend medical school at Harvard University, where he specialized in diseases of women and children. By the time he was 40, Delany had pursued successfully careers in both journalism and medicine, but his consuming interest remained the repatriation of Afro-Americans to Africa.[20] Consequently in 1852 he published his best-known work, *The Condition, Elevation, Emigration, and Destiny of the Colored People of the United States*, the first black nationalist book to be published. He was later to write, among other things, a novel, *Blake: or, the Huts of America*, several chapters of which were published in *Anglo-African Magazine* in 1859. This novel tells the story of a slave who escaped when his wife was sold and sent to Cuba. He then spent his life organizing a general uprising among slaves throughout the ante-bellum South. Still later Delany published a book on ethnology, *Principia of Ethnology: The Origin of Races and Color, with An Archeological Compendium of Ethiopian and Egyptian Civilization.*[21]

Early in his career Delany became disenchanted with the possibility of peaceful coexistence between blacks and whites in the United States. In 1852 he wrote, "We love our country [the United States], dearly love her, but she doesn't love us–she despises us, and bids us be gone, driving us from her embraces."[22] And, in a letter to the abolitionist William Lloyd Garrison, he wrote: "I am not in favor of caste, nor a separation of the brotherhood of mankind, and would as willingly live among white men as black, if I had an *equal possession and enjoyment* of privileges; but shall never be reconciled to live among them, subservient to their will–existing by mere sufferance, as we, the colored people, do, in this country."[23]

Delany's opposition to the American Colonization Society, which was especially intense, stemmed from his aversion to the colonization of Liberia, which he referred to as "a poor miserable mockery–a burlesque on a government." He saw the country as a colony of southern slaveholders, and it was his view that the society was determined to deposit so-called free blacks there in order to protect the institution of slavery. Of the society he wrote, "We look upon the American Colonization Society as one of the most arrant enemies of the colored man, ever seeking to discomfit him, and envying him of every privilege that he may enjoy."[24] Consequently, Delany became active in the Negro Convention Movement and was a principal figure in the national emigration convention of 1854.

It was at this convention that Delany made his impassioned speech, "Political Destiny of the Colored Race on the American Continent." He had expressed his opposition to colonization in Africa as early as 1852 (he preferred resettlement in the Western Hemisphere). However, in the appendix to *The Condition, Elevation, Emigration, and Destiny of the Colored People of the United*

States, entitled "A project for an Expedition of Adventure to the Eastern Coast of Africa," he advocated the establishment of an autonomous black state in East Africa to which Afro-Americans would emigrate. Nevertheless, it was not until the late 1850s that he championed the cause of Afro-American repatriation to Africa. At the 1854 convention his primary concern was resettlement in the Americas, in "that the continent of America was designed by Providence as a reserved asylum for the various oppressed people of the earth, of all races, to us seems very apparent." Several locations were suggested, including Canada, where he was later to live briefly, but Delany considered Canada a place of "temporary relief," because he was certain that Canada would ultimately become a part of the United States. He preferred the West Indies and Central and South America as permanent homes for the black people of the United States. "Upon the American continent, then, we are determined to remain despite every opposition that may be urged against us."

Convinced that blacks could never achieve equality with whites in the United States, Delany told the audience at the convention, "Let it then be understood, as a great principle of political economy, that no people can be free who themselves do not constitute an essential part of the *ruling element* of the country in which they live." He continued, "The liberty of no man is secure, who controls not his own political destiny. . . . A people, to be free, must necessarily be *their own rulers*: that is, *each individual* must, in himself, embody the *essential ingredient*–so to speak–of the *sovereign principle* which composes the *true basis* of his liberty."[25]

In this extraordinary speech, Delany said he was convinced that blacks should settle in an area where Anglo-Saxons were not the ruling element in the population, for "The Anglo-Saxon has taken the lead in this work of universal subjugation. But the Anglo-Saxon stands preeminent for deeds of injustice and acts of oppression, unparalleled perhaps in the annals of modern history." Consequently, he continued, "to be successful, our attention must be turned in a direction towards those places where the black and colored man comprise, by population, and constitute by necessity of numbers, the ruling element of the body politic."[26]

Delany emphasized again and again the racist nature of the United States. He told those gathered at the convention in Cleveland that the major problem facing Afro-Americans was not "a question of the rich against the poor, nor the common people against the higher classes; but a question of white against black–every white person, by legal right, being held superior to a black or colored person." He could not envision an end to black subjugation in the United States because "The rights of no oppressed people have ever been obtained by a voluntary act of justice on the part of the oppressors." Perhaps his most severe condemnation was reserved for the government of the United States, which through the enactment of the Fugitive Slave Act, "the crowning act of infamy," made it possible for any Afro-American to be enslaved at any time. "Any one of us, at any moment, is liable to be *claimed, seized* and *taken* into custody by the white as his or her property–to be *enslaved for life*–and there is no remedy, because it is the law of the land!" He urged all blacks to rise in rebellion whenever an attempt was made to enforce the provisions of the law.

Although the convention focused its emigration interests on the Western Hemisphere, its officials authorized Delany to travel to the Niger valley in Africa, while other representatives were to go to Central America and Haiti. Each was authorized to negotiate with governing officials of these territories and report back to future conventions. In 1859, Delany sailed for the Niger valley, during which time he traveled widely in West Africa for a year, negotiating treaties for the emigration of blacks to Africa. By this time he was a strong proponent of the repatriation of blacks to Africa. "Africa for the Africans" became his rallying phrase. From Africa he went to London, where he had been invited to attend the International Statistical Congress in July 1860.[27] While there he read a paper on his explorations in Africa before the Royal Geographical Society, and lectured on Africa in England and Scotland for more than six months. Upon his return he was convinced that because of the wealth of the continent, a powerful black nation could be established there. Thus, he championed the cause of black emigration to Africa, preferably to the Niger valley. However, he was unable to amass substantial support for his proposal.

When the Civil War commenced, Delany temporarily altered his emigrationist position, preferring instead to organize a unit of black troops.[28] He obtained a position as recruiting agent for black troops and examining physician. Toward the end of the war he met with Abraham Lincoln and proposed that a unit of black troops, led by black officers, be recruited. Lincoln arranged for him to meet the secretary of war, who commissioned him a major in the infantry, attached to the 104th United States Colored Troops. He was sent to Charleston, South Carolina, to aid in the recruitment and organization of another black regiment. After the Civil War he remained in Charleston.

There he worked in the Freedman's Bureau for three years, attempting to protect the rights of the newly freed blacks, and became engaged in local politics. He was a leader of the Colored People's Convention, held in Charleston in 1865 in an effort to solidify black political power. After leaving the Freedman's Bureau he held several political posts in Charleston, including that of customs house inspector. When a new political party was organized, he became its nominee for lieutenant governor, but lost the election by a narrow margin.

Delany thus abandoned emigrationism in favor of working for civil rights in the United States. This turn of events angered many of his followers. Among the incidents that caused greatest concern among South Carolina's black population was Delany's support of Wade Hampton, a Democratic candidate for governor, former Confederate general, and wealthy land owner who advocated the formation of vigilante groups to maintain white supremacy. Because of the antiblack climate of opinion in the state, Hampton was assured of the white vote, and with Delany's assistance he attracted enough black votes to win the election. As a reward for his support, Delany was appointed a trial justice in Charleston. Hampton died shortly after assuming office, and Delany left his post to resume his emigration activities. By this time he was a firm advocate of repatriation to Africa, even to Liberia. In 1878 he worked with the Liberian Exodus Association, which chartered a boat to carry 206 blacks from South Carolina to Liberia.

Delany returned to the practice of medicine for a short period before settling in Boston, where he worked as agent for a Central American mercantile firm. In 1885 he died at the age of 73 in Xenia, Ohio. The life and careers of Martin R. Delany amply illustrate the complexity of the man. The last two decades of his life are sometimes perplexing, and his actions frequently appear to have been contradictory. However, when viewed within the context of the times in which he lived, such contradictions appear to have almost been inevitable. And though he never commanded a mass-based following, Delany was one of the most influential black men in the last half of the nineteenth century. His careers and views on emigration changed from time to time, but he remained firmly committed to the cause of black liberation.

Bishop Henry M. Turner: "Home to Africa"

The failure of Reconstruction and the virtual reenslavement of blacks toward the end of the nineteenth century generated widespread interest in black nationalism in general and in the emigration of blacks from the United States in particular. Like Delany, many spokesmen had believed that the emancipation of the slaves signaled a new era in black–white relations in the United States, but they were soon to learn that racism was so deeply entrenched among white Americans that the prospect of racial equality appeared grim. Large numbers of blacks had worked diligently to defeat the Confederacy, and later in the Reconstruction, only to learn that in America white supremacy took precedence over social justice.

As W.E.B. DuBois has pointed out, had it not been for the efforts of blacks the Union forces would have encountered greater difficulty in defeating the Confederacy. Indeed, Afro-Americans were essential to the victory of the Union armies.[29] At the height of the fighting some 200,000 blacks assisted the Union forces as servants, cooks, and other laborers alone. More important, some 186,000 black troops were organized into 154 regiments. They participated in 198 battles and suffered 68,000 casualties. Without the participation of blacks it is doubtful whether the Union armies could have defeated the Confederacy; certainly the war would have been prolonged for many years. The Confederacy attempted to wage war in the midst of 4 million black slaves. Because of their role in the southern economy, the slaves were able to pose serious difficulties for the Confederacy by simply refusing to work. But the blacks' main contribution was the skill they displayed as soldiers in the infantry, cavalry, and artillery. And after the fighting ceased, their role in the Reconstruction was equally noteworthy.

Perhaps the most articulate and influential spokesman for black emigration to Africa between the Civil War and World War I was Bishop Henry M. Turner of the African Methodist Episcopal church.[30] Like Delany, Turner was born "free." And like Delany he was an officer during the Civil War and worked in the Freedman's Bureau during Reconstruction. When Delany died, he became the leading spokesman for the resettlement of blacks in Africa. As both a minister and a politician, Turner was among the first in a long line of blacks to attain national and international recognition as a leader who combined these two activities as a means of promoting black liberation. His mass following among poor southern blacks during one of the most difficult periods in a long and troublesome history indicates that he spoke to the needs of the people.

Born in South Carolina in 1834, Turner's early youth was spent in the cotton fields, from which he escaped to work as a janitor in a law office.[31] There he learned to read and write. At the age of twenty he was ordained an evangelist with the Southern Methodist church, which was controlled by whites but which permitted him to preach to both blacks and whites. In this position, as in the cotton fields, Turner met racial prejudice and discrimination. On a trip to New Orleans in 1858, however, he became acquainted with the African Methodist Episcopal church, a black religious group which had earlier become autonomous from its parent white church because of racial segregation. He immediately left the Southern Methodist church for the A.M.E. church. After training for the ministry of this church, he was assigned to a parish in Washington, D.C. While there he urged the Union forces to recruit black troops. When this policy was adopted he became a recruiter of black troops, and because of the success of these efforts, he was appointed chaplain to the black troops.

At the war's end, Turner was assigned as chaplain with the Freedman's Bureau in Georgia. There he again met discrimination and returned to the A.M.E. church, serving as organizer for the state of Georgia, where the church had not existed previously. Since he was well-known to government officials, the Republicans asked him to be their organizer among the newly freed blacks in the state. He promptly called the first Republican state convention ever held in Georgia and was elected to the Georgia Constitutional Convention in 1867 and to the legislature in 1868. But as soon as the legislature convened, the first order of business was to disqualify blacks from holding elective office. Although he was denied his seat, he made an impassioned speech from the floor:

The Scene presented in this House, today, is one unparalleled in the history of the world.... Never, in the history of the world, has a man been arraigned before a body clothed with legislative, judicial or executive function, charged with the offence [sic] of being a darker hue than his fellowmen.... Cases may be found where men have been deprived of their rights for crimes or misdemeanors; but it has remained for the State of Georgia, in the very heart of the nineteenth century, to call a man before the bar, and there charge him with an act for which he is no more responsible than for the head which he carries upon his shoulders. The Anglo-Saxon race, sir, is a most surprising one.... I was not aware that there was in the character of that race so much cowardice, or so much pusillanimity.... We [blacks] have pioneered civilization here; we have built up your country; we have worked in your fields, and garnered your harvests, for two hundred and fifty years!.... We are willing to let the dead past bury its dead; but we ask you now for our RIGHTS.... The black man cannot protect a country if the country doesn't protect him; and if, tomorrow, a war should arise, I would not raise a musket to defend a country where my manhood was denied.[32]

Although he had been the organizer of the Republican party in the state, Turner was unseated by the forces determined to maintain white supremacy at all costs, by the people responsible for the Civil War in the first place. Blacks had voted in greater numbers than whites, but their chosen representatives were denied seats in the legislature. To the black delegates, Turner said, "White men are not to be trusted. They will betray you. . . . Do not fight for a country that refuses to recognize your rights. . . . Black men, hold up your heads. . . . This thing means revolution."[33] Once again white supremacy triumphed and the blacks were expelled.

After his expulsion, Turner received an appointment as postmaster of Macon, Georgia, the first black to hold such a position in the state. Again, the Georgia whites brought pressure to have him removed, and after a mere two weeks he was dismissed, having been falsely charged with fraud, counterfeiting, and theft. From Macon he was appointed customs inspector in Savannah, where he remained a short time before returning to the A.M.E. church.

Although he had hoped that the victory of the Union forces would improve the lot of black people, Turner had always envisioned emigration as a possible solution to the problems of blacks in the United States. After these bitter experiences, he was convinced that blacks should "return to the land of [their] Fathers." Although he was only in his early forties, repatriation to Africa was to remain his consuming interest throughout his long life. Having built up a strong mass following among the poor rural southern blacks, he was the dominant figure in the black nationalist, repatriation to Africa movement. He became publications manager for the church, an influential post he held for four years, and from which he was able to acquire a following among the younger ministers and members. Though he met bitter opposition in the church for his emigrationist views, his support was such that he was elected bishop in 1880. From this position, he constantly exhorted blacks to go "home to Africa," usually in the pages of the *Christian Recorder*, the influential weekly newspaper of the A.M.E. church. Most prominent black leaders, including Frederick Douglass and Benjamin T. Tanner, editor of the *Recorder*, opposed him.

Convinced that powerless blacks could never achieve freedom in the United States, Turner focused his efforts on establishing a powerful black nation in Africa to which Afro-Americans would emigrate. His criticisms of the United States were severe, but meticulous. When the Supreme Court ruled in 1883 that the Civil Rights Act of 1875 was unconstitutional, he considered that this ruling absolved Afro-Americans of allegiance to the United States. He declared that black men would no longer enlist in the armies of the United States and denounced the Constitution as "a dirty rag, a cheat, a libel and ought to be spit upon by every Negro in the land."[34] He urged blacks either to relocate or prepare for extermination.

Turner was among the few prominent Afro-Americans to support a bill introduced in Congress by Senator Matthew Butler of South Carolina. This bill proposed that the U.S. government provide transportation for any Afro-American who wished to leave the South if the applicant wished to become a citizen of the country of destination.[35] Although no mention of emigration was made in the bill, that was clearly its aim. A request for an appropriation of an initial $5 million was contained in the bill. The bill was attacked by blacks and whites alike, though for different reasons. Whites feared a mass exodus of cheap labor, while blacks felt it was a scheme to deport all Afro-Americans to Africa. Bishop Turner supported the bill because "it will enable at least a thousand self-reliant black men to go where they can work out their own destiny." Although the bill never came to a vote, it stirred a heated debate in Congress and throughout the country, and generated interest among blacks in Turner's campaign for black emigration to Africa.

In 1891, the Council of Bishops of the A.M.E. church authorized Turner to visit Africa. Several A.M.E. ministers had emigrated to Liberia, and his mission was to assist them in the organizational work of the church. However, he viewed the trip as one which would afford him the opportunity to prepare the groundwork for Afro-American repatriation. When he arrived in Sierra Leone, he is said to have wept. And when the people of Freetown heard of his impending arrival, they are said to have streamed to the waterfront to greet him. Though he was impressed with Sierra Leone, Turner preferred Liberia because it was an independent nation with a black government, and Sierra Leone was a colony.

Reports had reached the United States that most blacks who had emigrated to Africa had met death or disease, but for the bishop, Africa was all he had dreamed it would be. He was impressed with the people he met, the resources of the continent, and its potential for economic development. But most of all he was impressed with the liberty blacks enjoyed in Liberia. In one of his letters he wrote, "One thing the black man has here and that is manhood, freedom and the fullest liberty; he feels like a lord and walks the same way."[36]

After a month in Africa, Turner returned to the United States in February 1892, convinced that he would do whatever he could to convince blacks to emigrate to Africa. He was placed in charge of the overseas missionary of the A.M.E. church, and among his first projects was to establish a newspaper, the *Voice of Missions*, which was his mouthpiece for his emigration activities. He used the newspaper to promote a variety of emigration schemes, including the demand for "indemnity by the government for Afro-Americans desiring to resettle in Africa, as payment for services rendered during slavery." He wrote, "The way we figure it out, this country owes us forty billions of dollars, and we are afraid to ask for a hundred million." The $40 billion figure was based on an estimate of $100 a year for 2 million blacks for 200 years. He continued, "Congress, by its legislation, throws away over a hundred million annually, and we are so little, such contemptible pigmies, so insignificant that we shudder at the very idea of a hundred million."[37] The *Voice of Missions* became the foremost organ for the spread of sentiment for African emigration. In addition to information on Africa, the newspaper regularly contained denunciations of the treatment of blacks in the United States.

In 1893 the bishop again traveled to Africa, this time via Europe in an effort to encourage British businessmen in trade between the United States and Africa. European colonialism had already gained a foothold on the continent, and Turner urged both blacks and whites to save Africa for black people. On this trip he again visited Sierra Leone and Liberia. Liberia's President asked him to serve as the country's ambassador in Washington, an offer which he accepted. However, the appointment was so strongly opposed by the American Colonization Society that the Liberian government rescinded it. He then became Liberian counsul for the Southern states.

While in Africa, Turner continued to file glowing reports of the continent and its people in the form of weekly letters to both the *Christian Recorder* and the *Voice of Missions*, and upon his return he seized upon every opportunity to advocate emigration by blacks to Africa. To this end he sponsored a congress on Africa in Chicago during the exposition of 1893, and issued a call for a national convention of American blacks. The convention, held in Cincinnati, attracted some 800 delegates. Although conditions for Afro-Americans continued to deteriorate and emigration sentiment was strong among the poor, middle-class opposition militated against the success of the convention. Furthermore, it was Bishop

Turner's first attempt to extend his leadership to blacks outside the south.

The following year the bishop met with greater success. In January 1894 the International Migration Society was founded at his urging, and its object was to accelerate the emigration of blacks to Liberia. Among other things the organization incorporated the already existing African Steamship Company as a subsidiary. This move was made so that some 5,000 Afro-Americans could be resettled each year. Some ten months later the Migration Society found itself in financial difficulties. The country was in a depression, and the Society had been unable to transport any blacks to Africa. Therefore, as a gesture of its seriousness and to attract new members, the Society sent 13 of its members, who had paid their passage to Liberia via Europe. The plans of the organization to transport them on its own ships did not materialize, but it did manage to establish its first colony in Africa.

It should be noted here that part of the Society's difficulties stemmed from the large number of people posing as emigration officials, under various guises. Economic conditions were such that people throughout the South devised a variety of schemes to support themselves. One of the favorites was that of selling fraudulent tickets to Africa. And, of course, those blacks who enjoyed some measure of economic prosperity were willing to take their chances and remain in the United States. While they agreed with many of Turner's exhortations against the country, it was unlikely that they would meet physical violence as was so frequently the case of the poor blacks, especially in the rural South. Emigration interest, however, remained intense in the 1890s.

The Migration Society was able, after much difficulty and many delays, to charter a Danish ship to take a load of its members to Liberia. Some 2000 blacks departed from Savannah, Georgia, for Monrovia, Liberia, on March 19, 1895, and on April 7 they arrived at their destination. Although the passengers were excited about their new home, it seems that the cablegram the Society had sent to Liberia, to announce their arrival, had never reached the country. Consequently, the ship arrived to the surprise of Liberian officials.[38] Inasmuch as the emigrants were without funds, the government of Liberia assisted by providing food and lodging. The American Colonization Society, which had an agent in Liberia, also made its facilities and expertise available to the newcomers. Shortly after their arrival, Bishop Turner reached Liberia in his third trip to Africa. He visited some of the new settlers and was pleased with their adjustment. However, concern was voiced among many Afro-Americans when several of those who had made the trip returned to the United States out of disillusionment. It was in 1895 that Bishop Turner's emigration campaign met its most formidable opponent—Booker T. Washington. Washington's accommodation scheme and his strong opposition to black emigration were contained in his now famous "Atlanta Compromise" speech. Although he was opposed by many blacks, Washington's views made him acceptable to wealthy and influential whites, both in and out of government. Washington's exhortations did not stem the tide of interest in emigration among the poor southern blacks, many of whom lived in circumstances not significantly different from slavery. Consequently, the Migration Society initiated plans to charter a second ship in the autumn. As usual, difficulties developed and the ship with its 321 passengers did not leave until March 1896.

Several of the passengers returned to the United States by summer, and, according to one historian, "within a few months the majority of 'Laurada's' passengers were either dead or had left Liberia."[39] The returning passengers claimed that the promises contained in the Migration Society's propaganda had not been kept, that many had died of fever, and still others had starved to death. Some families remained and prospered, while others remained and endured hardships rather than continue to subject themselves to American oppression. But word of the disenchantment of the returnees with Migration Society and conditions in Liberia soon spread among Afro-Americans, and together with the depression, caused Turner's emigration campaign to lose its appeal among America's blacks.

Bishop Turner continued both his emigration activities and his missionary work for the A.M.E. church. In 1898 he went to South Africa, where he traveled for five weeks on official church business. But his main activity was spreading the cause of nationalism among black South Africans. This trip served to rekindle his enthusiasm for Afro-American emigration. By the time he returned, the United States had launched its imperialist war against Spain, and Turner denounced the action, urging other blacks to resist participation in the war. In his *Voice of Missions* he wrote, "The colored men would far better be employed in remaining at home, marrying wives and giving the race sons and daughters, and perpetuating our existence, than rushing into a death struggle for a country that cares nothing for their rights or manhood, and wait till they are wanted, and then the nation will feel and know his worth and concede to him the respect due the defenders of a nation."[40]

By the turn of the century, white supremacy had become so entrenched in the South, where the vast majority of blacks lived, that they had virtually been returned to servitude. The 1896 *Plessey* v. *Ferguson* decision of the Supreme Court meant that black subordination had become complete. It was impossible for blacks to improve their status through political action, because they had been disfranchised. Consequently, Turner renewed his efforts to get Afro-Americans to emigrate to Africa. In addition, he caused a stir in the A.M.E. church and throughout the country by preaching that "God is a Negro." In the *Voice of Missions* he wrote, "We have as much right biblically and otherwise to believe that God is a Negro, as you buckra or white people have to believe that God is a fine looking, symmetrical, and ornamented white man." He continued, "Every race of people since time began who have attempted to describe their God by words, or by paintings, or by carvings, or by any other form or figure, have conveyed the idea that the God who made them and shaped their destinies was symbolized in themselves, and why should not the Negro believe that he resembles God as much so as other people?"[41]

The International Migration Society did not survive the turn of the century, and the *Voice of Missions* ceased publication. However, the bishop started a new journal, the *Voice of the People*. In addition, he organized several emigration conferences sponsored by his newly formed Colored National Emigration Association. At one such meeting a resolution was passed, asking Congress to appropriate $500 million for Afro-American emigration to Africa. The resolution was ignored, and the members of the Colored National Emigration Association worked to purchase a ship for this purpose. By 1906, after many failures and little success, Bishop Turner "lost interest in the project and became deeply involved with local politics, trying to stop Georgia from disfranchising her black citizens."[42] Nevertheless, he continued to advocate the emigration of Afro-Americans to Africa.

The increasing prominence of Booker T. Washington as a leader who urged blacks to "stay at home," along with the militant opposition of middle-class blacks and the black press, and the fears of many blacks about Africa, led to the demise of the emigrationist movement. By the end of the first decade of the twentieth century emigrationist activity was virtually nonexistent. Bishop Turner died in 1915, still convinced that emigration was the only workable solution to the problems facing America's blacks. And though most black intellectuals disagreed with him, they also disagreed with Booker T. Washington's accommodationist policies. Throughout his long and full life, Bishop Turner provided dynamic and capable leadership to the Afro-American emigrationist movement in the United States. His black nationalist leadership has been increasingly recognized in recent years, and although he is responsible for the settlement of only a few Afro-Americans in Africa, he was almost single-handedly responsible for generating interest in Africa as the fatherland of black Americans for nearly half a century.

3

Marcus Garvey and
the Universal Negro
Improvement Association

When Marcus Garvey arrived in the United States in March 1916, he found a powerless and demoralized black population. Both Booker T. Washington and Bishop Henry Turner had died in 1915, and although W.E.B. DuBois was active in intellectual circles, he did not have a mass following among the poor blacks. Garvey arrived at a time when there was no black leader of national prominence who commanded a following among the masses of black people. Though not an immediate success when he arrived in Harlem, within a few years Garvey was able to build the largest organized black nationalist movement in American history, and indeed in world history, for the Universal Negro Improvement Association was worldwide in its organization.

Conditions among blacks in post-World War I America

Garvey's greatest successes were achieved in the United States, and the accomplishments of the movement he was to lead were in part the result of conditions facing black people in this country after World War I. The second decade of the twentieth century was one of massive black migration from the rural South to the urban North. Estimates on the number of persons leaving the South during this decade vary, but many put the number at about one million, or 10 percent of the total black population.[1] Blacks in the South had already been effectively disfranchised, and southern whites, with the approval or at least the acquiescence of the federal government, were determined that blacks would remain slaves in principle, if not in name. While many factors accounted for the great migration out of the South, violence played a crucial role.[2] Since blacks were no longer the private property of slaveholders, and thereby no longer important economic investments, lynching was deemed a suitable means of maintaining control over the powerless blacks. At the beginning of the second decade of the twentieth century, it has been modestly estimated that lynchings occurred at a rate of two a week. Lynch mobs, which included a cross-section of the white community, frequently advertised their activities in the newspapers, attracting thousands of gleeful spectators. Even black servicemen in uniform frequently were lynched during World War I. Milder forms of brutality, such as floggings and terrorism, were even more widespread. In general, every conceivable form of barbarous treatment awaited black people, the vast majority of whom lived in the rural areas, thereby simplifying the task for the heartless whites.

In addition to violence, the economic plight of blacks in the rural south was severe. Unemployment was high, and when these landless people were able to secure work, they were relegated to positions paying subsistence wages. Health and sanitary facilities, where they existed, were substandard. And while educational facilities for whites were limited, those reserved for blacks were in general deplorable.

With the entry of the United States into World War I, and the growing need for workers in industries in the North, blacks migrated to cities in the East and Midwest in large numbers. Prior to World War I, blacks had been systematically kept out of industrial employment, but with the flow of European immigrants virtually halted, their services were needed in industry. Furthermore, when white workers in big industries went on strike, blacks could always be used as strikebreakers. Black women could easily secure work as domestic servants for middle-class and wealthy whites. Although earning a livelihood was difficult, the task was somewhat easier outside the South.[3]

This decade, then, was one of massive redistribution of America's black population. The North, as any place outside the South was called, encouraged black migration because it needed a cheap labor supply, while the less than human conditions in the South repelled the blacks. The two major motivations for black migration, then, were economic improvement and the desire to escape violence directed against them. However, upon reaching the North, blacks soon learned that conditions there were only somewhat less harsh. Where they had faced lynch mobs in the South, in the North they encountered panic and fear from whites, which took the form of race riots. Major riots erupted in East St. Louis, Illinois, in 1917, and in Chicago and Washington, D.C., in 1919.

Indeed, the summer of 1919 has been called the "Red Summer" because 26 major race riots erupted between May and September. Hundreds of blacks were killed and thousands more were injured. In addition, gangs of whites frequently roamed through the black community, terrorizing its inhabitants. In virtually all cases the police and other law enforcement officials either assisted the mobs or ignored them.

Blacks were forced to live in the most squalid sections of cities, and attempts to move to other areas were met with mob violence. Though segregation did not carry the legal sanction it had in the South, it was the norm in all institutions affecting the lives of black people. It was the war-time President, Woodrow Wilson, who was instrumental in instituting the practice of racial segregation in federal employment and in public facilities in Washington, D.C.

In all industries, including those involved in the production of war materials, blacks were relegated to the lowest paying, segregated jobs. When a delegation of blacks attempted to protest these practices to Woodrow Wilson, he simply ignored them. Two national organizations, the National Association for the Advancement of Colored People and the National Urban League, had been established for the purpose of improving the legal, social, and economic conditions of black people, but they lacked the power and support necessary to effect any meaningful changes. White supremacy was the American credo and blacks were deemed hardly worthy of human treatment.

With the entry of the United States into World War I, a war which was allegedly fought to make the world "safe for democracy," some 400,000 blacks registered for military service, and many served in Europe. In typical American fashion they were forced to serve in segregated units, where they were often brutalized by white servicemen. Some were lynched and still more were simply beaten by mobs. And while black servicemen were fighting for "democracy" abroad, their families were fighting for physical survival in the streets of America.

The mood of the black community was one of despair. Government officials made no attempt to alleviate these conditions, but promised improvements after the war's end. When the war was over, white Americans settled down to business as usual, which meant a continuation of white supremacy. Lynchings continued in the South and race riots swept the country. For most blacks it was clear that in the minds of white Americans democracy and white supremacy were synonymous, and there appeared to be no hope of ever securing justice in the United States.

It was this mood of hopelessness that Marcus Garvey found among blacks, especially those in the urban North. He found a leaderless people, a people despised by whites at all levels, and a people in desperate need of assurance of their human worth.

The early Marcus Garvey

Garvey, who arrived in New York at the age of twenty-eight, was able to understand the mood of blacks in the United States, for conditions in his native Jamaica were equally dismal. Furthermore, the population of Jamaica was highly stratified into three categories along color lines, with whites enjoying the highest status, followed by mulattoes, and blacks (like Garvey himself) at the bottom. Although blacks constituted some 80 per cent of the population, and Anglo-Saxons approximately 2 percent, the mulattoes effectively served as a buffer group, sustaining the dominant group's position at the top, and at the same time preserving their own middle position.

Garvey was born August 17, 1887, the youngest of 11 children, to Marcus and Sarah Garvey in the small town of St. Ann's Bay in Jamaica.[4] The Garvey family was able to live in rather comfortable circumstances because the father, although lacking formal education, was a master mason and was able to amass extensive property holdings in the town.

Of the eleven children, only Marcus and a sister lived to adulthood. Both maintained close relations with the mother, for the father spent his free time in his library reading books and newspapers. At an early age young Marcus Garvey read the materials in his father's library and longed to travel to see the world beyond St. Ann's Bay, to which many ships from distant lands came for cargoes. According to his widow, the younger Marcus Garvey's mother was kind and considerate to her son, while his father was "engrossed in himself and his brooding." His brooding resulted from feelings that his property was unjustly being taken from him. For example, the owner and publisher of a newspaper had mailed him a free subscription for 20 years, but after the owner died the executors sent a bill for the newspaper, which the elder Garvey refused to pay. He was sued but refused to pay the claim, and a court ordered some of his property sold at a price considerably less than its real value.[5] A series of similar court actions led to his losing all his land except that on which his house stood.

At the turn of the century agricultural conditions in the West

Indies were undergoing a change from the cultivation of sugar to growing bananas, a shift which left thousands of Jamaicans jobless. This forced some to become contract laborers in Central America. Others migrated to Cuba and to the United States.[6] Garvey's hometown experienced the economic crisis, and at the age of fourteen he cut his education short and migrated to Kingston.

One incident of crucial importance to his later thinking occurred before he left St. Ann's Bay.[7] During his childhood he had maintained friendly relations with the white children among whom he lived and with whom he went to school. As he was later to record, "To me at home in my early days, there was no difference between white and black." He had played with children of a Wesleyan minister whose church his family attended and whose property was adjacent to theirs. Garvey had been especially friendly with one of the minister's daughters. The two parted at the age of fourteen; her parents decided it was time for them to separate their daughter from this black youth. "They sent her and another sister to Edinburgh, Scotland, and told her that she was never to write or to try to get in touch with me, for I was a 'nigger.' It was then that I realized that there was some difference in humanity, and that there were different races, each having its own separate and distinct social life." Even the white boys who were his friends in childhood went their separate ways when they reached adolescence.

Garvey had hoped to continue his education in Kingston but was forced to work as an apprentice in a printing plant owned by his godfather. The printing plant was small, and his godfather had an extensive library, which not only facilitated his reading but also enabled him to learn all aspects of the printing trade. Though his earnings were meager, he fulfilled his promise to bring his widowed mother to Kingston. She did not enjoy city life and soon died.

Unlike his mother, Garvey found life in Kingston an exciting experience. The many street debates fascinated him, and he adopted the practice of attending various local churches to learn the techniques of oratory. By the age of twenty he was a master printer and foreman of one of the largest printing companies in Kingston. When the printer's union struck the company for higher wages, Garvey was elected leader of the strike, and since he was the only foreman to join the striking workers, he was fired.[8] Because of his leadership role in the strike and his increasing involvement in political activities, he was unable to secure private employment. He then went to work for the government printing office, and in 1910 commenced publishing his own periodical, *Garvey's Watchman*.

This first publishing venture was not successful, and since he wanted to get involved in political organizing on behalf of black workers, a task which required more money than he was able to earn in Kingston, Garvey traveled to Costa Rica, where an uncle was able to secure work for him as a timekeeper on a United Fruit Company banana plantation. The oppressed workers on the plantation were mainly immigrants from Jamaica, and recognizing their plight, he left the plantation job to publish a newspaper, *La Nacionale*, which was devoted to awakening the black workers to their collective plight. This newspaper, like his previous venture, was unsuccessful.

From Costa Rica he traveled to Panama, where he was outraged at the inferior working conditions of his fellow Jamaicans on the Panama Canal. There he published for a brief period another newspaper, *La Prensa*. From Panama he traveled to Ecuador, Nicaragua, Honduras, Colombia, and Venezuela. In each of these countries he attempted to organize the West Indians in an effort to improve their working conditions. But his efforts were unsuccessful. According to his widow, he became ill with fever, "and sick at heart over appeals from his people for help on their behalf, but decided to return to Jamaica in 1911, and contend with the government there, as well as to awaken Jamaicans at home to the true conditions of the Spanish mainland."[9]

Back in Jamaica, Garvey was unable to interest the government in the conditions facing Jamaican subjects in other countries. He then traveled to Europe and settled in London, after traveling through half of the continent, where he attempted to enlist the support of African students and black seamen in his effort to improve the conditions of the world's black people. While in London he learned of the conditions facing blacks in Africa and the United States through conversations with Africans and reading. Among other books, he read Booker T. Washington's *Up From Slavery*. These experiences caused him to ask penetrating questions regarding the universal plight of black people. "Where is his King and kingdom? Where is his President, his country, and his ambassador, his army, his navy, his men of big affairs?" Unable to find them, he declared, "I will help to make them."[10]

During his stay in London, Garvey met an Egyptian nationalist and scholar, Duse Mohammad Ali, the publisher of a monthly, *African Times and Orient Review*. Garvey worked with Duse Mohammad Ali, from whom he learned of the conditions facing black colonial subjects throughout Africa. He also attended Trinity

College for a short period, and then decided to return to Jamaica to start an organization to unify the black people of the world in a first step toward their liberation from oppression.

Five days after his arrival in Jamaica in July 1914, he organized, along with some friends, the Universal Negro Improvement Association (UNIA) and African Communities (Imperial) League, with a program, as he described it, of "uniting all the Negro peoples of the world into one great body to establish a country and Government absolutely their own."[11] The aims and objectives of the organization, as Garvey defined them were:

To establish a Universal Confraternity among the race; to promote the spirit of pride and love; to reclaim the fallen; to administer to and assist the needy; to assist in civilizing the backward tribes of Africa; to assist in the development of Independent Negro nations and communities; to establish a central nation for the race, where they will be given the opportunity to develop themselves; to establish Commissaries and Agencies in the principal countries and cities of the world for the representation of all Negroes; to promote a conscientious Spirtual worship among the native tribes of Africa; to establish Universities, Colleges, and Academies and Schools for racial education and culture of the people; to improve the general conditions of Negroes everywhere.[12]

Garvey soon discovered that in Jamaica the word "Negro" in the title of an organization brought forth reactions of hostility and resentment from those of his countrymen who preferred to be called "colored." Furthermore, as leader of the organization, he was resented by the mulattoes because of the blackness of his skin. Consequently, in the two years before his arrival in the United States, he was unable to enlist any mass support for the Association.

In an effort to bring the program of the UNIA to the United States, Garvey communicated with Booker T. Washington in Tuskegee, Alabama. Washington invited him to visit Tuskegee and promised to appear with him on speaking tours throughout the country. But by the time Garvey arrived, Washington had died. He met with other black leaders instead and made a tour of 38 states. He had planned to return to Jamaica after informing some leaders of the aims and objectives of the UNIA, but decided to remain in Harlem, because he feared that some of the political leaders in the community were attempting to use the organization for personal gain. Consequently, he resigned as president of the Jamaica chapter and remained in New York. He was elected president of the New York chapter and initiated a campaign to gain members.

Organization of the UNIA

Using the motto "One God! One Aim! One Destiny!" Marcus Garvey spoke on the streets of Harlem to enlist members in the UNIA. In three weeks he claimed to have recruited 2,000 new members in Harlem. By 1920 he claimed 4 million members, the following year 6 million members in some 900 chapters throughout the world. These figures have been disputed by scholars, most of whom estimate peak membership in the association at between one and two million.[13] Whatever the official membership, it is clear that the UNIA counted thousands and perhaps millions among its supporters who were not official dues-paying members.

Guiding the organization was an eight-point platform:

1. *To champion Negro nationhood by redemption of Africa.*
2. *To make the Negro Race conscious.*
3. *To breathe ideals of manhood and womanhood in every Negro.*
4. *To advocate self-determination.*
5. *To make the Negro world-conscious.*
6. *To print all the news that will be interesting and instructive to the Negro.*
7. *To instill Racial self-help.*
8. *To inspire Racial love and self-respect.*[14]

During its prime years the national office of the UNIA, as well as its many branches throughout the world, included an elaborate array of officers. Garvey himself was president general of the UNIA and provisional president of Africa. Assisting him were a secretary general, several ministers (for labor, industries, and legions), a chaplain general, a surgeon general, a registrar, and an auditor general. There was a counsel general with several assistants, a publicity director, a muscial director, agricultural specialists, many high commissioners, several potentates and deputy potentates (residents of Africa), and many more officials of lesser rank. Such an elaborate structure was necessary because of the scope of the activities of the UNIA.[15] The association was active not only in every major city in the United States, but throughout North America, the Caribbean, Central and South America, Africa, Asia, and Europe. The policies and activities of the hundreds of chapters differed, depending upon local conditions, but each was required to comply with the procedures prescribed in the constitution of the association.

In order to reach this mass, the UNIA established, early in 1918, the *Negro World*, the leading black weekly of the period.

The *Negro World* was published each week between 1918 and 1933 and reached a peak circulation of 200,000.[16] It was disseminated throughout the world, with sections printed in French and Spanish for the benefit of those blacks who could not read English. It was through the pages of the *Negro World* that the philosophy of Garveyism was spread. The major emphases of the newspaper were pride in cultural heritage and the unity of black people throughout the world. Although the UNIA was ultimately to engage in other publishing ventures, the *Negro World* remained its official organ.

One of the more important accomplishments of the UNIA was the first International Convention of the Negro Peoples of the World, held in New York City during the entire month of August 1920 and attended by some 25,000 delegates from some 25 countries. Garvey issued the call for the convention from his headquarters in Harlem for black leaders from around the world to assemble and report on the conditions of blacks in their areas. It was at this convention that Garvey was elected provisional president of Africa.

The major project of the convention was the adoption of a Declaration of Rights of the Negro People of the World on August 13, to be presented to the various governments of the world.[17] The preamble to the declaration detailed the injustices suffered by black people throughout the world, including discrimination and brutality in the United States and the colonization of Africa by European nations. The Declaration of Rights contained 54 specific demands for the improvement of the status of black people. These included proclaiming Africa as the "Motherland of all Negroes," and calling for the "self-determination of all peoples." Also included were such demands as "the colors, Red, Black, and Green, be the colors of the Negro race" and that black children be taught "Negro History." In general, the declaration was an attempt to secure immediate justice and ultimate autonomy for blacks wherever they existed. Furthermore, it sought to unite and mediate the various factions existing among the world's black population.

The UNIA was a membership organization which collected monthly dues of 35 cents from its members, of which 25 cents remained in the local chapter and 10 cents went to the association's headquarters.[18] Furthermore, the Association developed multi-million dollar business enterprises, including the Black Star Line, the Negro Factories Corporation, a chain of cooperative grocery stores and restaurants, and a publishing house. But the activities of the UNIA were much broader; its ideology combined territoriality, cultural nationalism, and religious nationalism with economic nationalism. In short, the UNIA became the first black organization to embrace the complete spectrum of black nationalism, and its leader was the first black man to put forth a comprehensive ideology of black nationalism. In view of the current resurgence of black nationalism in the world and the renewed interest in Garvey, a brief description of the various aspects of his program seems in order.

Territoritality

One of the fundamental goals of the UNIA was "Africa for the Africans." "Africans" encompasssed all people of African descent throughout the world. The notion of territoriality was a significant aspect of the movement and was in part responsible for the support Garvey was to receive from millions of alienated blacks. Article 13 of the Declaration of Rights of the Negro Peoples of the World states, "We believe in the freedom of Africa for the Negro people of the world, and by the principle of Europe for the Europeans and Asia for the Asiatics; we also demand Africa for the Africans at home and abroad." In an essay entitled "Africa for the Africans," Garvey wrote, "It is only a question of a few more years when Africa will be completely colonized by Negroes, as Europe is by the white race. What we want is an independent African Nationality.... It is hoped that when the time comes for Americans and West Indian Negroes to settle in Africa, they will recognize their responsibility and their duty."[19]

In an essay, "An Appeal to the Soul of White America," Garvey suggested that repatriation to Africa was worthy of serious consideration as a solution to America's race problem. In repayment for centuries of unpaid service to building the country, he urged white Americans to "let the Negroes have a government of their own. We have found a place; it is Africa, and as black men built America, surely generous and grateful white men will help black men build Africa."[20] In another essay, "An Appeal to the Conscience of the Black Race to See Itself," he urged blacks to establish a homeland in Africa. "The Negro needs a nation and a country of his own, where he can best show evidence of his own ability in the Art of human progress.... The Negro will have to build his own government, industry, art, science, literature, and culture, before the world will stop to consider him."[21]

Garvey was not always clear as to whether he expected all blacks outside Africa to return. For example, at one point he indicated that a free and unified Africa under black leadership could "lend protection to the members of the race scattered all over the world, and...compel the respect of the nations and races of the earth."[22] This was then a call for international black solidarity rather than repatriation to Africa. And on occasion Garvey ruled out repatriation for all blacks. For example, in a speech delivered at Madison Square Garden in New York in 1924 in honor of the returning delegates who had been sent by the UNIA to Europe and Africa, he said, "We do not want all the Negroes in Africa. Some are no good here, and naturally will be no good there."[23] He included among the undesirables mulattoes in the United States.

In most of his speeches and writings, however, Garvey was adamant about blacks returning to Africa, for as he said, "Nationhood is the only means by which modern civilization can completely protect itself."[24] In order to gain nationhood he appealed to government officials in the United States and petitioned the League of Nations for assistance. Short of peaceful resettlement of blacks in colonized Africa, Garvey advocated the use of force. At the Second International Convention of Negroes in 1921, for example, he said, "George Washington was not God Almighty. He was a man like any Negro in this building, and if he and his associates were able to make a free America, we too can make a free Africa." He closed his address with these words: "It falls our lot to tear off the shackles that bind Mother Africa. . . . You did it in the Revolutionary War. You did it in the Civil War. . . . You can do it marching up the battle heights of Africa. Let the world know that 400,000,000 Negroes are prepared to die or live as free men."[25]

Since virtually all of Africa was under the colonial domination of European nations at the time, the UNIA established military organizations with the ultimate goal of the reconquest of Africa. These military units included the African Legion, a paramilitary group led by a former Army captain, and its female counterpart, the Ladies Brigade; the Black Cross Nurses, who would provide assistance to the wounded in battle; the Garvey Militia; the Black Eagle Flying Corps; and the Universal African Motor Corps.

Though some scholars have claimed that the literal movement of blacks "back to Africa" was the crux of Garveyism, the philosophy and program of the UNIA were considerably broader in scope. Indeed, on occasion Garvey himself was not clear on this point. But more often than any other theme, that of the repatriation of Afro-Americans to Africa and the establishment of a unified government there appeared in his speeches and writings.

Cultural nationalism

The creation of racial pride among blacks throughout the world was no doubt the most profound and lasting contribution of Garvey and the UNIA. Though he advocated racial purity, because he believed that assimilation was impossible, Garvey was foremost a humanitarian. Having observed the brutality inflicted on blacks around the world, Garvey strongly believed that racial purity offered the only possibility for black unity, and having been born in a country where mulattoes held higher status than their darker fellow-blacks and used these privileges to their own advantage, he was strongly opposed to racial amalgamation. "I believe in a pure black race just as how all self-respecting whites believe in a pure white race, as far as that can be," he said. "I am conscious of the fact that slavery brought upon us the curse of many colors within the Negro race, but there is no reason why we ourselves should perpetuate the evil."[26] And later he wrote, "Miscegenation will lead to the moral destruction of both races, and the promotion of a hybrid caste that will have no social standing or moral background in a critical moral judgement of the life and affairs of the human race."[27]

On the question of race prejudice, Garvey was clear: "Black and white are proportionately bad as well as proportionately good, living under the same conditions and environments of our imperfect civilization. . . . I would not wholesalely condemn any one group of the human race for the selfish good of another."[28] In stating the aims of the UNIA, he declared, "The organization believes in the rights of all men, yellow, white, and black."[29] On the question of world peace he said, "There can be no peace among men and nations, so long as injustice is done to other peoples, just so long will we have cause for war, and make a lasting peace an impossibility."[30]

Although charges of racism were frequently leveled against Garvey, they were usually unfounded, because his concern was the liberation of black people, not the oppression of others. But his concern for the oppressed black masses caused him to gain the support of racists, thereby adding to the charges of racism. For example, because of his outspoken views on racial purity, he was befriended by such avowed racist groups as the Ku Klux Klan and the Anglo-Saxon Clubs. In 1922 the UNIA entered into a tacit alliance with the Klan, and Garvey made a trip to Atlanta, Georgia, to confer with the Imperial Giant of that organization. Officials of the Anglo-Saxon Clubs were invited to speak at UNIA rallys in

New York. But, as Cronon has indicated, the meeting between Garvey and representatives of the Klan was "one of expediency, rather than mutual admiration," for he frequently deplored the antiblack violence and terror tactics of the Klan.[31] Nevertheless, such actions as these further alienated Garvey from bourgeois black leadership. After the meeting with the Klan he was roundly condemned in the black press and by black spokesmen. W.E.B. DuBois, for example, wrote in *Crisis*, the official organ of the National Association for the Advancement of Colored People, that "Marcus Garvey is, without doubt, the most dangerous enemy of the Negro race in America and the world. He is either a lunatic or a traitor."[32] To this charge Garvey responded, "I regard the Klan, the Anglo-Saxon Clubs and White American societies, as far as the Negro is concerned, as better friends of the race than all other groups of hypocritical whites put together."[33]

The major thrust of Garvey's cultural nationalism took the form of teaching pride in blackness, racial solidarity, and respect for the African heritage of black people. In the pages of the *Negro World* he wrote of the glorious past of black people, the heroism of leaders of slave revolts in the United States, of the history of the Ethiopian Empire, and of Toussaint L'Ouverture's leadership in the Haitian Rebellion. The masses of poor blacks knew little of their cultural heritage and history, and Garvey's movement served to instill black pride in them. As Ottley was able to write in 1943: "Concretely, the movement set in motion what was to become the most compelling force in Negro life—race and color consciousness, which is today the ephemeral thing that inspires 'race loyalty;' the banner to which Negroes rally; the chain that binds them together."[34]

Economic nationalism

Garvey sought to ameliorate the economic problems of American blacks by establishing business enterprises on a large scale. The foremost of these was the Black Star Line, a steamship company which ultimately included four vessels (a fifth vessel was purchased but never delivered).[35] The primary purpose of the Black Star Line was to join peoples of African descent throughout the world in commerce and industry, and a secondary goal was to provide transportation for those blacks seeking repatriation to Africa. In an effort to pursue these goals, the Black Star Line in 1919 secured a charter in Delaware authorizing the ownership of ships, the right to navigate throughout the world, and to carry passengers, mail, and freight. Some $800,000 in stocks in the corporation were sold to black people at five dollars a share.

The first ship purchased was the S.S. *Yarmouth*, which was rechristened the S.S. *Frederick Douglass*, for which the corporation paid $165,000. During 1920, two additional vessels were added to the Black Star Line: a river boat, the S.S. *Shadyside*, which was purchased for $35,000 and used for excursions on the Hudson River; and the S.S. *Kanawha*, which was rechristened the S.S. *Antonio Maceo*. The latter was a $60,000 yacht that was fitted out to join larger ships for another $25,000. The following year the Black Star Line agreed to purchase another ship through a white-owned exchange in New York. When the ship, for which a deposit had been paid, did not appear, the directors of the Black Star Line confronted the operator of the exchange, only to learn that the ship was in drydock in Indochina. The operator of the ship exchange agreed to purchase a German ship, the S.S. *Orion*, for the Black Star Line and apply the original deposit toward the purchase price. The *Orion*, offered for $225,000 by the United States Shipping Board, was to have been rechristened the S.S. *Phyllis Wheatley*. This ship was to have been used for African trade, since the *Yarmouth* sailed between the United States, the West Indies, and Central America. The *Phyllis Wheatley* was never delivered, however, because the operator of the ship exchange was unable to produce the $25,000 down payment, although Black Star officials had already given him more than $20,000. The integrity of the exchange was certainly questionable. Because of the failure of the exchange and other circumstances the ship was never delivered. Not the least of these circumstances was a declaration to the United States Shipping Board that the UNIA was a communist organization and affiliated with the Soviet Union. Upon hearing this allegation, the United States Board took six months to complete the paper work required for the sale and contract, and when completed they contained a demand for a performance bond of $450,000.[36]

In the meantime the *Shadyside* had been taken out of service and soon sank in the Hudson River. The *Kanawha* had been abandoned. And the once proud flagship *Yarmouth*, which completed a total of three voyages to the West Indies, was sold at a public auction at the direction of a federal district judge to satisfy a judgment against the Black Star Line. Then, in January 1922, Garvey was arrested on a charge of using the mails to defraud, in part because of complaints from Black Star Line stockholders. Postal officials claimed that Garvey and his associates had misrepresented the company and that the stock was deceptive. Within a month, Garvey and three other officials of the line were indicted on twelve counts of using the mails to defraud the public. The trial was postponed and the defendants were released on bail until a federal investigation into the case could be conducted. The failure of the Black Star Line can be attributed to many factors, not the least of which are the acts of unscrupulous shipowners who sold unseaworthy vessels to the company. Once again, the victim was blamed for the crimes committed against him. Garvey was found guilty by a jury but the other three were acquitted. Garvey was jailed for several months in New York, while his supporters arranged for his release on bail, pending appeal. During his appeal, in 1924, he organized the Black Cross Navigation and Trading Company, which purchased yet another ship, the *General Goethals*, later rechristened the *Booker T. Washington*. This ship was to be used for trade between the United States and the West Indies, the function that the *Yarmouth* had performed, but the ship never returned after its first voyage to the West Indies.

In addition to shipping, the UNIA entered other lines of business on a wide scale. One of its first purchases was Liberty Hall, a large auditorium in Harlem with a seating capacity of 6,000. Liberty Hall became the American headquarters of the UNIA and was used for a variety of functions. Garvey's widow described its function and that of "Liberty Halls" established later throughout the country as follows: "Liberty Halls... served the needs of the people: Sunday morning worship, afternoon Sunday Schools, Public Meetings at nights, and concerts and dances were held, especially on Saturday nights. Notice boards were put up where one could look for a room, a job, or a lost article."[37] Soup kitchens and temporary lodging were also available.

The UNIA organized the Negro Factories Corporation in 1919, and stock was offered to Afro-Americans at five dollars a share. The purpose of the company was "to build and operate factories in the big industrial centers of the United States, Central America, the West Indies, and Africa to manufacture every marketable commodity."[38] According to one writer, "The Black Star Line had been formed under a standard corporation charter, but the Negro Factories Corporation was both more amorphous and more socialistic. The factories were, in effect, cooperatively owned, staffed by UNIA members, and directly responsible to the minister of industries, who was in turn accountable to the international conventions and the supreme executive council."[39] Among the other business enterprises of the UNIA were the Universal Restaurants, the United Chain Stores, millinery stores, laundries, a hat factory, a moving company, hotels, a printing plant, and other factories to produce items for the organization, such as flags, lapel buttons, photographs of officials, and cigars. Because of the scale of these business enterprises and the lack of competent managerial personnel, many were failures. In addition, many of Garvey's associates were dishonest.

In publishing the UNIA was quite successful. After the establishment of the *Negro World*, two other papers were founded. *African World* was published in South Africa, and a daily, *Negro Times*, commenced publication in New York in 1922. But of all his publications, the *Negro World* was the most successful. In each of its issues Garvey wrote an editorial, "Fellowmen of the Negro Race," which was signed "Your obedient servant, Marcus Garvey, President General." The paper also contained a page devoted to poetry for the people.

The *Negro World* carried the motto of the UNIA: "One Aim, One God, One Destiny," and was described as "A Newspaper Devoted Solely to the Interests of the Negro Race." Its pages carried accounts of the glories of Africa and of the contributions of black people to world history. In other words, one of the functions of the paper was that of instilling pride in racial heritage among black people throughout the world.

Religious nationalism

The religious component of the UNIA was the African Orthodox Church, founded in New York in 1921. Earlier Garvey, like Bishop Henry Turner before him, had written, "If the white man has the idea of a white God, let him worship his God as he desires. If the Yellow man's God is of his race let him worship his God as he sees fit. We, as Negroes, have found a new ideal. Whilst our God has no color, yet it is human to see everything through one's own spectacles, and since the white people have seen their God through white spectacles, we have only now started out (late though it may be) to see our God through our own spectacles."[40] Garvey believed that for blacks to worship a white God meant that they would have to remain subservient to white people.

In an effort to build strength for the African Orthodox Church, Garvey appointed the Reverend George Alexander McGuire as chaplain general of the UNIA. At the 1920 annual convention of the organization, McGuire, who had been one of its chief organizers, impressed the delegates with a sermon in which he urged blacks to go as missionaries among whites to teach them about brotherhood. The delegates apparently liked the idea of the African Orthodox Church, for most of them were poor and had been reared in the fundamentalist religious tradition. When McGuire was appointed to head the new church, he was ordained as bishop in a service conducted by officials of the Greek Orthodox Church.

Bishop McGuire set out to build the church by urging his congregations to "burn all pictures of white Madonnas and white Christs" adorning their homes. He was not immediately successful, even within the UNIA, because of the strong opposition of black ministers who feared the loss of members should the African Orthodox Church succeed. But by 1924 the church had 21 congregations, with 2,500 communicants, spread throughout the United States, Canada, Trinidad, Cuba, and Haiti.[41]

The official organ of the church was the *Negro Churchman*, a monthly magazine that published news from all of the branches of the church. It served as a mouthpiece for Bishop McGuire who, by the time of the Fourth International Convention of Negro Peoples of the World in 1924, was preaching that Christ was black. He also preached beneath a large oil painting portraying a black madonna and child. And during UNIA parades (important features of the organization), members marched under a huge painting of the black madonna and child.

Problems and assessment

Marcus Garvey was convicted of the charge of using the mails to defruad; he was sentenced to a five year term, beginning in 1925. After serving two years, his sentence was commuted by President Calvin Coolidge, and he was immediately deported as an undesirable alien. He went to his native Jamaica, from which he visited UNIA offices elsewhere in the West Indies and Central America. Then he went to London to establish the European headquarters of the UNIA in 1928, and to Paris to open a branch office. He then went to Geneva, where he presented a "Petition of the Negro Race" to the League of Nations. After another brief stay in London, he visited Canada but was soon asked to leave the country. In the following years he convened several International Conventions of the Negro Peoples of the World in Kingston, but at the 1929 meeting a split in the UNIA developed over the location of the headquarters of the organization. Since he had been deported from the United States, Garvey argued that the headquarters should be located in Jamaica, but the New York contingent felt that it should remain there. This split was irreconcilable and led to the decline of the organization.

In 1933, after the demise of the *Negro World*, Garvey published a magazine, *Black Man*. Through the pages of this magazine he attacked his most severe American critics, especially W.E.B. DuBois and A. Philip Randolph. Support for the UNIA waned in Jamaica, and Garvey moved his headquarters to London in 1935. With the invasion of Ethiopia by Italy that year, the declining UNIA received a boost, but the organization was never able to recapture its broadbased support. In the late 1930s Garvey became ill with pneumonia, which continued until his death in London on June 10, 1940, at the age of 53. His remains were finally transferred to his native Jamaica in 1956. Probably the greatest irony is that in all these years the leader of the back-to-Africa movement never visited the continent.

Although Garvey was able to capitalize on the despair of the millions of blacks who had migrated from the rural South to urban areas throughout the United States, and those who migrated from the West Indies, and to build his black nationalist movement into the largest the world has known, many factors militated against his success. Some of these were structural, resulting from the nature of the society during the period in which he lived and worked in the United States; others were personal, stemming from his own inability to work with others; and still others resulted from a combination of these factors.

Garvey's greatest success was achieved in the United States, but his West Indian heritage, with its emphasis on determining status on the basis of skin color, served to preclude his acceptance of many Afro-Americans. In the United States, however, any person of Afro-American ancestry was considered black, no matter how remote his ancestry. In attempting to apply the Jamaican formula to the United States, Garvey managed to alienate large numbers of black people who otherwise might have supported his movement. As Harold Cruse has written, "Garvey's ultimate undoing was his blindness to many facts about America, particularly the differences in the psychologies of West Indian and American Negroes."[42]

At a time when racism was at its peak in the United States, Garvey met hostility from whites at all levels, especially those in positions of power. This is perhaps best illustrated by his difficulties with the Black Star Line. The ships purchased by the UNIA were clearly not seaworthy, yet he was forced to pay outrageous prices for them. As Cronon has written, "the real criminals were the white culprits who had unloaded the rusty hulks on unsuspecting and inexperienced Negroes."[43] The charges which finally led to his imprisonment were weak, and if Garvey had not been an important black leader, the government probably would not have been able to get a conviction.

Among the strongest of Garvey's opponents were leaders of organized labor and Communists. Garvey did not trust either, mainly because of his strong aversion to interracial movements. In a speech entitled "Beware of Greeks Bearing Gifts," he said, "If I must advise the Negro workingman and laborer, I should warn him against the present brand of Communism or Workers' Partnership as taught in America, and to be careful of the traps and pitfalls of white trade unionism, in affiliation with the American Federation of white workers and laborers."[44] Having experienced difficulty with organized labor during his youth in Jamaica, Garvey saw white workers as rivals rather than allies. At a time when black labor leaders were attempting to organize black workers, he advocated the rejection of trade unionism. At the same time Garvey was strongly opposed to communism. The UNIA had been branded communist by the Department of Justice, but Garvey publicly announced his opposition to communism because he felt that white Communists were insincere about Afro-American rights, and the Communist Party was dominated by whites. Of communism he said, "I am of the opinion that the group of whites from whom Communists are made, in America, as well as trade unionists and members of the Worker's party, is more dangerous to the Negro's welfare than any other group."[45] For Garvey, "Capitalism is necessary to the progress of the world, and those who unreasonably and wantonly oppose or fight against it are enemies of human advancement; but there should be a limit to the individual or corporate use or control of it."[46] Garvey even went so far as to claim credit for being the founder of fascism. "We were the first Fascists....Mussolini copied Fascism from me but the Negro reactionaries sabotaged it."[47] In the opinion of Harold Cruse, one of the chief flaws of Garveyism was his insistence upon capitalist economics while most of the colonial world was "passing from anti-imperialsim to anti-capitalism as a way of economic organization."[48]

Most of the leading black intellectuals in the United States opposed Garvey, as did the black press. His flamboyant style and questionable tactics led to a steady stream of denunciations. When any aspect of his movement was questioned by black intellectuals or the black press, Garvey quickly retaliated, usually charging their opposition to their mixed ancestry. After his publicized trip to Atlanta for a meeting with leaders of the Ku Klux Klan in 1922 and the criticism which followed the encounter, his response was a threat to ostracize W. E. B. DuBois from "the Negro race," because he was an enemy of the black people of the world. He expressed the view that every white man was potentially a Klansman, and that he was a more honest appraiser of the situation than the other black leaders. Though the bulk of the UNIA support came from the poor and the poorly educated, as Theodore Vincent has shown, the leadership of the organization consisted of many well-educated persons.[49] In general, however, Garvey was steadfast in his distrust of those he considered to be intellectuals.

The imprisonment and later deportation of Garvey were crucial factors in the decline of his organization. At the same time the depression of the 1930s was much more severe for Afro-Americans than for whites. Consequently, those who had been his strongest supporters were unable to continue to provide any financial support. In addition, as Edwin Redkey has noted, the organization lacked persons with the requisite business skills necessary to sustain its many ventures.[50] Because of lack of trust Garvey, in many cases, refused to employ personnel appropriate to the task, because of minor ideological differences, preferring to rely on the less competent but more loyal. His shortcomings were many. He was often arrogant and vain; he made enemies easily, and many whom he should have cultivated he alienated. He was completely unable to cooperate with those who disagreed with him. Furthermore, he was extremely sensitive to criticism and supremely egotistical. And often he was boastful and tactless.[51]

The accomplishments of Marcus Garvey and the UNIA were many. As Cronon put it, "The creation of a powerful feeling of race pride is perhaps Garvey's greatest and most lasting contribution to the American race scene."[52] And Vincent is no doubt correct in his assessment that in the twentieth century, "Garvey did more than anyone else to stimulate race pride and confidence among the black masses."[53] This important legacy has been passed on to the present generation of Afro-Americans and their counterparts in numerous African countries, including the Central African Republic, the Congo (Zaire), Ghana, Kenya, Nigeria, and Zambia, all of which have achieved political independence since his death and whose leaders have acknowledged his inspiration.

4

Malcolm X and the rise
of contemporary nationalism

The deportation of Marcus Garvey in 1927 and the depression that followed effectively ended the influence of the Universal Negro Improvement Association as a broadly based black nationalist organization. But it did not signal the end of black nationalist sentiment in the United States. W.E.B. DuBois was a member of the Socialist party and a leader of the movement for Pan-Africanism, an attempt at the political unification of Africa in an effort to free the continent from colonialism. On the domestic front DuBois was forced to resign his position with the National Association for the Advancement of Colored People, an organization he helped to establish, because of his nationalist position. As editor of the *Crisis*, the official publication of the NAACP, DuBois published an article in 1934 in which he took the position that Afro-Americans should organize themselves to obtain economic and social power "no matter how much segregation it involves." In this essay he made the distinction between voluntary separation for survival and imposed segregation. Although DuBois had been a bitter opponent of Garvey, he remained a leader with strong black nationalist convictions.

As a founding member of the NAACP, DuBois had championed the cause of integration and full equality for blacks. At the same time, he recognized the peculiar status of Afro-Americans in the United States. As early as 1897 he described the dilemma faced by blacks:

It is a peculiar sensation, this double consciousness, this sense of always looking at one's self through the eyes of others, of measuring one's soul by the tape of a world that looks on in amused contempt and pity. One ever feels his twoness–an American, a Negro; two souls, two thoughts, two unreconciled strivings; two warring ideals in one dark body, whose dogged strength alone keeps it from being torn asunder.[1]

57

In a speech published in 1935, DuBois advocated "a negro nation within the nation." In this speech he put forth the position that only through economic and political control over their lives could Afro-Americans achieve equality in the United States. He envisioned the unity of black people being accomplished through "careful autonomy and planned economic organization."

The demise of nationalist sentiment

The thirty-odd years following the deportation of Garvey was a period in which black nationalist sentiment reached an all-time low in the United States. DuBois never commanded the support of large numbers of people as had Martin Delany, Henry M. Turner, and Marcus Garvey. Furthermore, other social forces tended to militate against the pervasiveness of black nationalism. The depression of the 1930s, during which at least half of all Afro-Americans were forced to accept social welfare relief, forced black people to turn their attention to the question of economic survival. Most Americans, except the ruling class, suffered severe economic hardships, and black people who were at the bottom of the economic ladder were characteristically hardest hit.

The American Communist party, which was founded in 1919, made significant inroads in the black community, especially among intellectuals, but its appeal to the masses was minimal. Before 1928 the Communist party had opposed black nationalism because of its position on the international solidarity of all workers, regardless of race. But in that year, the Sixth World Congress of the Communist International issued a resolution, "On the Negro Question in the United States," in which a call was made for "self-determination of the Negroes in the Black Belt" of the South. In his study of world nationalities Lenin had earlier observed that Afro-Americans comprised a significantly large proportion of the American population to be considered an oppressed nation. But according to Theodore Draper, the concrete proposal for self-determination for American blacks originated with Joseph Stalin.[2] In 1935, however, the Communists, operating on the assumption that the proletarian revolution was imminent, abandoned its nationalist stand in favor of a policy of equal rights for blacks within the United States.

The American Communist party's proposal for self-determination in the black belt was never seriously considered by the black community. The NAACP, which had vigorously opposed Garvey's nationalism, continued to advocate a policy of assimilation. And the New Deal policies of Franklin D. Roosevelt were such that most blacks cast their lot with the NAACP. Whereas most of the New Deal policies operated within the framework of segregation, with blacks receiving a disproportionately low share of the social rewards, there were some indications that the policies meant a new deal for America's poor, including blacks.

Throughout the 1930s black nationalism manifested itself mainly through black solidarity in the realm of economics. "Buy Black" and "Don't Buy Where You Can't Work" were familiar slogans. Adam Clayton Powell led economic boycotts of stores in Harlem, and on one occasion led 6,000 blacks to New York's City Hall to protest discrimination in employment. As usual, DuBois was in the forefront of these campaigns. In addition, the invasion of Ethiopia by Italy in the 1930s served to sustain interest in black nationalism. American blacks pleaded for Ethiopian independence before the League of Nations. Several organizations, including the International Council of Friends of Ethiopia, the United Aid to Ethiopia, and the Ethiopian World Federation, were formed by Afro-Americans.

During Roosevelt's first years as President, blacks were skeptical becuase he was a Democrat inasmuch as the Republican party had been the party of Lincoln and of abolition. But the tide had turned by the election of 1936, when most black voters cast their ballots for the Democratic ticket for the first time. Roosevelt appealed to the underdog. The federal government built low-rent housing, and black farmers received assistance through the Farm Security Administration. Even black painters and writers were subsidized by federal funds. Perhaps most important of all, Roosevelt and his wife Eleanor expressed a friendliness toward blacks which had been uncharacteristic of presidents and their wives. Black people were appointed to advisory posts in government, and Roosevelt ultimately appointed what became known as his "Black Cabinet" to advise him on the problems of blacks.

Antiblack violence in the form of race riots and lynchings diminished in the second half of the decade, and in some areas of American life segregation and discrimination also diminished. The rise of industrial trade unionism proved to be an important factor. The Congress of Industrial Organizations, for the first time, adopted a general policy of integration in some unions, but retained segregation in others. For the first time some black and white workers were employed together in positions of equal status and equal pay. In general, interracial trade unionism became respectable.

Many black leaders thus saw integration as the solution to the problems faced by America's blacks. And as the United States became increasingly involved in World War II, jobs were plentiful. As usual blacks were employed in menial capacities in these industries, but they migrated in massive numbers from the rural South to the urban North to work. And though Roosevelt had expressed friendly attitudes toward blacks, he was content to see them subjected to segregation and discrimination in industries contracted to manufacture war materials.

It finally took the threat of a mass March on Washington, originated by A. Philip Randolph, the founder of the Brotherhood of Pullman Car Porters, with the assistance of the NAACP and the Urban League, to pressure Roosevelt into action against discriminatory employment practices. Roosevelt attempted to persuade Randolph to call off the demonstration in which 100,000 blacks were to march on the White House. When asked what he could do, Randolph told Roosevelt that he could issue an executive order barring discrimination in war industries and the armed services. Realizing the seriousness of the threat, Roosevelt issued Executive Order 8802 which ostensibly banned discrimination in war industries and all apprenticeship programs. In addition, he appointed a Fair Employment Practices Committee. The proposed march was cancelled, however, the demand for an end to discrimination in the armed forces went unheeded until after the war, when another executive order by President Harry S. Truman finally accomplished this goal in principle.

Although blacks in the armed services were rigidly segregated throughout World War II and antiblack violence in the form of race riots continued both in and out of the armed forces, several other events supported the position of the integrationists. Since the United States had declared itself a world power, the leaders of the country became increasingly concerned about its internal black colony. For the first time the plight of blacks became a social problem worthy of serious consideration. The American Council on Education commissioned several studies of rural and urban blacks in the North and South. The Carnegie Corporation financed the massive study which resulted in Gunnar Myrdal's *An American Dilemma*.

As early as 1935 the NAACP embarked on court tests of segregated graduate schools in the South, forcing the University of Maryland to admit Afro-American students. Then came a series of other favorable court decisions and administrative decrees in education, employment, and public accommodations, culminating in the *Brown* v. *Board of Education* decision of 1954, which held that segregated public education was unconstitutional. This decision overturned the *Plessy* v. *Ferguson* ("separate but equal") decision of 1896. There was widespread feeling in the black community and among liberal whites that black liberation would be achieved through racial integration. Though opposition to the ruling was expected, it was widely believed that such opposition would be short-lived and integration in education would lead to integration in other aspects of American life, thereby accelerating the process of assimilation.

Because of strong resistance by white legislators and rank-and-file citizens to the Supreme Court ruling, the violence generated by black children attempting to attend previously all-white schools, and continued segregation in virtually all aspects of American life, Afro-Americans and their white supporters organized a massive civil rights movement. This movement began in 1955 with the Montgomery bus boycott, which was triggered when a black woman who was occupying a seat on a public bus in the section reserved for blacks refused to relinquish her seat to a white man. The bus driver ordered her to move, and when she refused his order, she was arrested. Word of her arrest spread quickly through the black community, mainly through the medium of the church, and the boycott was launched. Since the poor black people of Montgomery, Alabama, were the principal users of public transportation, their mass act of solidarity crippled the bus company.

The Montgomery bus boycott was led by Martin Luther King, Jr., who, because of his dedication to nonviolent resistance as a means of effecting social change, soon became the acknowledged leader of the civil rights movement, and no doubt the best-known black man in the world at the time. King was an advocate of integration, which became the dominant ethos of the movement during the 10 years of its peak activity. He founded the Southern Christian Leadership Conference (SCLC), one of the major civil rights organizations. Another new organization, the Student Nonviolent Coordinating Committee (SNCC), grew out of the sit-ins of the early 1960s. In addition, the Congress of Racial Equality (CORE), the NAACP, and the Urban League joined forces with these two organizations in an attempt to abolish racial segregation and discrimination from American life, especially in the South.

During its 10 years of peak activity the civil rights movement made notable gains in improving the citizenship status of Afro-Americans. For example, it was responsible for the Civil Rights

Act of 1964 and the Voting Rights Act of 1965, which together abolished legal segregation and discrimination against blacks. But the civil rights movement was primarily based in the South and its accomplishments served to elevate the citizenship status of blacks in that region to the point that they shared a comparable status to those outside the South. At the same time, however, it did little to improve the plight of blacks outside the South, where nearly half of the blacks lived in urban areas. This is not to minimize the importance of the civil rights movement, for it served to heighten the political consciousness of blacks and give them a sense of dignity which they had not known before. However, its methods and goals were too limited to achieve black liberation. What the movement did was to achieve the legal equality of blacks *in principle*, but legal equality in principle did not make for justice in practice.

During the height of the civil rights movement black nationalists were still found in the United States, but they were overshadowed by the integrationists. In all the major civil rights organizations integration was the major thrust, and so pervasive was this theme that it often was viewed as an end in itself, rather than a means toward achieving the larger goal of black liberation. Any black nationalist who questioned the likelihood or desirability of integration was immediately denounced by the leaders of the civil rights movement or ignored. Meanwhile, the Nation of Islam, a black nationalist organization, was gaining members.

It might be said that integration was the dominant ethos of the black movement between 1930 and 1965. The last major campaign of the civil rights movement came in 1965 with the Selma to Montgomery march, which led to the enactment of the Voting Rights Act of that year. After this accomplishment, many of the supporters of the movement assumed, as had the abolitionists before them, that they had succeeded in achieving freedom for Afro-Americans. Consequently, the movement activists relaxed their concerns.

In spite of all the cries for "Freedom Now" and the gains that were made, blacks still remained a colonized minority in America, a nation within a nation, and disillusionment was widespread. This disillusionment manifested itself in a series of black rebellions, beginning in 1964 and continuing throughout the decade. Furthermore, the war of aggression waged by the United States in Indochina had an important impact on Afro-Americans, for they were being killed in disproportionately high numbers in a war against fellow Third World people. Blacks were among the first to clearly recognize the war as racist, and SNCC was the first of the civil rights organizations to take a public stand against the war, declaring that the legitimate stuggle for black people was against their oppression in the United States. Other organizations followed this lead, including SCLC, when Martin Luther King, Jr., made his heroic "Declaration of Independence Against the War in Vietnam" speech in April 1967.

The leaders of SNCC were among the first Afro-Americans to internationalize the struggle against American imperialism at home and abroad. Two of its officials traveled to Vietnam as members of the Bertrand Russell International War Crimes Tribunal in 1967. Stokely Carmichael, a former chairman of SNCC, was a guest of honor and delegate at the Havana meeting of the Organization of Latin American Solidarity, a conference of leading revolutionary movements in Latin America. At this meeting, Carmichael addressed the delegates with the following message:

We greet you as comrades because it becomes increasingly clear to us each day that we share with you a common struggle; we have a common enemy. Our enemy is white Western imperialist society; and our struggle is to overthrow the system which feeds itself and expands itself through the economic and cultural exploitation of nonwhite, non-Western peoples. We speak to you, comrades, because we wish to make it clear that we understand that our destinies are intertwined. We do not view our struggle as being contained within the boundaries of the United States, as they are defined by present-day maps.[3]

From Cuba, Carmichael traveled to North Vietnam, Algeria, Egypt, Guinea, Tanzania, and other countries, meeting with revolutionary leaders. In the same year James Foreman, another former chairman of SNCC, traveled to Zambia to attend the International Seminar on Apartheid, Racial Discrimination, and Colonialism in Southern Africa, sponsored by the United Nations.

The turning point in the civil rights movement came in June 1966 in the James Meredith March Against Fear through his home state of Mississippi. At the inception of this one-man march, Meredith was shot by a sniper. The leaders of the major civil rights organizations met to continue the march as a means of revitalizing the lagging civil rights movement. When the marchers reached Greenwood, Mississippi, Carmichael addressed a large crowd of poor blacks, during which time he proclaimed, "What we need is black power." The crowd cheered, but most of the leaders of the march were upset with the introduction of this controversial slogan. An ideological split thus developed within the civil rights movement, from which it was unable to recover.

The introduction of the concept of black power was the beginning of the current spread of nationalist sentiment among Afro-Americans, and signaled the decline of integration as the dominant thrust of the black movement. Although the concept was not new, it had special appeal at this time because 100 years after the Civil War the relative economic, political, and social statuses of black and white Americans remained virtually unchanged. It was clear that a more radical approach to the problems facing Afro-Americans was necessary, and the movement for black power served this purpose. It was the logical successor to the civil rights movement.

Although the concept of black power angered and frightened many black and white Americans, it was eagerly accepted by large segments of the black community. It was a call for black community control of businesses, education, police, and other institutions which had not been responsive to the needs of its inhabitants. Furthermore, it was a call for black unity, for as Carmichael and Hamilton have written, "The concept of Black Power rests on a fundamental premise: *Before a group can enter the open society, it must first close ranks.* By this we mean that group solidarity is necessary before a group can operate effectively from a bargaining position of strength in a pluralistic society."[4] The opponents of black power rightly recognized that this concept set the groundwork for black autonomy, thereby rejecting integration as both unnecessary and unlikely.

Throughout the era of the civil rights movement, one black leader had the courage to oppose the powerful coalition of integrationist leaders. Perhaps more than any other individual, Malcolm X was responsible for the incredible spread of nationalist ideology in the contemporary black community.

The influence of Malcolm X

Few leaders in recent history have been as misunderstood as Malcolm X, yet his speeches and writings were models of clarity. He was feared and hated by both blacks and whites, and often the same individuals who shared these sentiments admired him for his intellectual ability and candor. During his lifetime his appeal among Afro-Americans, especially the youth, was widespread, but he was constantly maligned by black integrationists and whites in general. After his assassination he finally achieved a position of respect from all segments of the black community and from younger white radicals.

Malcolm X was important to Afro-Americans in a way few white people can understand. He did not command a broadly based organization like Marcus Garvey; he was not a scholar in the formal tradition of W.E.B. DuBois; and he did not command the respect of poor blacks in the rural South and whites throughout the country as did Martin Luther King, Jr. But he was certainly one of the most influential black men in this century. The depth of Malcolm X's understanding, his leadership ability, and his keen intelligence were such that if he had lived and developed his ideas and organizational skills, he could very well have become the most important black man in American history.

During the last years of his life, Malcolm X was a popular speaker, not only on American college and university campuses but throughout the world. Like Garvey before him, Malcolm X was primarily a speaker, and one of exceptional ability. Therefore, what was written about him was usually done by others or from recordings of his speeches. At the time of his death, however, he had completed his autobiography, which was published posthumously. Since that time dozens of books and hundreds of articles about Malcolm X and his ideas have appeared.[5] Of all the works by and about Malcolm X, the *Autobiography* stands out, and must certainly be one of the most important books in recent years.

Inasmuch as the details of Malcolm X's life are set forth in his widely read autobiography and in other works about him, primary emphasis here is devoted to his nationalism, his message to black people. One of his principal biographers, George Breitman, maintains that during the last year of his life Malcolm X was questioning the ideology of black nationalism and was uncertain about applying the concept to his own ideological thinking.[6] However, a careful reading of Malcolm X's own writing reveals that although his position changed through time, black nationalism remained central to his thoughts and actions. Little attention will be devoted to the powerful forces and racism in American society which contributed to his development and death, or to his association and break with the Nation of Islam. However, a brief general statement about the man might serve to put what follows into perspective.

Malcolm X was born in Omaha, Nebraska on May 19, 1925. He was a member of a large family, which moved first to Milwaukee and then to Lansing, Michigan, where he spent most of his early years. His father, a Baptist minister and a follower of Marcus Garvey, was killed by a mob of racist whites when Malcolm X was only six years old. His father's murder, the care of eight children, harassment from the state welfare department, and inability to provide for the family finally overcame his mother and she was confined to a mental hospital, where she remained for 26 years. The children became wards of the state and the family was destroyed. He dropped out of school at the age of fifteen, although he ranked third highest in his class, and moved to Boston to live with an older half-sister. There he worked at a variety of tasks reserved for blacks–shining shoes, clearing tables in restaurants, and service work in hotels. He moved to New York and became a waiter in a night club in Harlem. There he learned such activities of the underworld as gambling, dealing in drugs, and burglary.

Later he returned to Boston, where he continued his activities and was finally arrested for burglary and sentenced to 10 years in prison at the age of 20. While in prison he read virtually all of the books in the well-stocked prison library, books which had been donated to the prison by a wealthy philanthropist. He became acquainted with the Nation of Islam and corresponded with its spiritual leader, Elijah Muhammad. Upon his release from prison in 1952 at the age of 27, Malcolm X went to Chicago to meet Elijah Muhammad. He was accepted into the movement and after a brief training period was assigned to the post of assistant minister of a mosque in Detroit. From Detroit he was sent to organize a mosque in Philadelphia, and in 1954 he became minister of the mosque in Harlem. In this position, Malcolm X was largely responsible for the increase in membership and prominence of the Nation of Islam.

After a dispute with Elijah Muhammad, which resulted from a speech Malcolm X made after the assassination of President John F. Kennedy, during which he termed the assassination a case of "The chickens coming home to roost," he was suspended from the Nation of Islam for a period of 90 days. (The reference here was to the alleged role of Kennedy in the assassination of President Ngo Dinh Diem of South Vietnam.) He finally withdrew from the Nation of Islam in 1964 and organized the Muslim Mosque, Incorporated, an orthodox religious organization; later he organized the Organization of Afro-American Unity (OAAU), a secular group dedicated to the unification of peoples of African descent in the Western Hemisphere and the projection of the contributions of black people to the world.

In the last year of his life Malcolm X made two trips to Africa and the Middle East, including a pilgrimage to Mecca. On these trips he attempted to project the struggle of Afro-Americans onto the international arena by lining up support among heads of state and diplomats for a petition to the United Nations charging genocide against America's black population. Shortly after his last trip, he was assassinated in New York on February 21, 1965, leaving his widow, Betty Shabazz, and six children.

Like Garvey before him, Malcolm X spoke to the needs of black people, but unlike Garvey he appealed to reason, not emotions. In this sense he was a teacher. He advocated black autonomy at a time when black leaders and their white liberal allies were demanding integration. Through the logic of his message he gained an international reputation as a speaker and debater. He willingly debated politicians, civil rights leaders, college professors, journalists, and all others willing and courageous enough to debate him.

In his analysis of American society Malcom X was severe but meticulous. At one point he said he advocated separation because "not only do I refuse to integrate with you, white man, but I demand that I be completely separated from you in some states of our own or back home in Africa; not only is your Christianity a fraud, but your 'democracy' a brittle lie." Both black and white integrationists were unable to answer such a charge; indeed, they never attempted to do so. Rather, they attacked him as a "racist," a "black supremacist," and "a dangerous fanatic," who advocated violence.

On the charge of racism, Malcolm X declared that he was not a racist, and that one should distinguish between white racism and black responses to it. In response to a question at the Harvard Law School Forum, he said, "If we react to white racism with a violent reaction, to me that's not black racism. If you come to put a rope around my neck and I hang you for it, to me that's not racism. Yours is racism, but my reaction has nothing to do with racism."[7] In a later interview with a newspaper reporter he discussed the OAAU. When asked if he planned to use hate to organize people, Malcolm X responded, "I won't permit you to call it hate. Let's say I'm going to create an awareness of what has been done to them. This awareness will produce an abundance of energy, both negative and positive, that can be channeled constructively."[8] On still another occasion he said, "I'm not a racist. I've never been a racist. I believe in indicting the system and the person that is responsible for our condition."[9] Finally, in 1965 he wrote, "the white man is *not* inherently evil, but America's racist society influences him to act evilly. The society has produced and nourishes a psychology which brings out the lowest, most base part of human beings."[10]

The charge of being a black supremacist, although widespread, was baseless. Malcolm X felt that the only possible way for people of African descent to achieve liberation was through unity. This, he felt, would instill in black people the dignity and the confidence to command freedom from oppression. It was his conviction that before blacks could become integrated into the larger society, it was necessary for them to unite among themselves. At a press conference in New York on March 12, 1964, speaking of his newly organized Muslim Mosque, Incorporated, he said, "Whites can help us, but they can't join us. There can be no black–white unity until there is first some black unity. There can be no workers' solidarity until there is first some racial solidarity. We cannot think of being acceptable to others until we have first proven acceptable to ourselves."[11] In 1965 he wrote, "In the past, yes, I have made sweeping indictments of all white people. I will never be guilty of that again—as I know now that some white people *are* truly sincere, that some truly are capable of being brotherly toward a black man. The true Islam has shown me that a blanket indictment of all white people is as wrong as when whites make blanket indictments against blacks."[12] While on his pilgrimage to Mecca he wrote letters which received wide publicity in the United States. In one of these letters he wrote:

Never have I witnessed such sincere hospitality and overwhelming spirit of true brotherhood as is practiced by people of all colors and races here in this Ancient Holy Land, the home of Abraham, Muhammad, and all the other prophets of the Holy Scriptures. For the past week I have been utterly speechless and spellbound by the graciousness I see displayed all around me by people of *all colors*.[13]

As a member of the Nation of Islam, Malcom X had, on occasion, made comments about white Americans and white people in general, which led to his being labeled a "black supremacist." But those who were so eager to condemn him failed to understand the context in which such statements were made and failed to acknowledge the changes in his position which had taken place. For them, he continued to be a black supremacist and a fanatic. For example, well after he had made the preceding statements, Carl Rowan, a black man who was director of the United States Information Agency, was irritated by the amount of publicity Malcolm X's death was receiving throughout the world. He referred to Malcolm X as "an ex-convict, ex-dope peddler who became a racial fanatic."[14]

During the 11 years that Malcolm X was the most influential spokesman for the Nation of Islam, he frequently condemned all white people, referring to them as "devils." But he always prefaced his remarks with the phrase, "The Honorable Elijah Muhammad teaches us that...." And once out of the Nation of Islam he was careful to repudiate these teachings and to speak for himself.

Because he was a black nationalist, Malcolm X believed strongly in black autonomy. He was not opposed to whites joining the struggle if they sincerely supported black liberation, but he maintained that they should work through organizations in their own communities, because the racism of American whites was responsible for the oppression of blacks. His advice to whites who asked what they could do was, "Work in conjunction with us–each of us working among our own kind." This position was indeed logical, because the racism of which Malcolm X is so often accused is endemic to the white community.

The charge that Malcolm X advocated violence is bizarre, especially when it is made by those who are themselves the greatest purveyors and advocates of violence in history. Furthermore, it was made during the height of the civil rights movement, when antiblack violence was rampant but when it was expected that Afro-Americans would remain nonviolent. In all his public speeches and writings Malcolm X never advocated the initiation of violence by blacks, but he was a strong proponent of black self-defense. In his autobiography he wrote:

They call me "the angriest Negro in America." I wouldn't deny that charge. I spoke exactly as I felt.... They called me "a teacher, a fomentor of violence." I would say point blank, "That is a lie. I am not for wanton violence, I'm for justice. I feel that if white people were attacked by Negroes–if the forces of law proved unable, or inadequate, or reluctant to protect those whites from those Negroes–then those white people should protect and defend themselves from those Negroes, using arms if necessary. And I feel that when the law fails to protect Negroes from whites' attack, then those Negroes should use arms, if necessary, to defend themselves."[15]

Since virtually all of his speeches have now been published, the record is clear: although he was not an exponent of nonviolence Malcolm X advocated self-defense for blacks, but never did he encourage the initiation of violence, for he was aware that if blacks initiated violence, the forces in the society responsible for maintaining law and order would very likely embark on a campaign of genocide. The extermination of American Indians and Indochinese was ever present in his thinking, and he did not want to see Afro-Americans meet the same fate.

After he left the Nation of Islam, Malcolm X founded the Muslim Mosque, Incorporated, as a religious organization to serve the function of a spiritual force to rid the black community of the many vices which plagued it. Although he was an orthodox Muslim, he recognized that many Afro-Americans were not serious about religion and organized the mosque in such a way as to attract participation from a wide spectrum in the black community, especially the youth. The Muslim Mosque, Incorporated permitted blacks, regardless of their religious beliefs or lack of them, to participate in black nationalist economic, political, and social programs.

Shortly after announcing the formation of the Muslim Mosque, Incorporated, Malcolm X embarked upon a series of public speeches through which he formulated the philosophy of the new religious organization. He declared that the Muslim religion would be kept within the mosque, and after the religious services were over, the worshippers would become involved in community action—economic, civic, political, and social. He declared his intention to cooperate with other religions and civil rights organizations in an effort to achieve black unity.

Several months after the formation of the Muslim Mosque, Incorporated, Malcolm X announced the formation of the Organization of Afro-American Unity, a secular organization which he hoped would be flexible enough in its ideology and philosophy to attract a broad-based following among the less religious members of the black community. His dream, like that of Garvey, was to organize the 100 million Afro-Americans in the Western Hemisphere and unite them with the 300 million Africans. In so doing he hoped to project the cause of black liberation onto the international level and elevate the black struggle in the United States from one of civil rights to one of human rights.

The OAAU was patterned after the Organization of African Unity, established in Addis Ababa, Ethiopia, in May 1963. The "Statement of Basic Aims and Objectives" of the OAAU declared: "*Inspired* by a common determination to promote understanding among our people and cooperation in all matters pertaining to survival and advancement, we will support the aspirations of our people for brotherhood and solidarity in a larger unit transcending all organizational differences." Further, this statement declared that the organization was "*dedicated* to the unification of all people of African descent in this hemisphere and to the utilization of that unity to bring into being the organizational structure that [would] project the black people's contributions to the world."[16] The OAAU's goal was freedom from oppression. Its initial statement dealt with black control of education, economics, politics, and culture in the black community, and with self-defense. Above all, its major theme was unity among Afro-Americans. It pledged to "join hands and hearts with all people of African origin in a grand alliance by forgetting all the differences that the power structure has created to keep us divided and enslaved."

In an effort to demonstrate his concern for unity among Afro-Americans, Malcolm X, who had earlier expressed contempt for Martin Luther King, Jr.'s philosophy of nonviolence, came to King's defense when he saw on a television news broadcast that King had been knocked to the ground in one of his campaigns in Alabama early in 1965. It had been reported that the members of the American Nazi party were responsible for the act. Malcolm X dispatched a telegram to the group's leader, George Lincoln Rockwell, in which he threatened "maximum physical retaliation" if physical harm should be inflicted on King or other blacks attempting to exercise their civil rights. For his proposed alliance with all black organizations, he was accused by some of the more militant nationalists as having abandoned his black nationalist ideological position. Such a charge was baseless, because his primary concern was black unity, a theme he stressed throughout his lifetime.

Insofar as his ideology applied internationally, there is some evidence that Malcolm X was not only a Pan-Africanist, but also was moving toward a Third World socialist perspective.[17] He did not believe that Afro-Americans could be liberated as long as capitalism and its endemic exploitation persisted. In this sense, then, Malcolm X might be considered a revolutionary nationalist. But his first order of business after founding the OAAU was to internationalize the stuggle of Afro-Americans in the United States through a petition to the United Nations, charging genocide against 22 million black Americans. As ultimately outlined the petition charged the government of the United States with economic genocide, mental harm, murder, conspiracy, and complicity to commit genocide.[18] The petition declared that in its treatment of Afro-Americans, the U.S. government had violated not only its own Constitution, but also the Charter of the United Nations, the Universal Declaration of Human Rights, and the 1948 Draft Convention on the Prevention and Punishment of the Crime of Genocide.

While traveling through Africa and the Middle East, Malcolm X elicited the support of the leaders of many nations in his drive to place the case of Afro-American oppression before the United Nations. In addition, he represented the OAAU as an observer at the second conference of the Organization of African Unity in Cairo in July 1964. To the heads of state attending this conference, he submitted an eight-page memorandum in which he outlined the conditions under which blacks are forced to live in the United States and appealed for their support in bringing the petition before the United Nations. In the memorandum he declared that the human rights of Afro-Americans were violated daily. "It is not a problem of civil rights but a problem of human rights." He continued, "If South Africa is guilty of violating the human rights of Africans here on the mother continent, then America is guilty of worse violations of the 22 million Africans on the American continent." After a discussion of the U.S. government's violation of and failure to enforce its laws relative to blacks, he appealed to the conference leaders for their support: "We beseech the independent African states to help us bring our problem before the United Nations, on the grounds that the United States government is morally incapable of protecting the lives and the property of 22 million African-Americans. And on the grounds that our deteriorating plight is definitely becoming a threat to world peace." He concluded, "In the interests of world peace and security, we beseech the heads of the independent African states to recommend an immediate investigation of our problem by the United Nations Commission on Human Rights."[19]

The conference passed a resolution acknowledging that the U.S. Congress had just passed a civil rights bill, but it condemned the racism existing in the United States, and declared that the Organization of African Unity was "deeply disturbed" about the continued oppression of people of African descent. In additon, several of the leaders present agreed to support the petition of the OAAU in the United Nations. Needless to say, U.S. officials were distressed by the efforts of Malcolm X to bring the case of Afro-Americans before the United Nations.

Though the petition did not come before the United Nations in 1964 because of other organizational matters, the members of that organization debated the question of the Congo, during which several heads of African states condemned U.S. racial policies at home and abroad. The U.S. representatives maintained, as usual, that the treatment of blacks in the United States was a domestic issue and should not be debated in the United Nations.

Before the next session of the United Nations convened, Malcolm X had been assassinated. The opinion that his assassination resulted from his efforts to bring the case of black Americans before the United Nations is widely held by Afro-Americans. It is beyond the scope of the present work to attempt to posit blame for the assassination of Malcolm X. Theories abound: some maintain that the assassination was ordered by the Nation of Islam; others maintain that the U.S. Central Intelligence Agency was responsible; still others attribute his death to an internal dispute among his own followers; and finally, there are those who maintain that it was the work of self-appointed assassin(s).[20] Regardless of who was responsible, three black men were ultimately convicted of the murder in a jury trial.

The assassination of Malcolm X came at a time when he was developing the ideological position he thought would best serve the cause of black liberation. His death occurred less than one year after the founding of the OAAU, thereby precluding the possibility of that organization's development into a vehicle with which the masses of black people could identify.

It is impossible to ascertain how far Malcolm X's depth of understanding, fierce opposition to oppression, keen intellectual powers, and charisma would have taken him. There are those who maintain that had he lived, Malcolm X would have become the most important black leader in American history.

Malcolm X was a complicated man, and in spite of his many gifts, there remain many inexplicable aspects of his actions. Perhaps the most perplexing is his insistence on condemning the Nation of Islam and its spiritual leader, while at the same time proclaiming a rapprochement with all black groups and leaders. During the last year of his life, Malcom X persisted in making serious charges against the Nation of Islam and its leader in the media. These charges often reached a level out of character for one in his position and with the ideas he proclaimed. To many these had a ring of "sour grapes" after his break with the Nation of Islam. In addition, he repeatedly predicted that he would be murdered on the orders of Elijah Muhammad. There is some evidence that he intended to make peace with the Nation of Islam at the meeting at which he was assassinated. For example, he told Alex Haley:

I'm going to tell you something brother–the more I keep thinking about this thing, the things [threats on his life] that have been happening lately, I'm not at all sure it's the Muslims. I know what they can do, and what they can't, and they can't do some of the stuff recently going on. Now I'm going to tell you, the more I keep thinking about what happened to me in France, I think I'm going to quit saying it's the Muslims.[21]

The incident in France to which Malcom X referred occurred early in 1965. He was barred, without explanation, from entering the country to give a scheduled speech before a Congress of African Students. It was his opinion that the incident resulted from high-level cooperation between the French and U.S. governments and probably the Central Intelligence Agency.

Before he was assassinated in 1965, Malcolm X had won admiration and respect from large segments of the black community, especially the youth. Since his death he has earned a lasting place among Afro-Americans as a black nationalist leader. Even the more conservative black leaders recognize that his influence was such that government officials at all levels were forced to negotiate out of fear that Malcolm X would exert too much of a radical impact on the black masses. In this respect, Malcolm X set the stage for greater political consciousness in the black community. More than any other individual, he changed the direction of the black movement from an emphasis on assimilation through integration to black liberation through black nationalism.

Shortly before his death, Malcolm X admitted that his life had been "chronology of *changes*."[22] His concern for the problems of Afro-Americans and Africans spread to the Third World in general and toward a type of revolutionary international socialism, a position which prompted many of his supporters to suggest that he had virtually abandoned black nationalism. For example, he was strongly anticapitalist. In an interview in 1965 he said, "it is impossible for capitalism to survive, primarily because the system of capitalism needs some blood to suck. Capitalism used to be like an eagle, but now it's more like a vulture. . . . As the nations of the world free themselves, then capitalism has less victims, less to suck, and it becomes weaker and weaker. It's only a matter of time in my opinion before it will collapse completely."[23]

George Breitman concludes that Malcolm X was "a revolutionary internationalist on the way to becoming a liberator of his people."[24] Yet he maintained a strong black nationalist ideology. The statement of aims and objectives of the OAAU does not include the concept "black nationalism," but in the areas of self-defense, education, politics, economics, and culture, it is clear from this statement that his ideological position was that of black nationalism.

On the question of repatriation of Afro-Americans to Africa, he declared in December 1964, that "this is what I mean by a migration or going back to Africa—going back in the sense that we reach out to them and they reach out to us. Our mutual understanding and our mutual effort toward a mutual objective will bring benefit to the African as to the Afro-American. But you will never get it relying on Uncle Sam alone. You are looking in the wrong direction."[25] Consequently, more than emigrationism, he advocated international solidarity of peoples of African descent, with Afro-Americans controlling the institutions in the black community.

At least one writer maintains that the appeal of Malcolm X among Afro-Americans resulted from "his racism, his celebration of blackness, his promise of vengeance."[26] But he possessed many other qualities which account for his exalted position in the black liberation movement: intelligence, incorruptibility, ability to synthesize ideas, selflessness. Most of all Malcolm X was totally dedicated to the liberation of Afro-Americans. As Ossie Davis said in the eulogy delivered at his funeral: "Malcolm was our manhood, our living, black manhood! This was his meaning to his people. And in honoring him, we honor the best in ourselves."[27]

Since his death Malcolm X has attained the status of patron saint of the black nationalist movement, regardless of the many ideological differences. His autobiography has become a standard work in Afro-American studies programs throughout the country, and his theories, though they represent more a synthesis of other thinkers than original ideas, are studied in courses on black social thought. Many memorials bear his name: educational institutions such as Malcolm X College in Chicago, public schools, parks, and streets. His autobiography has been made into a major movie; recordings of his speeches have been widely disseminated; his memory is honored in the hundreds of books and articles written about him or dedicated to him. Each year thousands of people honor the memory of Malcolm X by making a pilgrimage on the anniversary of his birth to Ferncliff Cemetery in Hartsdale, New York, where he is buried. Others quietly pay tribute to him by remaining at home instead of working or going to school. The work of the OAAU is carried forth by the sister of Malcolm X, Ella Collins, and the organization presents annual awards in his honor. Many black nationalist groups, including organizations of black servicemen, bear his name. And a group made up primarily of Asians, called "Chickens Come Home to Roost," honors his memory. Similar groups exist throughout many parts of Africa and the Caribbean.

5

The impact
of contemporary nationalism
on the black community

Expressions of unity and solidarity by a people in their struggle for
self-determination are fundamental components of nationalism.
Obviously such expressions assume different forms, depending
upon a variety of circumstances. In the case of people of African
descent in the United States, these expressions have varied widely
over a period of more than four centuries. The extraordinary
degree of unity prevailing in the contemporary black community,
while unique in many ways, nonetheless stems from a history of
more than 400 years of struggle (see Chapter 2).

It is perhaps in the period of the 1960s and 1970s, however,
that nationalism, manifested in the form of unity and black solidarity, has made its greatest impact on the black community. While
there is no single organization comparable in size and scope to
Marcus Garvey's Universal Negro Improvement Association,
which reached its peak membership and influence in the 1920s,
elements of black nationalism have penetrated the entire black
community; few families or individuals have escaped its influence.
Furthermore, expressions of black nationalism cut across age,
educational, and regional lines.

Because of the dearth of empirical evidence on individual
expressions of nationalism in the black community, the concern
here is primarily with the impact of collective manifestations,
although it is not limited to those. Even within this limited scope,
the propositions put forth are largely speculative, and it is frequently difficult to distinguish between those groups I have
loosely defined as nationalist and those that are essentially integrationist in approach. Therefore, I have limited the discussion to
those groups that expressly promote black unity and solidarity.

In addition to the proliferation of local, national, and international black nationalist organizations, ranging anywhere from the Black Liberators of St. Louis, to the Nation of Islam, to the Congress of African Peoples, collective expressions of black nationalism are found throughout U.S. society on a wider scale than in any previous period of a long and difficult history. These activities cover all aspects of Afro-American life and culture in the United States. Black nationalist organizations and caucuses are found among high school and college students, in prisons, and in the military; among artists, politicians, and scholars; and in virtually all professional and lay organizations that have black members. Some of these groups, such as the National Medical Association, which was founded in 1895, have long histories and have attempted to reflect the increasing nationalist sentiment among Afro-American people. Others, such as the Black Academy of Arts and Letters, which was formed in 1969, are recent in origin and resulted from this mood of nationalism. In order to illustrate the impact of such groups, I have selected five areas for brief discussion: the arts, law enforcement, the military, the professions, and politics. In each of these areas one is able to witness the growing solidarity of Afro-American peoples in the United States.

The arts

It is in the arts, especially creative writing, the theater, and music, that the contributions of black people have perhaps been most notable and innovative, and at the same time least recognized and rewarded in the larger society. At the present time blacks in these areas are having a significant impact on the consciousness of the black community. They are in the forefront of the movement to create self-awareness, self-respect, and self-direction. As Marcus Garvey said half a century ago, "Action, self-reliance, the vision of self and the future have been the only means by which the oppressed have seen and realized the light of freedom."[1]

One of the major difficulties black artists have faced in the United States is that artistic standards historically have been set by the larger white society and these most often have been antithetical to the experience of black people.[2] At the same time many black artists have adopted the standards set by the larger society, especially the norm which holds that art must somehow be separate from politics. That is, art should not be used an as ideological weapon to raise the consciousness of a people in their pursuit of liberation. Historically, even in Western culture, there has not been a consistent clearcut dichotomy between art and protest.

Recent experiences in China, Cuba, North Vietnam, and other revolutionary Third World countries have demonstrated that art can serve as a powerful weapon in the liberation of the oppressed.

Within the last decade there has been a vigorous effort on the part of black artist, especially those loosely identified as cultural nationalists, to redefine black art and reshape the thinking of black people. In so doing there has been a rejection of white American standards. In the foreword to his novel *The Cotillion*, John Killens reflects this mood when he announces that the book does not fit the conventional criteria of a novel, although he is aware of these norms. He writes that he "got all screwed up with angles of narration, points of view, objectivity, universality, composition, author-intrusion, sentence structure, syntax, first person, second person. I said to hell with all that!"[3]

In much the same way other black artists have rejected conventional white artistic standards in their attempt to create political consciousness among black people. This is not a new development; examples can be found in black art generations and even centuries ago. It is the present period, however, in which the ideology of black nationalism has had its greatest impact on black artists. Younger black creative writers today, unlike many of their predecessors, are writing specifically for the black community. And if the opening of black bookstores and the sale of books directed toward the black community are indications of success, black people are reading the works of black authors to a greater extent than ever before. For example, three volumes of poetry by Don Lee, *Black Pride, Think Black!* and *Don't Cry, Scream*, had sold more than 80,000 copies early in 1970.[4] Most of the major black communities now contain at least one bookstore specializing in books by and about blacks, and in the last few years at least 15 new black publishing houses have been established to meet the growing needs of black writers and readers.[5] Black studies programs in colleges and universities no doubt account for much of the success of books by young black writers, but increasingly these books are read by rank-and-file members of the black community.

Black playwrights, like black novelists and poets, are rejecting not only the content of traditional American theater, but also its form. In so doing they are using one of the oldest educational institutions, the theater, as a vehicle for promoting self-awareness, self-respect, and self-direction. Throughout American history the image of black people presented in the theater has been controlled by whites, and the result has been that the world, including the black community, has received a distorted view of the lives and aspirations of black people. The dominant ethos among contemporary black playwrights, directors, and producers is that black theater must not only entertain black people, it must educate them.

Within the last few years black theater groups have emerged in cities and towns throughout the country. Some of these emphasize works which are clearly revolutionary in approach, but even the more conventional groups, such as the Free Southern Theater, emphasize black pride and black unity. One of the most inovative of black theater groups is the National Black Theater. Its founder-director, Barbara Ann Teer, defines its purpose as the creation of an alternative system of values for the black community. "Ours is to open up, liberate, regain, and reclaim our spiritual freedom," she said in an interview. "If we are successful, people watching will feel this."[6] Actors in the National Black Theater are called "liberators." Before they can become members of the group, they are required to study black culture, black economics, and black politics.[7] Each performance is a combination of music, drama, and the dance, adapted from life in the black community, particularly from religious services.

Such groups as the National Black Theater, the New Lafayette Theater, and the Afro-American Studio for Acting and Speech in Harlem; the Black Arts theaters in Washington and Milwaukee; the Performing Arts Society of Los Angeles; and the Arena Players in Baltimore have demonstrated that when the theater speaks to black people, audiences can be attracted and performances sustained.

Inasmuch as the new black theater addresses itself to the black community and rejects conventional white norms, white reviewers frequently find it impossible to understand what is presented. For example, in reviewing Imamu Amiri Baraka's *Slave Ship*, Clive Barnes of the *New York Times* had this to say: "This is a propaganda play. It is a black militant play. It is a racist play. It purports to counsel black revolution. Its attitudes are ugly and prejudiced, and its ... total condemnation of the white American is as sick as a Ku Klux Klanner at a rally."[8] And in the pages of *Commentary*, George Dennison wrote of Baraka's plays: "I would like to identify these plays, especially *The Slave*, as part of the rot of America, particularly the racist rot that flickers back and forth, north and south, east and west."[9] Whereas white reviewers respond with anger, black audiences react approvingly, for they understand that a response on the part of blacks to white racism is not necessarily racist.

Aside from American Indian culture, Afro-American music is widely regarded as perhaps the only serious art form indigenous to the United States, and this music has long served as a unifying force in the black community. From the work songs of the early ante-bellum period to the revolutionary new black jazz, music has given substance to the experiences of black people. And it is through music that the essence of black life in the United States is revealed.[10]

The nationalist element in black music is not new; Duke Ellington's compositions "Black Beauty" and "For My People" reflect the sentiment of race pride, as do the earlier religious songs "Before I'd Be A Slave" and "Let My People Go." But it is in the new black music that black nationalism has found its clearest expression. Black music, like all other elements of black popular culture, has historically been controlled by whites, but many of the younger musicians are committed nationalists and have joined with others in producing records controlled and distributed by the artists themselves.[11] In addition to controlling their music, many of these musicians make themselves available for benefits in support of radical black organizations and black candidates for political office. Furthermore, others have formed organizations to provide financial support for young musicians so that they will not have to depend on white foundations and city and state art commissions for their survival. The African Jazz Arts Society and Studio in New York and the Afro-Arts organization in Chicago are representative of this trend.

Black musicians today, more than in any previous period, are sharing a sense of community with their fellow blacks and are attempting to unify the black community in its pursuit of self-determination. Because they realize that the arts alone cannot replace politics and economics, they demonstrate their political commitment by activities in the community as well as in their music.

As a means of giving recognition to black artists and scholars, the Black Academy of Arts and Letters was formed in 1969. In the first years of its existence the Academy has honored many blacks, including those who for political reasons have been denied recognition commensurate with their contributions by the larger society. These include Imamu Baraka, W.E.B. DuBois, Paul Robeson, and George Jackson. The members of the academy appear to be saying to the society as a whole that black people will no longer permit white people to be the sole judges of black accomplishments in the arts and letters.

Law enforcement

In a society which has created and thrived on institutions fostering conflict between individuals and groups, the law enforcement official is necessarily subjected to stresses and strains. Far more than his white counterpart, the black policeman, because of his blackness, has historically been trapped in a network of contradictions that seemingly defy resolution.[12] Within the past decade, however, black policemen around the country have attempted to reconcile some of their role conflicts through organizing themselves into black nationalist groups within police departments.

Nationally there are approximately 30,000 black policemen, or 7 percent of the total 420,000 policemen in the United States. In every major city they are vastly underrepresented proportionately when compared with the black population in urban areas. For example, the proportion of black policemen varies anywhere from 36 percent in Washington, where blacks comprise 71 percent of the population, to 2 percent in both Birmingham and Dallas, where blacks make up 42 percent and 25 percent of the population respectively.[13] And, although blacks are overwhelmingly an urban people and are generally forced to live in conditions which are said to breed conventional crime, their communities are guarded by police who are insensitive to their needs and prejudiced against them. Indeed, the National Advisory Commission on Civil Disorders reports that of all the grievances expressed by blacks in a survey conducted in 1967, police brutality ranked highest, surpassing unemployment, substandard housing, and inadequate education.[14]

This is not the place to discuss the role of the white policeman as a member of the army of occupation in the black community or the traditional function of the black policeman as a mercenary in a colonial situation. The relevant point here is that in recent years black nationalism has had its effect on the consciousness of the black policeman and that he sees himself as a black man first and a policeman second. This development has had far-reaching consequences for the black community and for the society as a whole. There are two national organizations of black policemen in the United States, the National Council of Police Societies, founded in 1960, and the National Society of Afro-American Policemen, founded in 1964. These organizations have chapters in major cities throughout the country, and in cities where the number of blacks on the police force is too small for a formal organization, black policemen organize themselves around specific issues. For example, in Omaha when a white policeman killed a 14-year-old black girl, the white policemen started a defense fund for the officer, and the black policemen started a fund to assist the girl's family.[15] Although the National Council of Police Societies is a somehat more conservative organization than the National Society of Afro-American Policemen, the rapid growth of the latter has forced the former into a more radical position. For example, at its 1970 convention the National Council adopted several resolutions, including one which stated, "We urge that police departments rapidly acquire nonlethal weapons such as the tranquilizing instruments developed at the Carnegie-Mellon University in Pittsburgh. Such weapons are now used by animal handlers in national parks and zoos, indicating that the nation considers animals more important then some human beings."[16] They also agreed to prevent the killing of blacks by white policemen even if it meant arresting them.

The growing black nationalism of policemen results from many factors. Perhpas the most important is the spread of black pride and black solidarity throughout the society. The new black policemen wear Afro haircuts and greet each other as "brother." Furthermore, they identify with and frequently reside in the communities they serve. As the pledge of the National Society of Afro-American Policemen reads: "We will no longer permit ourselves to be relegated to the role of brutal pawns in a chess game affecting the communities in which we serve. We are husbands, fathers, brothers, neighbors, and members of the black community. Donning the blue uniform has not changed this."[17] Increasing numbers of young blacks are entering police departments. Most often they come from slum communities, where they have either been the victims of police brutality by white officers or have at least witnessed such acts. Upon entering police work they find that such practices have not ceased; rather, they appear to have accelerated with increasing black militancy. For example, although no accurate statistics are available, the number of black youths killed by white policemen outside the South has steadily increased in the last decade. And milder forms of brutality are also on the increase. The younger black policemen respond to these incidents differently then those who preceded them. Recently a black policeman in Chicago removed his gunbelt and told a white policeman, "I'm going to beat your brains out." He was angry because he had witnessed a white policeman club a black youth to the ground without provocation as he hauled him from a paddy wagon. Three other black policemen moved in and separated them.[18] Incidents such as this are commonplace in police departments around the country.

Furthermore, concurrent with the spread of nationalism among blacks, there has been an increase in antiblack, right-wing conservatism among white policemen. They have supported conservative political candidates such as Barry Goldwater and George Wallace. In 1968 the president of the Fraternal Order of Police, the largest organization of policemen in the country, with 90,000 members and affiliates in more than 900 communities, publicly endorsed George Wallace for President.[19] Black policemen are forced to use locker rooms with antiblack racial slurs on the walls, and frequently white police unions use dues from black members to lobby against legislation designed to assist black people, such as open housing bills and bills to create civilian review boards. In addition, the antiblack prejudice of white policemen is translated into discriminatory practices within police departments.

Not all black policemen are members of nationalist police organizations, but their numbers are increasing rapidly, especially in large cities. In New York City, 75 percent of all the black policemen are members of the Society of Afro-American Policemen; in Chicago 50 percent of all black policemen are members of the Afro-American Patrolmen's League; and in San Francisco all black police officers are members of the Officers for Justice. The rapidity with which the movement is spreading is especially disturbing to white policemen; they are no longer free to commit brazen acts of brutality against blacks without feeling the wrath of militant black policemen who are no longer blindly loyal to the forces responsible for the oppression of black people.

Virtually all big city police departments have become racially polarized as a result of the growth of Afro-American police organizations. Chicago, a city long noted for maintaining "law and order," is a case in point. It is the city where in 1968 the long-term mayor issued orders to policemen to "shoot to maim looters, shoot to kill arsonists." It is also on the most rigidly segregated cities in the country, and one which has historically experienced widespread racial violence. In 1968 a young black policeman with an outstanding four-year record of service, including an efficiency rating of 97 percent and 50 departmental citations for outstanding work, organized the Afro-American Patrolmen's League. In its charter the league resolved "that the black community and the black police officers will be mutually supportive of efforts to bring about a new community where unity of purpose and recognition of the nobility of the black heritage will be a deterrent to crime;

where moral authority imposed from within will govern human relationships rather than technical legalism; and where those of us who are black will be able to live lives of beautiful fulfillment."

After several months membership in the Afro-American Patrolmen's League increased substantially, and resentment from white policemen at all levels was strong. The Chicago's Fraternal Order of Police, a white-dominated police union noted for its support of "stop and frisk" laws and the Mayor's "shoot to kill or maim" orders, was one of its strongest opponents. The organizer of the league was suddenly suspended, the lives of his children were threatened, white policemen refused to serve with members of the league, and throughout the city there were fistfights between black and white policemen. Nevertheless, the members of the League pressed their campaign against police brutality. They petitioned for the establishment of an independent, nonpolice agency to investigate complaints against the police, and they proposed that there be greater civilian involvement in all levels of police work. They also embarked on a series of community services—legal aid, free investigation of charges of police brutality, and general advice to blacks on police-related questions.

Within the brief time of its existence Chicago's Afro-American Patrolmen's League has had a positive impact, not only on the consciousness of black policemen, but on the black community as a whole. Membership in the league has increased, and mutual trust and respect between the police and members of the black community are in greater evidence than at any previous time. What has happened among Chicago's black policemen has been repeated in cities throughout the country.

The military

Increasing solidarity among blacks has had its impact on the military, and as in police departments, the armed services have become racially polarized. Although the military services have technically been integrated since 1948, statistics show that blacks have not reached parity with whites. By the end of 1970, when blacks made up 11.2 percent of the total population, they accounted for 9.3 percent of all servicemen. Within the armed forces, however, whereas black enlisted men were 13.6 percent of all enlisted men, black officers accounted for only 2.1 percent of the total number of officers. Furthermore, blacks accounted for 10 percent of all troops in Southeast Asia, and 12.7 percent of all military fatalities in Vietnam.[20] Prior to 1970 the casualty rate among blacks was even higher. For example, between 1961 and 1966, blacks accounted for 16 percent of all servicemen killed in action in Southeast Asia, but constituted only 10.6 percent of troops there.[21]

Once blacks enter the armed forces, they face a series of acts of discrimination on and off military installations in the United States and abroad. And like their civilian counterparts, they have formed black nationalist groups in order to express their anger and to improve their lot. The names of some of these organizations are indicative of the problems black servicemen face: the Black Action Group, the Black Defense Group, the Black United Soldiers, Blacks in Action, the Malcolm X Association, and the Unsatisfied Black Soldier.

Since World War I black men have been sent abroad to fight in wars aimed a preserving America's position of economic dominance in the world. During each of these many wars blacks have been expected to close ranks in support of the war effort and delay appeals for justice until the end of the war. Only then would they have their grievances redressed. Predictably, at the end of each war the nation maintained business as usual, that is, white supremacy. The war of aggression in Southeast Asia, however, has had a different impact on the black community than previous wars, coming as it did at a time when the civil rights movement was being transformed into the black liberation movement. Furthermore, because of the increased political consciousness of black people, the issues involved in this cruel and barbaric war were clear. That black people should be expected to march off without resistance to fight fellow Third World people for the benefit of the ruling class indicates once more the insatiable arrogance of white America.

The younger blacks in the armed forces are no longer willing to prove that they can be as efficient about killing those defined by the State Department as the "enemy" as their white counterparts. Many of them are veterans of uprisings in such places as Los Angeles, Newark, and Detroit. The general propagation of nationalist ideology in the black community has endowed them with pride in blackness and strong feelings of black solidarity. Throughout the United States, Asia, and Europe this development has led to racial conflicts, some resulting in deaths. A survey of American servicemen in Vietnam indicates that on a wide variety of issues black servicemen hold different attitudes from their white counterparts.[22] A large majority of those questioned said they had no business fighting in Southeast Asia; nearly half (45 percent) expressed a willingness to take up arms at home to secure justice; and only 14 percent said they would follow orders without reservation to put down black rebellions at home.

In West Germany, where black servicemen are especially well organized, incidents of racial friction resulting from highly publicized incidents of black oppression in the United States and from discrimination in the military and by tavern owners and landlords, occur almost daily.[23] After several race riots in 1970 the Department of Defense dispatched a race-relations team to investigate. Upon their arrival members of this team invited officials of the Black Action Group, the Black United Soldiers, and the Unsatisfied Black Soldier to meet with them. The meeting was boycotted because the soldiers felt that it was an insult and a waste of money inasmuch as the problems they face in Germany are well-known.[24] Instead, the black groups organized a "Call for Justice" rally at Heidelberg University, which was attended by 1,000 black servicemen.

Many black servicemen in Germany are affiliated with the Black Panther party, and several of them have defied military orders and have joined German youths in marches in support of Angela Davis. White servicemen have responded by establishing chapters of the Ku Klux Klan, and several cross-burning incidents have been recorded. A 19-year-old black soldier who is the leader of one of the black nationalist groups summed up what appears to be the mood among blacks in Germany when he said, "We think now, we read. We think and we think black. We live here just to go back to the world and fight for ourselves and our people."[25]

In South Vietnam friction between the black activist servicemen and their white counterparts was also widespread. For example, at a military stockade in Longbinh in 1968, some 200 black inmates went on a rampage that left one white inmate dead, many more injured, and the stockade wrecked.[26] Early in 1970 a military survey defined the extent of racial polarization and friction in South Vietnam as a " 'most serious and dangerous trend,' as reflected in the number of cases in which mobs of blacks had attacked white military police."[27]

South Korea and Okinawa have not been free from racial friction resulting from increasing consciousness among black troops. Black soldiers stationed in South Korea rebelled after several of them were arbitratily denied passes by officers. They burned five buildings housing officers' quarters to the ground, causing an estimated $50,000 in damages.[28] In Kosa, Okinawa, black soldiers have responded to off-base discrimination by refusing to permit white soldiers to enter bars they frequent.[29] In addition to rebelling against discrimination on and off military installations in Asia, black soldiers have expressed racial solidarity by establishing drug treatment clinics for black addicts.[30]

The Department of Defense appears to be more tolerant of black nationalism in the military abroad than at home. However, each branch of the armed forces–Air Force, Army, Marines, and Navy–has had to contend with increasingly militant young black servicemen at home. There have been attempts to curb both individual and collective manifestations of black nationalism. Black servicemen have received jail sentences for wearing their hair "natural,"[31] and when black airmen attempted to form an organization in 1970 for the purpose of promoting cultural awareness, they were forced to meet off the installation.[32] As early as 1968 a group of 43 black soldiers refused orders to go to Chicago as part of the force assigned to guard the Democratic National Convention, for fear that they would be used to supress Chicago's blacks.

Although military spokesmen contend that blacks are less likely to face discrimination in the armed forces than in civilian life, racial polarization and friction are constant reminders that the armed services face the same problems as the society at large. In the military, as in police departments, black nationalist groups are made up mainly of younger men, and their actions are viewed with skepticism by those who are older and who are career military personnel. The older career serviceman or policeman is more likely to be individually oriented, whereas the younger tends toward collective orientation. At Camp Lejeune, North Carolina, a black marine staff sergeant who had completed 18 years in the Marine Corps complained to a newspaper reporter that he could not "go along with the 'new brother' stuff." He said, "I don't understand it. When I came into the corps 18 years ago, all the colored marines wanted was a chance to prove ourselves as marines–green marines. Now some of these Negro youngsters are saying that they want to be black first and marines second–it can't be done."[33] This marine was referring to a situation in which a black marine had been courtmartialed when he refused to serve as a sergeant upon his return from Vietnam because of the continued oppression of black people. Many of the younger marines formed a committee, so that the officials would be forced to confront them collectively rather than individually.

In the fall of 1972, the U.S. Navy, the branch of the armed forces which has historically been the most intransigent in its antiblack racial policies, found itself experiencing difficulty with black sailors on an unprecedented scale. On two of the largest aircraft carriers, the *Kitty Hawk* and the *Constellation*, black sailors revolted against the inferior treatment they received, and in the case of the *Constellation* the Navy experienced its first full-scale mutiny in history.[34] The *Kitty Hawk* incident occurred on October 12, while the ship was en route to Vietnam from the Philippines. A Marine riot squad, armed with tear gas, was called in because of friction between black and white sailors, and with its intervention, a six-hour riot erupted between black and white sailors and left 50 persons injured, 44 of them white. Twenty-eight sailors were arrested, all but one of them black.

The incident aboard the *Constellation*, which was nearly two months in the making, occurred off the coast of San Diego, California. It reached its peak on November 3, when about 80 black sailors (there were no black officers aboard) engaged in a sit-down strike to protest such discriminatory practices as differential shipboard discipline and work assignments and refused an order to return to work. When the carrier reached San Diego, on an unscheduled return caused by the incident, 130 sailors were put ashore. When ordered to return, 120 of them defied the order, for as one of their spokesmen put it, "We fear for our lives unless these matters are settled on shore." They were charged with being absent without leave and other minor infractions, because Navy officials refused to admit that they had indeed experienced a mutiny.

Although the Navy attributes the difficulties with black sailors on the *Kitty Hawk* and the *Constellation* to lowered educational and character qualifications, initiated in an effort to recruit additional personnel from minority groups, the black sailors complained of persistent discrimination: more stringent punishment than white sailors for comparable infractions, inferior work assignments, and other practices. The Navy has had a long history of discrimination against blacks, both in assignments and in its recruitment practices. For example, by its own admission blacks accounted for 5.8 percent of its enlisted men in 1972, but only 0.7 percent of its officers were black. Several official inquiries have supported the charges made by the black sailors, but Navy officials have denied them, maintaining that its equal opportunity policy has been effective and that such incidents have resulted from increased "permissiveness" in the Navy.

Since the structure of the armed forces is somewhat more authoritarian than that of the society as a whole, military officials have attempted to contain expressions of nationalism by young black servicemen through disciplinary acts. Black servicemen are somehow expected to forget the oppression they faced for the first 18 years of their lives and become transformed into "good troops." But for most, if not all of them, this is no longer working. They understand that the forces responsible for their status in the larger society are the same ones responsible for their being in the armed forces, and that these forces will have their places designated for them upon their release.

The professions

Inasmuch as black nationalist movements in the United States have historically depended upon the working class for support, it is not surprising to find expressions of black unity and solidarity on a wide scale among police and servicemen. What is atypical about the movement today, however, is that it cuts across class lines. Middle-class blacks have been noted for their attempts to escape from the world of their less fortunate fellow blacks. As E. Franklin Frazier noted, "The black bourgeoisie have shown no interest in the 'liberation' of Negroes except as it affected their own status or acceptance by the white community."[35] The civil rights movement of the 1950s and early 1960s, which developed after the publication of Frazier's study, attracted large numbers of middle-class blacks, because its integrationist thrust posed no serious threat to their status. And while it is no doubt true that at the present time black nationalism has greater appeal to the working class than to the middle class, there is considerable evidence to support the proposition that the black community has a greater sense of oneness than ever before.

Groups which have adopted some elements of black nationalist ideology are found in virtually all the professions. These usually take the form of parallel organizations or black caucuses within larger, predominately white organizations. The National Conference of Black Lawyers, formed in 1969 by black attorneys and law students throughout the country, is one such parallel organization. According to its constitution, the National Conference of Black Lawyers was formed to "make use of legal tools and legal discipline for the advancement of economic, political, educational, and social institutions for black people," among other things. During its short existence this organization has engaged in several projects designed to assist black people, including a challenge in federal court of the binding and gagging of Chairman Bobby Seale of the Black Panther party and a challenge of the jailing and discontinuing indefinitely pretrial hearings in the New York Panther 21 case. This group has also won dismissal of charges against 13 black Cornell University students charged with the occupation of the student union building, and some of its members testified before the Senate Judiciary Committee in opposition to the nomination of Harrold Carswell to the Supreme Court.

One of the major activities of the National Conference is the defense of unpopular black clients. At a time when public officials are engaged in a campaign of repression against black militants, it is crucial that black lawyers expose the nature of these activities and defend the victims. Government officials attempt to maintain the facade of democracy by jailing black leaders, ostensibly on criminal charges, when in fact they are jailed for their political views. Perhaps the best known of such cases in recent years is that of Angela Davis. The National Conference responded to this challenge by selecting a panel of 12 black law professors from 11 different universities to provide advice and counsel to Angela Davis's defense. Since the appointment of law professors to this type of case was unprecedented in this country, large numbers of individuals and organizations characteristically expressed amazement and discomfort at this development. In response to this anxiety, the chairman of the panel publicly announced that "the time is gone forever when middle-class blacks who have certain expertise will sit back and allow our leadership to be destroyed by those who believe that a contrary opinion is a dangerous force. . . . No longer will we stand by and allow our community to be deprived of the best of our brains or our political dissenters. . . . We are saying no, never again, will a black man be persecuted simply because he disagrees with a majority political belief or engages in activities which are not in conformity with majority values."[36]

In a related development, the 130 black judges attending the annual meeting of the National Bar Association in Atlanta in 1971 formed the Judicial Council, the first formal organization of black judges in American history.[37] The purpose of this group is to focus upon problems of "race and class prejudice in administering justice." The Judicial Council elected as its first president Judge George W. Crockett, Jr., of Detroit, who received national attention when he summarily released at the police station 140 of the 142 persons arrested by Detroit policemen in a raid on a church where members of the Republic of New Africa were holding their first anniversary conference. This action was taken because Crockett determined that the constitutional rights of those arrested had been violated.[38] As result of his actions, however, it was necessary for Crockett to be driven to and from his office by police escort for four months, and the Michigan Senate passed two motions of censure against him.

The election of Crockett by his peers was an important expression of confidence in, and solidarity with, a black judge who refused to accommodate to political pressures in protecting the rights of black people. As he said in an interview, "I'm a *black* judge and I never allow myself to forget that fact. If I did, I'd be lost."[39] Throughout the country black judges and lawyers are expressing solidarity with their fellow blacks on a scale never before achieved in American history.

Like their counterparts in law, black physicians are expressing solidarity with their fellow blacks in a variety of ways. The National Medical Association, the oldest black professional organization in the country, announced at its annual meeting in 1971 that it was opposed to all of the national health insurance plans under consideration by Congress and that it would offer its own plan. This action was being taken, the president announced, because the major proposals which had been offered for consideration were primarily concerned with payment of doctors, while the National Medical Association is concerned with the delivery of health care to all people.[40] The group called upon the estimated 6,000 black physicians in the United States to support the Black Congressional Caucus in attempting to change the dominant value system of the society from one emphasizing private profits to one emphasizing social justice. And during the revolt of prison inmates at Attica, the National Medical Association petitioned to participate in the negotiations and to inspect the medical facilities.

Within the last decade black caucuses have been formed in virtually all the professional organizations in the conventional academic disciplines. One such organization is the Caucus of Black Sociologists which was formed in 1968. This caucus represents the approximately 400 practicing black sociologists in the country, and although it was initially concerned with promoting the professional interests of black sociologists, especially in relation to the activities of the American Sociological Association, its objectives and activities are now much broader. One of its functions is the "transmission of relevant sociological knowledge to black communities for their utilization in community development." At the 1969 annual meeting of the American Sociological Association, the black caucus expressed its opposition to the political oppression of the Black Panther party, to the treatment accorded sociologist

Nathan Hare at San Francisco State College, and to the scheduled execution of Ahmed Evans in Cleveland.[41]

Two of the most significant achievements of the Caucus of Black Sociologists to date relate to the contributions of black sociologists and the type of research conducted in the black community. At the 1970 meeting of the American Sociological Association, the black caucus introduced a resolution, which was approved by the voting membership, that the long-standing contributions of W.E.B. DuBois, Charles S. Johnson, and E. Franklin Frazier be recognized by the creation of an award to honor their intellectual traditions and contributions. Such awards have been made to honor white sociologists for some time, but the DuBois-Johnson-Frazier award was first made in 1971. The association also approved a resolution sponsored by the black caucus that sociological research in the black community should be concerned with validating social humanism, liberation, and the legitimacy of oppressed people for self-determination.[42] If implemented, this resolution will reverse a well-established tradition of research geared toward social control and the containment of the black community.

Unlike black sociologists, their counterparts in psychology and social work have established separate black organization. Among other things, members of the Association of Black Psychologists in the San Francisco area provided assistance to the team of defense lawyers in the murder-kidnap-conspiracy trial of Angela Davis in 1972.[43] During the two and a half weeks of jury selection, pairs of these psychologists regularly visited the courtroom, observed the prospective jurors being questioned, and reported their observations to the defense lawyers during recesses and at night. Their major concern was whether, in their professional judgement, prospective jurors were likely to be objective in their appraisal of the evidence presented by the defense and the prosectuion, and whether they appeared to be relatively free of racial prejudice. The prosecution lost its case against Angela Davis. The extent to which the black psychologists aided in her acquittal is not known, but the chief defense attorney feels that their efforts probably succeeded in "minimizing racism and prejudice in juror selections."

The National Association of Black Social Workers, one of the more militant groups of black professionals, has some 50 chapters throughout the country. Some of their accomplishments, in the short history of the organization, include the establishment of family service centers, adoption centers, and day care centers in the black community. In addition, pressure from the group has been responsible for curriculum changes in schools of social work, especially the introduction of courses on black and other minority communities. At its fourth annual meeting in April 1972, the National Association of Black Social Workers became embroiled in a controversy which reached national attention when it adopted a resolution opposing transracial adoptions, declaring that its members were "in vehement opposition to the practice of placing black children with white families."[44] Such adoptions are seen as a growing threat to the preservation of the black family, and since there are not enough eligible black families to give homes to all the black children available for adoption, the association recommended single and grandparent adoptions and special recruitment programs for black adoptive and foster families, with financial subsidies provided when necessary.

In addition to black lawyers, physicians, sociologists, psychologists, and social workers, other black professionals have been forming black nationalist organizations since the late 1960s. Such organizations have sprung up among economists, historians, political scientists, psychiatrists, urban planners, and others. However, it is probably in the area of politics that greatest advances have been made.

Politics

With the possible exception of the period of Reconstruction, Afro-Americans have played a minor role in conventional politics in the United States. Between the Reconstruction and the enactment of the Voting Rights Act of 1965 few blacks living in the South could exercise the franchise and were precluded from all but token participation in elections. Those who lived in the populous regions outside the South were too few in number to make a significant impact on politics in other regions. Consequently, no Afro-Americans served in the U.S. Congress between 1901 and 1931. The redistribution of the black population since 1931, and its concentration in metropolitan regions outside the South, enabled increasing numbers of Afro-Americans, usually from nonsouthern states to serve in Congress. Since the enactment of the Voting Rights Act of 1965, however, significant numbers of blacks have been elected to public office in the South.

According to the Joint Center for Political Studies in Washington, D.C., as of 1973 more than 3,000 black elected officials were serving on the local, state, and national levels. These include one U.S. senator, 16 congressmen, and 227 state legislators in 38 states. All of the southern legislatures include black members, with Georgia leading the Deep South with a total of 15. In addition, two U.S. Representatives were elected from the South in 1972, the first since Reconstruction. There are also hundreds of black mayors serving in large cities and small towns throughout the country. Despite the large number of black elected officials, Afro-Americans still account for less than 1 percent of all elected officials.

Contemporary black politicians, like policemen and servicemen, but unlike other generations of black politicians, are increasingly nationalistic in outlook. Rather than utilizing their positions for personal gain, many have cooperated in seeking legislation that best serves the interests of the black community. And like so many other blacks, they have formed Afro-American caucuses or groups, ranging anywhere from a national organization of black elected officials to the seven-member Alabama Conference of Black Mayors. Each state legislature with enough blacks to form a caucus has such an organization.

The Black Caucus of the California State Legislature investigated conditions of Soledad Prison in 1970 and issued a report on the treatment of black prison inmates. After extensive interviewing they concluded that "if even a small fraction of the reports received are accurate, the inmates' charges amount to a strong indictment of the prison's employees (on all levels) as cruel, vindictive, dangerous men who should not be permitted to control the lives of the 2,800 men at Soledad."[45]

In New York, members of the black caucus in the state legislature were active in attempts to mediate between the inmates and the officials at Attica before the massacre there in 1971. Black caucuses in state legislatures throughout the country have been active in supporting legislation in the interest of the black community and in opposing antiblack legislation.

Perhaps the most active and effective of these organizations is the 16-member Congressional Black Caucus, formed in 1970 after a black Congressman was denied a requested meeting with the President to discuss the plight of blacks and the poor. When the President refused to meet him, the black members of the House of Representatives met and formed the Caucus. Since that time its members have engaged in many collective actions, the first being a boycott of the President's State of the Union Message in January 1971.

The Caucus sees its primary function as concentration on legislation concerning the problems of the black community. More recently, members of the Caucus, in a series of speeches before the

House of Representatives, criticized the budget submitted to Congress by the President in 1973 and portions of his inaugural address.[46] The President had urged Americans to ask "not what will Government do for me but what can I do for myself." Representative Louis Stokes of Ohio, the chairman of the caucus, led the attack by saying, "Over the past four years we have learned that selfreliance is a virtue demanded only from minorities, the poor, and the disadvantaged. No one has told Lockhead [Aircraft Corporation] and Penn Central [Railroad] to pull themselves up by their bootstraps."

Members of the Congressional Black Caucus were active in organizing the National Black Political Convention in Gary, Indiana, in 1972. This convention issued a report, *The National Black Political Agenda*, in which a call was issued for the social transformation of American society: "Here at Gary we are faithful to the best hopes of our fathers and our people if we move for nothing less than a politics which places community before individualism, love before sexual exploitation, a living environment before profits, peace before war, justice before unjust 'order,' and morality before expediency."[47] The 88 recommendations made by the convention include community control of the police, schools, and other institutions in the black community; the release of all political prisoners; reparations for black people because of the legacy of slavery and discrimination; parallel black labor unions where established unions discriminate against blacks; national health insurance for all Americans; a guaranteed annual income of $6,500 for a family of four; cooperation with African liberation movements; and home rule for the District of Columbia.

The Congressional Black Caucus has held several hearings and conferences pertaining to problems of the black community. These include health, as well as racism in the armed forces, the media, and education. Each year the caucus sponsors a dinner at which an award is given to an outstanding black leader. This award is made in honor of the memory of the late Representative Adam Clayton Powell.

The problems facing Afro-Americans in the United States are of such a magnitude that the few black elected officials are powerless to effect significant changes. However, in the absence of an individual leader who commands a mass following in the black community, the Congressional Black Caucus has served as a national spokesman for Afro-Americans. In doing so its members have been supporters and sponsors of the most enlightened and progressive legislation to come before Congress.

As might be expected, complete unity among black politicians is still lacking, but on the local, state, and national levels black politicians have demonstrated that by solidifying their efforts they have become a powerful force in American politics. For example, the members of the Congressional Black Caucus, utilizing the recommendations contained in *The National Black Political Agenda*, presented to the Democratic leadership a "black bill of rights" before the Democratic National Convention in June 1972. Though the Democrats lost the Presidential election, their candidate had accepted in principle these recommendations and had committed himself to the appointment of additional blacks to the Supreme Court, proportionate representation in federal jobs, and financial assistance for voter registration in the black community.

Black politicians, like their white counterparts, often place political expediency above the interests of their constituents. In the case of black politicians their constituents are usually black, and though they are now more inclined to support legislation beneficial to the black community, there are notable exceptions. Inasmuch as they are relatively few in number, the impact of black politicians as a group has not been great. In addition, many of them are new to politics, and there are always those whose interests are purely personal gain. This was quite evident during the 1972 campaign and the following two years, when many announced support for candidates whose positions on issues were clearly not in the best interest of the black community.

In recent years the Congressional Black Caucus has lost some of its effectiveness, which no doubt reflects the general decline of overt nationalist activity. Its members, however, did put forth a solid front in favor of the impeachment of Richard Nixon.

The point being made here is not that today's black politicians have achieved total unity or that they can rightfully be considered black nationalists. Rather, the pervasiveness of nationalist sentiment is reflected among black politicians to a degree never before witnessed in the United States. Though their accomplishments to date might be minimal, with increasing numbers gaining elective offices, especially in the South, black politicians will be forced to become even more responsive to the needs of their black constituents.

The major postulate put forth in this chapter is that the ideological impact of contemporary nationalism has served to unify the black community as has no other force in history. This does not mean that widespread disharmony does not exist; disharmony will no doubt continue, but the unprecedented degree of unity which the black community has attained is growing. The major differences remaining, whether between the integrationists and the nationalists or between cultural and revolutionary nationalists, appear to center on selection of the means most likely to bring about the desired goal of black liberation. It seems clear that the spread of black nationalist ideology in the 1960s and 1970s has served to give the black community a sense of unity never before attained in the United States. This unity is clearly manifested in a decline in the self-hatred so characteristic of blacks for centuries. To a significant degree black people are rejecting conventional white standards of physical beauty, most notably in hair styles and dress. No longer do black people feel the need to adhere to standards set by the oppressor in other aspects of behavior. Furthermore, black people in all social strata—the unemployed, factory workers, white-collar workers, and professionals—have come to share pride in their cultural heritage.

The individual symbols of unity have been projected into collective expressions of solidarity. Hence, the hundreds of local and national groups which espouse at least some elements of black nationalist ideology, and the widespread support in the black community for such figures as Muhammad Ali and Angela Davis, or the outrage expressed at the murders of Fred Hampton and George Jackson. The remarkable unity demonstrated by inmates at Attica before the massacre would have been unlikely a decade ago.

To credit the black nationalist movement with generating a striking degree of unity in the black community is not to minimize the accomplishments of its immediate predecessor, the civil rights movement. It is possible, even likely, that the black nationalist movement would not exist on its present scale without the successes and lessons of the civil rights movement, for they were many. The goals of the movement, however, were too limited to accomplish the task of black liberation. The failure of the civil rights movement to effect significant changes in the lives of the black masses was one of the crucial factors contributing to the spread of nationalist sentiment.

Freedom from external domination, that is, self-determination, is the essence of liberation. When a people have lived under external domination for centuries, the nature of their existence calls for solidarity if they are to extricate themselves. In a society where status is ascribed on the basis of physical characteristics, individualism among the oppressed is a luxury which the group can ill afford. And individual instances of social mobility become a major method of cooptation. Unity, therefore, is a necessary precondition for liberation. It is not sufficient, for a unified people are not necessarily free from outside control, but without unity it is unlikely that liberation can be achieved.

6

Revolutionary nationalism:
The Black Panther Party
and other groups

In the few years of its existence the Black Panther party has become one of the leading revolutionary nationalist organizations in the United States. Although some black nationalists maintain that it is not an authentic black nationalist group, the officials and rank-and-file members of the party have always considered their organization a nationalist one. The ideology of the party embraces some aspects of other revolutionary movements and ideologies, particularly Marxism–Leninism, but black unity and black autonomy are at the core of its platform and program. Furthermore, its cofounder, Huey P. Newton, has championed the cause of black self-determination from the outset. He viewed the party as the successor to Malcolm X's Organization of Afro-American Unity. The writings of black revolutionaries such as Malcolm X and Frantz Fanon were as crucial to the party's ultimate ideological position as those of Marx, Engels, Lenin, Mao, Ho, Guevara, and Debray. Furthermore, virtually every item in the party's platform addresses itself to the cause of self-determination for the black community. And although the Black Panthers are at odds with some aspects of black nationalist ideology, especially cultural nationalism, they have embraced some of the principles of cultural nationalism, particularly those of the Afro-American student groups.

Although the nationalism of the Black Panther party differs sharply from that of some of the other contemporary black nationalist groups, it is difficult to see how one could fail to acknowledge its preeminence as the leading revolutionary black nationalist group in the United States at the present time. The party has constantly changed aspects of its program, depending upon circumstances, but this has also been true of many of the world's revolutionary movements. And the history of black nationalist movements in the United States illustrates the necessity for adaptations to changing circumstances.

Origins, program and organization of the party[1]

The Black Panther party was founded by two young black militants, Huey P. Newton and Bobby Seale, in Oakland, California, in the fall of 1966. At the time Newton was 24 and Seale was 30. The two met while studying at Merritt Junior College in Oakland, four years before the party was formed. They had both been members of the student Afro-American Association on campus, and later of the Soul Students Advisory Council there. The major purposes of these organizations were to press for the introduction of Afro-American history courses at the college and the employment of additional black teachers.

Newton was a student leader on campus. When Seale heard Newton speak at a rally, he was impressed by Newton's knowledge of Afro-American history and his criticisms of the civil rights movement, which was at its peak at the time. The two young militants left the college in 1965, preferring to set up their own organization in Oakland's black community. To ascertain the needs of the community, they surveyed its residents. Based on the results of this survey, they began to design a program to meet the needs of the black community.

In the fall of 1966, while working for a poverty center in Oakland, Seale and Newton began to develop the program of the Black Panther Party for Self-Defense. The black panther had been the symbol of the Lowndes County Freedom Organization, formed by the Student Nonviolent Coordinating Committee in Alabama in 1965. SNCC selected the black panther as the emblem of its organization, and the Black Panther party chose the name because the panther is reputed to be an animal that never makes an unprovoked attack but will defend itself vehemently when attacked.

Police brutality was one of the main grievances of Oakland's black residents, and point seven of the platform Seale and Newton developed stated: "We want an immediate end to POLICE BRUTALITY and MURDER of black people." The plank continued, "We believe we can end police brutality in our black community by organizing black self-defense groups that are dedicated to defending our black community from racist police oppression and brutality. The Second Amendment to the Constitution of

the United States gives a right to bear arms. We therefore believe
that all black people should arm themselves for self-defense." To
implement this part of the platform, the newly organized party set
up a system of armed cars to patrol the black community. (Money
for the initial purchase of weapons was raised by the founding
members of the party through the sale of copies of "the Little Red
Book," *Quotations from Chairman Mao Tse-Tung*, to students at
the University of California at Berkeley.) When black people were
stopped by the police, the patrols would intercede to assure that
constitutional rights were not violated. Since the carrying of
firearms openly was not illegal in California, the angry police were
unable to prohibit these activities. Newton had studied law after
leaving Merritt Junior College, and law books were carried along
with the weapons in the patrol cars. The patrol squads had the
effect of reducing the incidence of police brutality against black
people, but at the same time the incidence of harassment of
Panthers intensified, ultimately leading to a nationwide campaign
of repression against them.

The armed patrols met with the approval of residents in the
black community and attracted the attention of young blacks on
the West coast and throughout the nation. Early in 1967, the party
attracted the first noted personality to its ranks. When Betty
Shabazz, Malcolm X's widow, arrived in San Francisco for an
appearance at Black House, she was met, escorted, and guarded
by Black Panthers, including Newton and Seale. Eldridge Cleaver,
who had recently been released from prison and who was working
as a writer for *Ramparts* at the time, observed these events and
was moved to join the party. "The most beautiful sight I had ever
seen," he said later. "Four black men wearing black berets,
powder-blue shirts, black leather jackets, black trousers, and shiny
black shoes—and each with a gun! In front was Huey P. Newton.
Beside him was Bobby Seale. A few steps behind him was Bobby
Hutton. Where was my mind at? Blown."[2] Cleaver then joined the
party and became minister of information. His wife, Kathleen,
became communications secretary. Shortly thereafter Cleaver's
best-selling book *Soul on Ice* was published, giving the party
nationwide publicity.

During the same period a young black man, Denzil Dowell, of
Richmond, California, was killed by a county deputy sheriff. The
Dowell family asked members of the Black Panther party to come
to Richmond to investigate the killing. Several cars of armed
Panthers went to Richmond, where there were several encounters
with the local police, but the Panthers demanded their right to

hold street rallies with local residents.[3] During the investigation they discovered that two other black men had been killed by the police. They went to the sheriff's office to demand that the murderer of young Dowell be apprehended. The meeting was of no avail, but by the time they left Richmond, the Panthers had recruited several young people who had been impressed by their display of courage.

Upon their return to party headquarters in Oakland, they decided that the party needed its own newspaper to counter the adverse publicity they were receiving in the white-owned press. The first issue of *The Black Panther, Black Community News Service* appeared April 25, 1967. The issue was completely devoted to the murder of Denzil Dowell.

The decision was made, also in the spring of 1967, to drop "for Self-Defense" from the party's title, because party activities had broadened. Among other things, the Panthers were engaged in several programs in Oakland's black community, including apprising welfare recipients of their rights, teaching black history, protesting evictions, and demanding the installation of traffic lights at school crossings. All these activities won them the respect of the residents of Oakland's black community.

In the meantime, however, a bill designed to disarm the Panthers had been introduced in the California legislature.[4] It called for the banning of loaded weapons within incorporated areas of the state. The night before the debate on the bill, Newton devised a plan whereby Panthers would journey to Sacramento in a caravan of cars to observe the assembly debate in action. Before the departure Newton (who was persuaded to remain in Oakland) drafted Executive Mandate Number One, which was to be read to the press in Sacramento.[5] The mandate ended with the following paragraph:

The Black Panther Party for Self-Defense believes that the time has come for Black people to arm themselves against this terror before it is too late. The pending Mulford Act brings the hour of doom one step nearer. A people who have suffered so much for so long at the hands of a racist society must draw the line somewhere. We believe that the Black communities of America must rise up as one man to halt the progression of a trend that leads inevitably to their total destruction.

On the morning of May 2, 1967, a caravan of cars carrying 29 Panthers, 20 of whom were armed, and one reporter (Cleaver represented *Ramparts* because of his parole status) journeyed to the state capitol at Sacramento. When they reached the outside stairs, Seale read Executive Mandate Number One to the assembled newspaper and television reporters. They then entered the building surrounded by reporters, passed the office of Governor Ronald Reagan, who had seen them outside while he was speaking to a crowd of youths gathered on the lawn, and went upstairs in search of the Assembly. There they were stopped by a guard, who said they could not enter. As they brushed past the guard, Seale demanded that the constitutional rights of citizens be protected. Inside the Assembly the guards confiscated some of their weapons, which were later returned. After reading the Mandate again for reporters, the Panthers left the building, only to be arrested elsewhere in Sacramento on trumped-up charges, including conspiracy and disturbing the peace. Cleaver and a local black woman were also arrested. Two of the group were bailed out, whereupon they returned to Oakland. The following day Newton went with them to Sacramento for the court hearing, bailed out some of the others, and held a press conference.

The episode in Sacramento was widely reported in the media throughout the world, and the Black Panther party became well-known. New chapters were established in Los Angeles, New York, Georgia, and Michigan. Hundreds of black youth from the streets were thereby attracted to the fearless Black Panther party. But the event in Sacramento set off a nationwide campaign of hysteria against the party.

Because they had no previous convictions, Seale and several other Panthers accepted prison sentences for as long as six months. While they were in prison an event occurred which was of major significance for the Black Panther party. The police throughout the country had intensified their harassment of Panthers, particularly in the Oakland area. Newton was a special target for such harassment. In the early morning hours of October 28, 1967, Newton, then the party's minister of defense, and another member were driving in an automobile and were stopped by a white policeman. The policeman radioed to the police station, "I have a Panther car." A second police car was dispatched to the scene, and within a brief time the original arresting officer had been killed and Newton, who suffered serious gunshot wounds in the stomach, was under arrest for murder. The other officer was also wounded.[6] When he recovered from the wounds, Newton was incarcerated at the Alameda County Jail without bail.

The events surrounding the shootout are vague. According to the surviving policeman, the arresting officer recognized Newton and ordered him into the police car. Although shots were fired, one policeman was killed, and the second was wounded, the surviving policeman reported that Newton did not have a weapon. Newton is said to have forced a passing motorist to drive him to a hospital, where he was treated for his wounds, and where he was beaten by other policemen.

Although Newton steadfastly proclaimed his innocence, he was tried for murder, assault with a deadly weapon, and kidnapping.[7] At the trial he was represented by a white lawyer, Charles Garry, who was known for his defense of controversial clients, especially radicals. The trial began on July 15, 1968, and the verdict was handed down on September 8. Throughout his stay in prison Newton was held in solitary confinement. A massive defense effort had been put forth on his behalf, including testimony from several sociologists, in an effort to show that the jury was not devoid of racism and that the slain policeman had a reputation for being a racist. The jury, which finally consisted of ten white persons, one black (the foreman), and one Japanese person, declared him not guilty of assault, but guilty of voluntary manslaughter. The charge of kidnapping had been dropped. Newton was sentenced to an indeterminate term of from two to fifteen years. This verdict was appealed, but the judge denied bail. The Oakland police had expected Newton to be sentenced to die in the gas chamber, and when the compromise verdict became known, they were so enraged that they attacked the Panther headquarters, riddling it with bullets.

Although he was sentenced to a term of from two to fifteen years on the compromise charge of voluntary manslaughter, Newton had served three years in prison when finally released in 1970. The judicial litigation continued for a total of four years, during which time he was tried three times. The first conviction was reversed by the California Court of Appeals, and the following two retrials ended in deadlocked juries. The district attorney finally dismissed all charges against him. During his incarceration, however, the party continued to grow, as did the campaign of repression against it. By the end of 1969 virtually all of its national leaders had been killed, jailed, or forced into exile. Charles Garry, the party's chief defense lawyer, reported that in the two years between December 1967 and December 1969, 28 Panthers had been killed by the police, and hundreds more were arrested on charges which were so blatantly false that in 87 cases they were dropped by the courts. Garry reported that in over 30 years of law practice, "I have never experienced the type of persecution forced on the Black Panthers."[9] J. Edgar Hoover, then director of the Federal Bureau of Investigation, initiated the wave of repression by declaring the Black Panther party the "greatest threat to the internal security of the United States."

Two days after the assassination of Martin Luther King, Jr., on April 4, 1968, the Oakland police opened fire on a house where a Panther meeting was being held. The attack was unprovoked, and as two Panther officials left the house with their hands in the air, the police opened fire on them. Bobby Hutton, the first person to join the party after Newton and Seale, was killed, and Eldridge Cleaver was wounded.

In the meantime the Black Panther party mounted a massive "Free Huey" campaign, in which thousands of black and white youths demonstrated daily for Newton's freedom. At the same time the Panthers formed coalitions with several groups, both locally and nationally. The most important coalition was that with Peace and Freedom party, which originated in California but which soon spread throughout the country. Members of the Black Panther party succeeded in collecting enough signatures to put the Peace and Freedom party on the ballot in California and several other states. The Peace and Freedom party, which consisted mainly of antiwar white liberals and radicals, was organized mainly as an alternative to the established Democratic and Republican parties, and part of their agreement with the Panthers was that they would join forces with the "Free Huey" drive. In addition, the Peace and Freedom party agreed to run Newton, Seale, and Kathleen Cleaver for state offices in California. Eldridge Cleaver became the Presidential candidate in 1968, running on a platform of black liberation and opposition to the war in Vietnam. None of the candidates was elected, but the Black Panther party became well-known throughout the United States and abroad.

In February 1968 at a "Free Huey" rally, the Panthers announced a merger with the Student Nonviolent Coordinating Committee, appointing leaders of that organization to important posts in the Black Panther party. H. Rap Brown became minister of justice, Stokely Carmichael was appointed field marshal, and James Foreman assumed the position of minister of foreign affairs. This merger was short-lived, because of a bitter dispute between Panther and SNCC officials. The major point of disagreement was the opposition of SNCC officials to alliances and coalitions with white groups.[8]

The Black Panther party continued to provide services to the black community: free breakfasts for children, free health clinics, free clothing distribution centers, petitions for community control of the police, and liberation schools. Their influence spread at home and abroad. Black Panther parties were established in England, France, and Israel. At home, Chicanos, Chinese Americans, Puerto Ricans, and poor whites emulated the Panthers by forming parallel organizations. But the nationwide campaign of repression, coupled with internal strife, served to weaken and virtually destroy the Black Panther party.

The 10-point platform and program of the party, prepared by Newton and Seale in the first weeks of October 1966, reads as follows:

1 We want freedom. We want power to determine the destiny of our black community.

2 We want full employment for our people.

3 We want an end to the robbery by the white man of our black community.

4 We want decent housing, fit for shelter of human beings.

5 We want education for our people that exposes the true nature of this decadent American Society. We want education that teaches us our true history and our role in the present-day society.

6 We want all black men to be exempt from military service.

7 We want an immediate end to POLICE BRUTALITY and MURDER of black people.

8 We want freedom for all black men held in federal, state, county, and city prisons and jails.

9 We want all black people when brought to trial to be tried in court by a jury of their peer group or people from their black communities, as defined by the Constitution of the United States.

10 We want land, bread, housing, education, clothing, justice and peace. And as our major political objective, a United Nations-supervised plebiscite to be held throughout the black colony in which only black colonial subjects will be allowed to participate, for the purpose of determining the will of black people as to their national destiny.

The 10 points of the platform and program of the Black Panther party are clearly not revolutionary. Indeed, many of the points could well be supported by such nonrevolutionary, integrationist groups as the National Association for the Advancement of Colored People and the Urban League. At the same time, the leaders of the party characterize it as a revolutionary Marxist-Leninist party. For example, the national office issued the following statement:

The Black Panther party stands for revolutionary solidarity with all people fighting against the forces of imperialism, capitalism, racism, and fascism. Our solidarity is extended to those people who are fighting these evils at home and abroad. Because we understand that our struggle for our liberation is part of a worldwide struggle being waged by the poor and oppressed against imperialism and the world's chief imperialist, the United States of America, we–the Black Panther party–understand that the most effective way that we can aid our Vietnamese brothers and sisters is to destroy imperialism from inside, attack it where it breeds.[10]

Newton sees no contradiction between the rather modest call for decent housing for black people and advocacy of the overthrow of capitalism. Indeed, he sees the 10-point program as essential to black survival at the present time: "A Ten-Point Program is not revolutionary in itself, nor is it reformist. *It is a survival program.* We, the people, are threatened with genocide because racism and facism are rampant in this country and throughout the world. And the ruling circle in North America is responsible."[11]

Furthermore, the ideology of the Black Panther party has changed since its inception. Initially its leaders stressed racial oppression of black people, but at the party's "United Front Against Fascism" conference in July 1969, Seale stressed that the party was committed to the class struggle. Consequently, alliances were made with white and other Third World revolutionary groups in the United States. In a speech following his release from prison, Newton told his Boston College audience, "In 1966 we called our Party a Black Nationalist Party. We called ourselves Black Nationalists because we thought nationhood was the answer. Shortly after that we decided that what was really needed was revolutionary nationalism, that is, nationalism plus socialism."[12]

In an attempt to explain its ideological position, the Black Panther party in 1969 disseminated a booklet, written by the minister of information (Eldridge Cleaver at the time). Acknowledging that the party was in the process of refining its ideology, Cleaver wrote, "When we say that we are Marxist–Leninists, we mean that we have studied and understood the classical principles of scientific socialism and that we have adapted these principles to our own situation for ourselves. However, we do not move with a closed mind to new ideas or information."[12]

The Panthers have liberally adopted aspects of revolutionary ideology from other Third World leaders and spokesmen, because classic Marxism–Leninism fails to deal with the problems faced by Afro-Americans. Prior to the founding of the People's Republic of China and the Democratic People's Republic of Korea in the late 1940s, Marxism-Leninism was almost exclusively European.

Hence, the ideology of the Black Panther party combines revolutionary black nationalism with Third World adaptations of

Marxism–Leninism. Aspects of its ideology are from Frantz Fanon (the cleansing force of violence which frees one from despair and feelings of inferiority); from Mao Tse-Tung (the power of the gun); from Che Guevara (death with honor, and many Vietnams); from Ho Chi Minh (feed on the brutality of the occupying army); from Al Fatah (terrorize, disrupt, and destroy); from Kim Il Sung (autonomy, integrity, and responsibility of the party).

Panther leaders believe that their focus of interest should be on the black lumpenproletariat (those outside the labor force because of their inability to find employment), or the so-called street blacks. These people, they maintain, have been locked outside the economy, and within capitalist society this means that they have no institutional input into the system. Since they are not part of the labor force, they are not represented by organized labor. Therefore, they have been forced to create their own forms of rebellion which are consistent with their relationship to the means of production and the institutions of the larger society which oppresses them.

In keeping with its changed ideological position, the Black Panther party revised its 10-point program and platform on March 29, 1972. In most cases "oppressed people" and "oppressed communities" were added to "black people" and "black community," but there were other changes. For example, point six, on the exemption of blacks from military service, was deleted, and free health care for blacks and other oppressed people was substituted. Similarly, points eight and nine were combined to form point nine; point eight now calls for an end to aggressive wars. Finally, the political objective calling for a United Nations-sponsored plebiscite in the black community has been deleted and "community control of modern technology" substituted. The revised 10-point program reads as follows:

1 *We Want Freedom. We Want Power to Determine the Destiny of Our Black and Oppressed Communities.*

2 *We Want Full Employment for Our People.*

3 *We Want an End to the Robbery by the Capitalists of Our Black and Oppressed Communities.*

4 *We Want Decent Housing, Fit for the Shelter of Human Beings.*

5 *We Want Education for Our People that Exposes the True Nature of this Decadent American Society. We Want Education that Teaches us Our True History and Our Role in the Present-Day Society.*

6 *We Want Completely Free Health Care for all Black and Oppressed People.*

7 *We Want an Immediate End to Police Brutality and Murder of Black People, Other People of Color, All Oppressed People inside the United States.*

8 *We Want an Immediate End to All Wars of Aggression.*

9 *We Want Freedom for all Black and Poor Oppressed People now held in U.S. Federal, State, County, City, and Military Prisons and Jails. We Want Trials by a Jury of Peers for All Persons Charged with So-Called Crimes under the Laws of this Country.*

10 *We Want Land, Bread, Housing, Education, Clothing, Justice, Peace and People's Community Control of Modern Technology.*

In addition to the 10-point program, the Panthers have adopted a set of 26 rules for members of the party, ranging anywhere from prohibiting the use of narcotics "while doing party work," to requiring all branches to submit weekly reports to the national office. In addition, there are eight "Points of Attention," including such courtesies as "Speak politely," and three "Main Rules of Discipline," including such prohibitions as stealing from the oppressed.

The Black Panther party is headed by a central committee, under the leadership of Huey P. Newton, its co-founder and formerly minister of defense, who is now servant of the people. Bobby Seale, the party's chairman is second in command, followed by the minister of information. The central committee also contains the chief of staff, a field marshal, a minister of education, a minister of foreign affairs, a minister of justice, a prime minister, a communications secretary, and a minister of culture. On the local level, the 38 chapters (as of August 1972) parallel the national organization, with a deputy chief of staff and deputy ministers. Because of internal strife, especially in 1971, the party has undergone some reorganization, but the basic structure remains.

Panthers, police, and American "justice"

In its short history the Black Panther party became one of the major targets of the respressive machinery of the American judicial system. In addition to the apparently police provoked shootout between Newton and the Oakland police in October 1967 and the murder of young Bobby Hutton in April 1968, in the two years between 1968 and 1970 members of the party throughout the country were subjected to many brutal assaults by law enforcement personnel. Dozens of Panthers were killed, and thousands were arrested on such trumped-up charges as "attempted murder" and "resisting arrest."[14]

The harassment of the Panthers was often blatant. For example, the New York Panther 21 were kept in jail for two years, charged with plotting to murder policemen, bomb police stations, department stores, subway and railway installations, the Bronx Botanical Gardens, and a Board of Education building. After a trial which lasted eight months and which cost the taxpayers in excess of $300,000, the Panthers were acquitted of all these charges by a jury. Meanwhile, the bail for the defendents had been set at $2.1 million.

In the early morning hours of December 4, 1969, the party offices in Chicago were raided by 15 members of the Cook County State's Attorney's office, who were armed with submachine guns, shotguns, and revolvers. When they left, the chairman of the Illinois chapter, Fred Hampton, and a Panther leader from Peoria, Illinois, Mark Clark, had been murdered. Four others, including a woman, were injured. Although police officials claimed that these deaths and injuries resulted from a gun battle between the police and the Panthers, all evidence from independent investigations indicates that the Panthers had been killed by the police while sleeping.

Bobby Seale and another official were charged with murder and kidnapping in New Haven, Connecticut, in 1969. A man said to have been a member of the party was murdered on May 21. Seale went to New Haven to fulfill a speaking engagement at Yale University on May 19 and left the morning of May 20. After a trial which lasted six months, including four months to select a jury, the case was finally dismissed, because the jury was deadlocked.

These are but three of the most widely publicized cases of judicial harassment of members of the Black Panther party, but they are typical of the problems faced by the party throughout the country. Such behavior caused the American Civil Liberties Union to issue a report detailing 48 major police–Panther incidents in the years 1968–1969.[15] And, on December 29, 1969, the ACLU reported, "The record of police actions across the country against the Black Panther party forms a prima facie case for the conclusion that law enforcement officials are waging a drive against the black militant organization resulting in serious civil liberties violations."[16] Finally, a staff report by the National Commission on the Causes and Prevention of Violence had this to say about police–Panther relations:

The Black Panther Party has remained defensive, and has been given credit for keeping Oakland cool after the assassination of Martin Luther King, but this has not stemmed from any desire on their part to suppress black protest in the community. Rather, it has stemmed from a sense that the police are waiting for a chance to shoot down blacks in the streets. Continued harassment by the police makes self-defense a necessary element of militant action for the Panthers.[17]

The police actions against the Panthers were part of a nation-wide campaign to destroy the party. Support for this allegation was provided by the mayor of Seattle, when he disclosed that he had refused a federal request to stage a raid on that city's Panther headquarters. Said Mayor Wes Uhlman, "We are not going to have any 1932 Gestapo-like raids against anyone."[18]

The party was initially organized to curb police violence against Afro-Americans. It espoused an ideology opposed to the American economic system, thereby becoming a logical target for official persecution. Furthermore, in addition to educating black people to the nature of American society, it served to educate others, including white youth, to the nature of American racism, imperialism, sexism, and economic exploitation.

Internal weaknesses

Official harassment was sufficient to keep the Panthers diverted from their planned agenda, for it was necessary for them to defend themselves continually. However, the party suffered from intraparty strife. Because of the nature of the party, it was organized along paramilitary lines, with power concentrated at the top and policies dictated by the central committee. There were no elections, and individual members were liable to summary purge without appeal. At the same time, because of its militant posture, including the right to bear arms, it attracted a varied lot of people, some of whom were seeking adventure. These members of the lumpenproletariat were often eager to confront the police against whom they had always been powerless. They had spent their lives as victims of police brutality, but were forced to suppress their feelings of hostility. Consequently, they saw in the Black Panther party a chance to stand up to the arbitrary authority exercised over them by the police. There was no other organization which provided such an outlet, and they needed the organizational support provided by the Black Panther party.

Although the party rules were explicit, and each member was forced to memorize them, enforcement of the rules has been somewhat lax, and on occasion individual chapters have developed their own working relationships with the police and other community groups. Some members with past arrest records, for example, were simply opportunists who sought favors from the police, such as the dropping of charges, in exchange for information on party activities. Others simply did not live up to the code of behavior adopted by the organization. Consequently, according to one investigator, two members whom the party claims were murdered by the police were killed otherwise; one by his wife, and another by a merchant in an attempted robbery.[19] Both of these acts were clear violations of the party rules.

The party refused to inquire into past politics and activities of members, relying instead on strict adherence to rules, and thus police infiltration of the party was widespread. For example, in the New York Panther 21 case, the prosecution rested its case on testimony from three undercover agents who had been assigned to infiltrate the New York branch of the party.[20] Although the prosecution called a total of 65 witnesses, none of the others was able to corroborate the testimony of the agents.

The Panther trials in New York and New Haven occurred at roughly the same time, and this was shortly after Huey Newton had been released from prison on bail. Charges were made by the New York chapter that Newton was ignoring the New York trial, focusing all his attention instead on that of Chairman Bobby Seale. By this time Eldridge Cleaver and his wife, Kathleen, had become exiles in Algeria, where they established the headquarters of the International Section of the Black Panther party.[21] By the beginning of 1971 the party found itself hopelessly split from within. Members of the New York chapter openly expressed their hostility toward Newton and what they perceived as yet another change in the ideological position of the party.

During the trial of the New York Panther 21, two of the defendants failed to appear at the trial, forfeiting bail totaling $150,000. When this occurred, Newton denounced them as "enemies of the people" and expelled them and seven other defendants from the party. Members of the New York chapter had signed an open letter to the Weatherpeople, an organization of white revolutionaries, criticizing the Black Panther party leaders for not being militant enough.[22] Newton charged that the two missing defendants had given court officials an opportunity to revoke the bail of their codefendants, including one who was four months pregnant; had jeopardized the chances of bail for the others; and had "propped up the dying case" of the prosecution. Newton's private secretary disappeared with the missing defendants, taking with her information which he charged was crucial to the defense of Seale and Ericka Huggins in New Haven and which included such other materials as his list of speaking engagements.

On February 26, 1971, the internal dispute within the party intensified when Newton appeared on a San Francisco television show in which Cleaver participated by telephone from Algiers. Cleaver was critical of Newton for his expulsion of the nine Panthers and called on Newton to expel David Hilliard, the party's chief of staff, whom he called a "revisionist," who had taken over the operations of the party when all the other leaders had been jailed or forced into exile. Surprised by the request from Cleaver, Newton responded by expelling Cleaver and the entire international section of the party.[23] Cleaver, in turn, expelled Newton from the party and reinstated the members Newton had expelled. Among other things, Cleaver declared that Hilliard's activities were calculated to "destroy the most valuable piece of machinery [the Black Panther party] that has been produced by revolutionaries inside the United States."[24] He also charged that Newton had used party funds to rent a $650-a-month penthouse apartment in Oakland.

The party's internal dispute became so intense in the following weeks that the party appeared to be disintegrating. The two Panthers who had skipped bail and Newton's former secretary appeared in Algiers and held a video-taped news conference, which was later replayed in New York. During this news conference they declared that the international section and the New York chapter had seceded from the Black Panther party. They charged that Newton was no longer in command, and that their new organization represented the official Black Panther party.[25] In the meantime, both factions struggled to control the party's newspaper, and two days after an article appeared in the paper alleging that Cleaver had killed a Panther in Algiers, a member of the party loyal to Newton was killed in Harlem while selling the newspaper.[26] It was rumored that he was killed by Panthers supporting Cleaver.

By the end of 1972, the activities of the Black Panther party were different from those of the preceding five years. A general reorganization had taken place. Perhaps the most fundamental change was a reemphasis on working in the black community and maintaining a low profile nationally. Seale became a candidate for mayor of Oakland, and Ericka Huggins, who had been acquitted with him in New Haven, was elected to Oakland's Community Development Council, an antipoverty agency. Elaine Brown, the deputy minister of information, became a candidate for councilwoman in Oakland. In addition to Ericka Huggins, three other members of the party were elected to the Community Development Council's Board of Directors.[27] There were fewer incidents with the police, and the party concentrated on voter registration drives and other activities in the black community. In addition to endorsing the Presidential campaign of Representative Shirley Chisholm of Brooklyn and supporting her campaign financially, the party cooperated with civil rights organizations as well as religious groups.

Cleaver and the New York branch had been unable to gain control of the party, although they continued to denounce it as counter-revolutionary for "working within the system." When asked in an interview if the Black Panther party had retreated from its revolutionary stance in favor of working within the community, Newton replied, "I think the Panthers have to participate in every community institution. We believe in intercommunalism–the relatedness of all people. We want to be part of the whole. That's what gives the motion to matter, and you can't very well drop out of the system without dropping out of the universe. So you contradict the system while you are in it until it's transformed into a new system."[28] Though the party's major activities are concentrated in the Oakland area, many of its community activities are conducted by chapters in every major city in the country.

Black community services and support

During its peak popularity the Black Panther party's best-known community service was its free breakfast program, through which children in the black community were given a free, hot breakfast each morning before school. Within the last few years, however, the survival program of the party has expanded to include 11 different services, with 8 other programs still in the process of being implemented at the end of 1972.[29] In addition to the nationwide free breakfast program, the Panthers operate a Free Food program for black and other oppressed peoples. Their Liberation Schools, which developed out of point five of the new platform, provide free educational facilities for black and other oppressed children "to promote a correct view of their role in the society." The Panthers also sponsor the Samuel Napier Youth Intercommunal Institute in East Oakland. The institute is an accredited school, designed to serve as an alternative to regular public schools. Along with teaching conventional basic skills by licensed teachers, the students are taught political awareness.

When they graduate from the institute, it is expected that they will become the political organizers in the high schools to which they are assigned.

In several cities the Panthers conduct legal aid educational programs. These programs give free legal assistance to those in need of such services, as well as legal aid classes. One of the more recent programs which has been successful in the black community is the Free Busing to Prisons Program. This program has achieved a considerable amount of success because virtually everyone in the black community has either a relative or friend in prison, and frequently they are unable to provide their own transporation for visits. In addition, there is the Free Commissary for Prisoners Program, which provides money for imprisoned men and women to purchase necessities from commissaries within prisons.

The Panther survival program includes the distribution of free shoes and clothing to the needy in the black community. There are two such programs: the People's Free Clothing Program and the David Hilliard Free Shoe Program. In order to support the free shoe program, the Panthers have opened the David Hilliard Free Shoe Factory.

Two of the party's most successful nationwide programs are aimed at improving the quality of health care in the black community. The George Jackson People's Free Medical Research Health Clinics provide medical treatment and preventative medical care to those in need. These clinics are staffed by physicians who volunteer their services. The People's Sickle Cell Anemia Research Foundation was established to test individuals for traits of the disease, to create better educational programs about the disease, and to coordinate the research of physicians already working in the area.

Finally, the Intercommunal News Service, of which *The Black Panther* is the principal organ, provides news and information about such conditions in the black community as police brutality and other liberation struggles throughout the world. The paper regularly reports on advances being made in such revolutionary countries as the People's Republic of China (which Newton and other officials visited in October 1971), the Democratic People's Republic of Korea, and the Democratic Republic of Vietnam. The party maintains close ties with revolutionary movements in Africa, Asia, and South America. Reports on these struggles are regular features of the paper.

In the Oakland area the party has initiated voter registration drives. During the first two weeks of the first drive, the party was able to register some 27,000 new voters. Newton justified the registration campaign on the grounds that it is necessary to be concerned about the day-to-day needs of the people. "We did this not because our program is a scheme to get into office," he said, "but because it is an attempt to tell the people we care a lot about them. It's to tell them that we have to develop a strong voting bloc so the people will have a voice in spending tax money and in the employment practices of various financial institutions and the city administration."[30]

Not all the Panther survival programs have been put into effect throughout the country, but many are regular service programs in the black community in most metropolitan areas. In addition, several programs are in the process of being implemented. These include the People's Free Ambulance Service, to operate on a 24-hour basis for those in need of emergency medical care; the People's Free Dental Program, to provide dental treatment and examinations, as well as preventive dental care; the People's Free Optometry Program, to offer eye examinations, treatment, and correctional lenses for those in need.

Four programs in the process of implementation are concerned with the housing needs of the black community, in accordance with point four of the revised program and platform. These include the People's Free Plumbing and Maintenance Program, geared to improve housing conditions; Community Cooperative Housing Program, to provide cooperatively owned housing by its residents; the People's Free Furniture Program, an effort to improve living standards; and the People's Free Linen Program, "to make daily living more healthy and comfortable."

Finally, the Panthers are moving to implement the People's Free Community Employment program. This service will secure employment for those who experience difficulty finding work.

Because of its service to the black community, the Black Panther party has won the support and respect of many of its residents. Though a considerable amount of their support resulted from their persecution by law enforcement officials, that is only part of the story. For example, the *Wall Street Journal* assigned four of its reporters to sample opinion among blacks in San Francisco, New York, Cleveland, and Chicago. Among other things, this survey showed strong backing for the party because of its programs. The paper reported that "a sizeable number of blacks support the Panthers because they admire other, less publicized activities of the party such as its free-breakfast program for ghetto youngsters, its free medical care program, and its war on narcotics use among black youth."[31]

In a survey conducted for *Time* magazine, Louis Harris and

Associates reported that 25 percent of a cross-section of Afro-Americans respected the Panthers "a great deal." This amounts to more than 5 million people.[32] And yet another poll of blacks in Baltimore, Birmingham, Detroit, New York, and San Francisco showed that 62 percent of those interviewed admired what the Panthers were doing.[33]

After the murders of Fred Hampton and Mark Clark in December 1969, editorials appeared in virtually all the major American newspapers.[34] The views of most of the white-owned press were indicated by the titles of their editorials. For example, the *Wall Street Journal's* (December 29, 1969) editorial was called "Warped Perceptions," its description of those sympathetic to the view that the war by the police against the Panthers was one of genocide. The *Phoenix Gazette* (December 10, 1969) entitled its editorial "They Promise Us Death," and it praised the Chicago police for the raid which resulted in the two deaths. The *Detroit Free Press* (December 11, 1969) called its editorial "Undesirables, but Citizens." *The New York Times* (December 17, 1969) declared that the police raid on the Panthers "raised anew the question of whether the authorities there and elsewhere are engaged in a search-and-destroy campaign rather than in legitimate law enforcement." It went on to say that "the doctrine and tactics of the Panthers are offensive, provocative, and neofascist." The *Los Angeles Times* (December 10, 1969) complained that "the operational code of the Panthers makes violence almost unavoidable." The *Chicago Tribune* (December 10, 1969) advised black citizens to "Put your faith in the law and the sensitivity to justice which motivates the overwhelming majority of all American citizens."

The black press approached the police-initiated war with the Panthers from a different perspective. The *Boston Bay State Banner* (December 11, 1969) called the Clark-Hampton Killings "legal murder" and went on to say, "It is interesting to note that no violent extralegal methods have been used to rid this country of its greatest threat–organized crime.... But of course these criminals are white." While condemning the "drive by police throughout the country to wipe out the Black Panthers," the *New York Amsterdam News* (December 13, 1969) commented: "And when we talk about the Black Panthers, we are always reminded that nothing was ever done about the white off-duty policemen who attacked a group of them in the hallways of a Brooklyn court." The *Chicago Daily Defender* (December 17, 1969) published a poem by Don L. Lee, entitled "One Sided Shoot-Out." It was dedicated to the memory of Fred Hampton and Mark Clark, and it ended with these lines:

the seeing eye should always see.
the night doesn't stop the stars
& our enemies scope the ways of blackness in three
bad shifts a day.
in the AM their music becomes deadlier.
this is a game of dirt.
Only blackpeople play it fair.

Shortly after the Hampton-Clark murders, a similar raid took place in Los Angeles. A columnist for the *Los Angeles Sentinel* (December 11, 1969), Booker Griffin, entitled his column, "Panther Genocide Plot Arrives in L.A." He wrote that "a mass national plot to commit genocide upon the Black Panther party has reared its ugly head in our community." He then asked, "Could it be that the Panthers are making some attempt to program a silent feeling that beats in the hearts and souls of a great cross-section of the black community?" In a column in the *Baltimore Afro-American* (December 20, 1969), entitled "How to Create 20 Million Black Panthers," David E. Sloan wrote, "They had been telling us so all along, but the reaction of the average black American to the allegation by militants that 'Whitey' was preparing to commit racial genocide was not to take it seriously. Now, apparently, the evidence is presenting itself to affirm that what the militants were saying is indeed true."

Dan Aldridge, writing in the *Michigan Chronicle* (December 13, 1969), began his column by discussing the massacre at My Lai and the mass murder of black students at Orangeburg, South Carolina, and then turned to the Hampton-Clark murders. He asked, "What do all the above incidents have in common? Well, they represent some examples of the way in which white America is carrying on her war against persons of color." An editorial in the *West Side Torch* (December 5–12, 1969), a Chicago newspaper, declared, "In a manner reminiscent of the slaughter of Little Big Horn, Fred Hampton, Chairman of the Black Panther Party, and Mark Clark were brutally and sadistically murdered by a band of legalized executioners."

Historically the black press has been reluctant to support revolutionary black groups, and the outrage expressed in the editorials and columns at the campaign to annihilate the Panthers is not meant to imply that the Panthers enjoy universal support in the black community. However, these expressions of support are indications of increasing solidarity in the black community. Furthermore, since the party has become engaged in so many projects in the black community, beginning in 1972, they have won the support of middle-class blacks as well as the so-called street blacks.

For example, Jesse Jackson was cheered at the annual meeting of the National Association for the Advancement of Colored People in Detroit in July 1972 when he declared that the black community needed the energy of the Panthers as well as the wisdom of the leaders of the NAACP.[35] The executive director of the Urban League, Vernon Jordan, has said that the Panther community program is good for the black community and good for the Panthers. And on June 24, 1972, the Panthers sponsored the massive Anti-War, African Liberation, Voter Registration, and Survival Conference in Oakland. At this meeting, attended by thousands of black people, expressions of solidarity came from several black ministers and black politicians, and the Bay Area Urban League presented the party an award for its Free Breakfast Program for Children.[36]

Alliances, coalitions, and influence on other groups

The appeal and influence of the Panthers have spread far beyond the black community in the United States. Alliances and coalitions have been effected with revolutionary black groups, with other Third World groups in the United States and abroad, and with white groups. Furthermore, many other groups have modeled their programs and activities on the pattern established by the Black Panther party. Newton made the position of the Black Panther party quite clear when he wrote in 1969 that "the only way that we are going to be free is to wipe out once and for all the oppressive structure of America. We realize we cannot do this without a struggle, without many alliances and coalitions, and this is the reason that we are moving in the direction we are, to get as many alliances as possible of people that are equally dissatisfied with the system."[37] Cleaver, while he was minister of information, wrote in his open letter to Stokely Carmichael in 1969, "One thing they [the enemies of black people] know, and we know, that seems to escape you, is that there is not going to be any revolution or black liberation in the United States as long as revolutionary blacks, whites, Mexicans, Puerto Ricans, Indians, Chinese, and Eskimos are unwilling or unable to unite into some functional machinery that can cope with the situation."[38]

The first coalition (actually a merger) took place between the Black Panthers and the Student Nonviolent (later, National) Coordinating Committee, early in 1968. This merger was short-lived because of ideological differences between the two groups on the role of whites in the black liberation struggle. Later, the Republic of New Africa, a black revolutionary nationalist group which advocates the partitioning of the United States into two separate nation states, one for blacks and one for whites, asked the Black Panther leaders for clarification of its stand on geographical separation. In response, while inviting the Republic of New Africa to join with the Panthers, Newton made it clear that the Panthers did not share their position on separation at the time. He wrote, "We are isolated in the ghetto area, concentrated in the North, in the metropolitan areas, in the industrial areas, and we think that this is a very good location as far as strategy is concerned in waging a strong battle against the established order."[39] At that time the Panthers called for a United Nations-supervised plebiscite for blacks to decide whether they wanted to secede from the United States or not. However, the Panthers offered whatever support they could provide to the Republic of New Africa, and asked for whatever support this organization could give to the Panthers.

The Black Panther party worked closely with black student unions in colleges and universities, especially on the West coast, and many of these groups adopted, almost verbatim, the program and platform of the Panthers, except those points concerned with the black community in general.[40] Also, the party formed coalitions with black revolutionary trade union groups and established black caucuses within other unions. For example, a Black Panther caucus was established in the United Automobile Workers' local in Fremont, California, and the Panthers assisted the black members of the Transport Workers Union in New York City in establishing an independent union.

The first working alliance between the Panthers and a white group was, of course, that with the Peace and Freedom party in 1968. In addition, in 1969 several other alliances with white groups were established. The Students for a Democratic Society, a revolutionary white group, passed a resolution in March of that year at its national council meeting, declaring that "within the black liberation movement the vanguard force is the Black Panther party."[41] The resolution went on to say that SDS declares "its support for the Black Panther party and their essentially correct program for the liberation of the black colony; its commitment to defend the Black Panther party against the vicious attacks of the racist pig power structure; its commitment to join the Black Panther party and other black revolutionary groups in the fight against white national chauvinism and white supremacy; its total commitment to the fight for liberation in the colony and revolution in the mother country." Chapters of SDS were urged to develop

and strengthen informal and formal relations with the Black
Panthers. In July the Panthers issued a call for a conference to
form a united front against fascism in America, to be held in
Oakland. To this conference they invited all groups interested in
attending, including the Yippies, and out of this developed the
predominately white National Committee to Combat Fascism.
This group established many chapters throughout the country, and
they served as subsidiary groups to the Black Panther party. In the
meantime, a White Panther party was founded in Ann Arbor,
Michigan. Its founder was arrested and sentenced to a term of
from 9-1/2 years to 11 years for allegedly passing marijuana to an
undercover agent. He was released after serving two years.

Although no formal alliance or coalition was ever effected between the Communist Party and the Panthers, an article, entitled
"On Establishing a United Front With Communists" appeared in
the party newspaper.[42] The article reviewed the traditional arguments put forth by groups around the world against cooperation
with Communists and ended with the assertion that "these excuses
will not hold water. The international proletariat has known all the
bitterness of tribulation caused by the split in the working class,
and becomes more and more convinced that the united front, that
the proletariat's unity of action on a national and international
scale are both necessary and perfectly possible." The following
year, however, Newton, in a response to William Patterson of the
Communist Party, U.S.A., declared that the American Communists were revisionists who were opposed to armed struggle.[43]
In 1972 the Black Panther party issued a call to Angela Davis to
"Come Home Angela," declaring that she had apparently "de-
serted black people under the dictates of the racist and reactionary
Communist party of America." The appeal ended with the question: "Is Angela Davis so blind as not to see that the Communist
party of America does not want her to work with other progressive
blacks because it would be in the interest of black people in
America and not in the interests of the reactionaries of Moscow?"[44]

On the other hand, the Panthers formed coalitions with the
peace movement, the women's liberation movement, and the gay
liberation movement, all of which are predominately white. Newton called for communication with and support for the peace
movement, because "if peace were to come about it would re-
volutionize the basic economic composition of the country.... If
the peace movement is successful, then the revolution will be
successful. If the peace movement fails, then the revolution in the
mother country fails."[45] On August 15, 1970, Newton issued a call

for "a working coalition with the gay liberation and women's liberation groups." These groups were invited to participate fully at Panther conferences, rallies, and demonstrations. Speaking to fellow Panthers, he said, "Whatever your personal opinions and your insecurities about homosexuality and the various liberation movements among homosexuals and women (and I speak of the homosexuals and women as oppressed groups), we should try to unite with them in a revolutionary fashion."[46] At the plenary session of the Panther-sponsored Revolutionary Constitutional Convention in Philadelphia on September 5, 1970, both homosexual and feminist groups were represented in large numbers. There were special groupings for women, lesbians, and male homosexuals, as well as many other categories of people. In addition, there were workshops dealing with self-determination for women and sexual self-determination, in which the participants themselves were given responsibility for drafting specific items for a new constitition for the United States. This alternative constitution was believed to be necessary, because the present Constitution was not designed to meet the needs of the people. At this meeting Newton called for a constitution "which will guarantee that within the socialist framework all groups will be adequately represented in the decision-making and administration which affects their lives."[47] (The Revolutionary People's Constitutional Convention was scheduled to be ratified at a meeting to be held at Howard University, Washington, D.C., November 27–29, 1970, but for a variety of reasons the Panthers maintain that they were unable to get a meeting place in Washington, although thousands of delegates arrived in the city from throughout the country.)

For these alliances and coalitions with predominately white groups, the Panthers have been sharply criticized by other black nationalists, especially the cultural nationalists. However, the Panthers have formed alliances with other Third World groups in the United States and have inspired the formation of several others. These include the Young Lords Organization, a group of young Puerto Ricans formed to fight for the "liberation of all oppressed people." The Young Lords have adopted a 13-point program and platform which closely parallels that of the Panthers, except that they emphasize independence for Puerto Rico and self-determination for Latin Americans inside the United States. The Young Lords also publish a newspaper, *Palante*, through the Latin Revolutionary News Service, and use the same format as *The Black Panther*.

In the Chicano community, the Brown Berets, a group of

militant young Mexican Americans, formed their community's counterpart to the Black Panthers. They are organized along the same lines as the Black Panther party, with which they have formed a coalition. The Patriot Party, also inspired by the Panthers, is a revolutionary organization of oppressed white people. It grew out of the Young Patriot organization in the poor white community of Chicago, but quickly spread to cities throughout the country. In virtually every respect the Patriot Party parallels the Black Panthers, in both goals and programs, and its leaders work closely with the Panther party.

Finally, the Panthers formed a coalition with a group of militant Chinese Americans, the Red Guards (later called I Wor Kuen), which was also inspired by the example of the Panthers. Starting out in San Francisco's Chinatown, they have incorporated chapters in New York and elsewhere and publish a newspaper, *Getting Together*, in both Chinese and English. The organization was formed after friction erupted between Chinese American youth and the police in San Francisco. The group calls for unity among Chinese American groups and for cooperation with blacks and Puerto Ricans. In February 1970 a call was issued for young Chinese to fight "against the real enemy–the rich whites who run this country and who profit from the war against Asian people." And when the delegates from the People's Republic of China arrived at the United Nations in 1971, members of I Wor Kuen were on hand to welcome them at the airport.

On cultural nationalism

The issue of forming alliances and coalitions with groups other than those of Third World peoples is not the only one on which the Panthers and other nationalist groups are at odds. Clearly one of the greatest divisions in the black nationalist movement is that between cultural nationalism and revolutionary nationalism.[48] In addition to the question of alliances and coalitions with white groups, which the Panthers encourage and which the cultural nationalists reject, there are ideological differences and such other strategic differences as the use of revolutionary force separating the two nationalist camps. Of all the differences, however, the ideological one is paramount. Whereas the revolutionary nationalists see the black struggle for liberation as basically one of class over race, race is the crucial factor in American life for the cultural nationalists. Since the transformation of the civil rights movement into the black nationalist movement in the second half of the 1960s, the leaders of the different camps have been at odds with each other. The cofounders of the Black Panther party, Newton and Seale, along with other Panther leaders, have constantly denounced cultural nationalism. In their days at Merritt Junior College, before the Black Panther party was formally organized, Newton and Seale left the school's Afro-American Association because of disagreements with the cultural nationalists' position on the question of race. According to Seale, Newton was criticized by black students because he held a door open for a white woman. In Seale's words, "They were so engrossed in this cultural nationalism, they just *hated* white people simply for the color of their skin." They later encountered difficulties with the cultural nationalists in the Soul Students Advisory Council at Merritt Junior College on the question of arming black people. Newton and Seale favored arming people, but their idea was rejected by the cultural nationalists.[49]

Newton spelled out his opposition to cultural nationalism in an interview on May 15, 1968. At this time he distinguished between what he said were two kinds of nationalism: revolutionary nationalism and reactionary nationalism. For him the Panthers are revolutionary whereas the cultural nationalists are reactionary. He continued:

Cultural Nationalism, or pork-chop nationalism as I sometimes call it, is basically a problem of having the wrong political perspective. It seems to be a reaction to, instead of an action against, political oppression. The cultural nationalists are concerned with returning to the old African culture and thereby regaining their identity and freedom. In other words, they feel that assuming the African culture is enough to bring political freedom. Many cultural nationalists fall into line as reactionary nationalists.[50]

He cites François Duvalier, former president of Haiti, as an example of reactionary nationalism. And in an article written for *Ebony* magazine the following year, he charged the cultural nationalists with impeding the struggle for black liberation. "The cultural nationalist seeks refuge by retreating to some ancient African behavior and culture, and he refuses to take into consideration those forces that are acting both on his own group and on the world as a whole.... We [the Black Panthers] feel no need to retreat to the past, although we respect our African heritage."[51]

Bobby Seale equates cultural nationalism with black racism. He accuses members of the US Organization, a cultural nationalist group in Los Angeles, of murdering two members of the Panthers.

"Alprentice 'Bunchy' Carter was killed because a group of black racists and cultural nationalists from Ron Karenga's US organization became enemies of the people and, in essence, sided with the capitalist power structure."[52] The other Panther party member killed at the same time was John Huggins, deputy minister of information for the southern California chapter of the party. Both were killed in an all-black student meeting at the University of California at Los Angeles.

Linda Harrison of the East Oakland office of the Panthers has perhaps best summarized the position of the party on cultural nationalism. She wrote: "Cultural nationalism manifests itself in many ways but all of these manifestations are essentially grounded in one fact: a universal denial and ignoring of the present political, social, and economic realities and the concentration on the past as a frame of reference. . . . And cultural nationalism is most always based on racism. We hear 'Hate Whitey' and 'Kill the Honkey.' . . . In all cases cultural nationalism in the midst of struggle seeks to create a racist ideology."[53]

The split between the Panthers and the cultural nationalists is such that any form of reconciliation appears unlikely. Both categories of nationalists posit their goal as the liberation of black people, but they differ sharply on how the goal is to be achieved. Recent evidence indicates that on at least one tactical point that formerly separated the Panthers and other revolutionary nationalists, the gap is being bridged. The cultural nationalists have been deeply involved in black community organizational activities for some time, and since 1972 such activities have been a major thrust of the Black Panther party.

Since this chapter was completed, Black Panther party leader Huey P. Newton is reported to have disappeared. In July and August 1974, Newton was arrested on three felony charges. The first occurred on July 30, when he was arrested by two black plainclothes policemen, who charged that a fight resulted when they refused Newton's offer to buy them a drink. Then, on August 17, the Oakland police charged that Newton's bodyguard pistol-whipped a tailor who appeared at Newton's apartment to show him some suit samples. Finally, after searching the apartment, the police charged Newton with having shot a young woman on August 6, claiming that evidence found in the apartment linked him with the crime. When he failed to appear in court, his attorney, Charles Garry, said, "I'm satisfied Huey doesn't intend to show up. I think he got a belly full of six-and-one-half years of intimidation and harassment by the Oakland Police."[54] Since being charged with the murder of an Oakland policeman in 1967, Newton has been constantly harassed by the police, although he has made infrequent public appearances.

This chapter has been devoted entirely to the Black Panther party as the vanguard of revolutionary nationalism in the black liberation movement. Other groups which may appropriately be described as revolutionary nationalists in orientation have been active, but they have been overshadowed by the Panthers. One such group, the League of Revolutionary Black Workers, grew out of the Dodge Revolutionary Union Movement, which was organized in 1968 to oppose racist oppression in the United Automobile Workers union and the management of the various plants. As of 1971 there were seven black unions, each representing a major automobile plant, affiliated with the league.[55] According to its constitution, the league is "dedicated to the relentless struggle against racism, capitalism, and imperialism. We are struggling for the liberation of black people in the confines of the United States, as well as to play a major revolutionary role in the liberation of all oppressed people in the world." Its ultimate objective is the creation of a society "free of race, sex, class, and national oppression, founded on the humanitarian principle of from each according to his ability, to each according to his needs."

The Republic of New Africa was formed in Detroit on March 31, 1968, when 200 black people from all over the United States met and signed a declaration of independence, proclaiming Afro-Americans "forever free and independent of the jurisdiction of the United States." The Republic of New Africa was proclaimed by its leaders to be "the government for the non-self-governing blacks held captive within the United States."[56] Among other objectives, the Republic of New Africa demands that the territory of the United States be partitioned into two separate states, one for blacks and one for whites, because its leaders feel that the two groups cannot live peacefully as equals within the same nation–state. The new black state would be organized according to the principles of socialism. Furthermore, this group has demanded that the U.S. government provide the new nation with $400 billion in reparations.

Since its inception the Republic of New Africa has encountered friction wherever it has attempted to operate. The headquarters of the group was moved to Bolton, Mississippi, in March 1971, where a group of 150 citizens and friends gathered on a 20-acre farm, which its members purchased for the nation's capitol and named El Malik, in honor of Malcolm X. In August the headquarters was raided by Mississippi policemen and agents of the Federal Bureau of Investigation. During the raid two policemen were wounded by gunfire. One of the policemen subsequently died of his wounds, and in May 1972 a member of the Republic of New Africa was sentenced to life in prison.[57] Several other officials of the group were arrested on a variety of charges, ranging from possession of illegal weapons to murder. The incident in Mississippi has apparently signaled the demise of the Republic of New Africa.

Finally, the Student National Coordinating Committee (formerly the Student Nonviolent Coordinating Committee), the first of the major civil rights organizations to embrace black nationalism through "black power," adopted a revolutionary nationalist ideology under the chairmanship of H. Rap Brown. Brown has set forth the ideological position of SNCC: "We cannot end racism, capitalism, colonialism, and imperialism until the reins of state power are in the hands of those people who understand that the wealth, the total wealth of the country and the world, belongs equally to all people."[58] In addition, in its monthly newpaper, *SNCC Monthly*, the leaders of the group declared: "We want equal status in a society that does not exploit and murder other people and smaller nations. We will fight for a socialist system that guarantees full, creative, nonexploitive lives for all human beings, fully aware that we will never be free until all oppressed people are free." Since the arrest and imprisonment of H. Rap Brown and the involvement of James Foreman with the League of Revolutionary Black Workers, the activities of SNCC have virtually ceased.

7

Cultural Nationalism

Within the context of black nationalism, the concept of cultural nationalism assumes that peoples of African descent share a way of life, or culture, which is fundamentally different from that of Europeans and other non-Africans. This way of life, it is assumed, is permitted greater freedom of expression on the continent of Africa than in the Western Hemisphere, but it is shared by Afro-Americans as well. Generations of American social scientists have rejected this notion, preferring instead the positions that Afro-American culture did not exist, that it represented a "pathological" version of the larger American culture, or that it was part of the larger "culture of poverty."[1]   One noted exception to the general practice of rejecting the validity of Afro-American culture was the work of Melville J. Herskovits, who as early as the 1930s put forth the theory that African cultural traits survived in the Western Hemisphere. Herskovits, a cultural anthropologist, maintained that aspects of African culture have had a marked effect on blacks in the United States, especially in religion, music, family life, language, dance, and mutual aid societies.[2] At about the same time, the most persistent critic of the Herskovits's theory was E. Franklin Frazier. Unlike Herskovits, Frazier maintained that the Afro-American's way of life derived largely from the circumstances under which they were forced to live in the United States, especially during the era of slavery and the first decades following emancipation.[3]

In many regards the theories of Herskovits and Frazier are not contradictory. The differences in formulation are found in differing approaches to the subject. Herskovits based his theory on ethnographic evidence resulting from extensive field research in both Africa and the Western Hemisphere, whereas Frazier relied heavily on written records. It is possible that African cultural traits survived in the United States without the carriers of these traits being aware that such a process was taking place. In defending the existence of black culture in the United States Blauner concludes: "if black Americans are an ethnic group, then they possess an ethnic culture; and just as the Jews explain to the world what Jewish culture is about and Italians define Italian-American culture, we will learn what Afro-American culture is from American blacks–when they are ready to tell us–rather than from our own dogmas and fantasies."[4] In addition to the African heritage, Blauner sees black culture originating from such diverse sources as the southern heritage of black people, slavery, emancipation, the migration of black people to the North, and the pervasiveness of white racism. He regards the cultural nationalist movement as a form of cultural revitalization.

In recent years, however, scholars have seriously studied Afro-American culture, or as some prefer, the black subculture in the United States.[5] This recognition of the reality of black culture resulted from the interest generated in Afro-American studies programs by black students and others as the black nationalist movement gained impetus in the late 1960s.

Two of the leading figures in cultural nationalism in the United States were Imamu Amiri Baraka (also known as LeRoi Jones) and Maulana Ron Karenga. Although national figures, Baraka's work has centered on the East coast, primarily in Newark and New York, and Karenga has maintained a base in California.

Imamu Amiri Baraka

Born in Newark, New Jersey, in 1934, and educated at Howard and Columbia universities, Baraka lived in New York City's East Village until 1965. There he wrote plays, poetry, reviews of jazz, fiction, and social history. Early in 1965 he moved to Harlem, where he organized the Black Arts Repertory Theater School. With the founding of this school he literally launched the black arts movement, which quickly spread throughout the country.

The school did not last long, and Baraka moved back to Newark, where he established Spirit House, a theater group which became the nucleus around which he was later to build a broadly based organization–Black Community Development and Defense. This organization later joined 38 others to form the Committee for a Unified NewArk, a political organization, because, as he put it, "Bloods are interested in traditional politics and anyone serious about organizing has to eventually recognize that we have to have the sentiment of the great numbers of black people. We must be *their* functionaries."[6] The goal of the Committee for a Unified

NewArk is securing political power for the black and Puerto Rican communities.

Community organizing was a new venture for Baraka. In the spring of 1967, he went to San Francisco State College to teach. While on the West coast he met Maulana Ron Karenga, who had built a well-disciplined organization called the US Organization, which stressed cultural nationalism. When Baraka returned to Newark, he used the US Organization as a model for organizing black people around concrete issues. Out of these organizational efforts developed the Black Community Development and Defense organization. One of its crucial functions was the creation of a new value system for the black community.

A Black Value System. Utilizing the seven concepts established by Karenga as the core of "scientific principles" necessary for the formulation of nationalism among Afro-Americans, Baraka has outlined what he calls "a black value system" based on the religion of *Kawaida*, or traditional black values and customs and a common code of morality.[7] These seven principles are:

1 Umoga, *or unity. This principle advocates unity in the family, community, nation, and race. Afro-Americans must strive to maintain both physical and mental unity and think of themselves collectively if liberation is to be achieved.*

2 Kujichagulia, *or self-determination. Afro-Americans must define themselves, name themselves, and speak for themselves instead of having these things done by outsiders. Self-determination develops out of unity and furthers the cause of liberation.*

3 Ujima, *or collective work and responsibility. This principle means that Afro-Americans must be at harmony with each other. The problems of any individual become the problems of the group, and they must be collectively solved. Through collective work and responsibility comes the internal unity which is necessary before blacks can deal effectively with the outside world.*

4 Ujamaa, *or cooperative economics. Rather than depending upon European systems of economics, ujamaa advocates a system in which blacks utilize the traditional African method of distributing wealth. Within the black community business enterprises would be maintained collectively and the profits shared equally.*

5 Nia, *or purpose. The collective aim of black people should be the development of the black community in order to build a nation which restores them to "traditional greatness."*

6 Kuumba, *or creativity. Baraka feels that black creativity or black art should be geared toward devising a method for black liberation. A*

> *cultural revolution is necessary before a political revolution is possible. In this regard, the minds of the people are crucial, and it is through art that people are prepared for liberation.*
>
> 7 Imani, *or faith. In order to create a new value system in the black community, it is necessary for the people to have faith: faith in leaders, teachers, and parents; faith in blackness; faith in nationalism; faith that blacks can build themselves into a conscious nation once again.*

Baraka maintains that black survival depends on the creation of a new value system, one which is radically different from that imposed by Europeans. "The internalization of a white value system will always militate for white decisions about the way things should be. Whether it is a national anthem or an economic system." Furthermore, "If we do not consciously create a new value system, one that is quite different from the rest of crazy America's–you will be exactly what crazy America is and die the way she dies."[8] And, "If you internalize the white boy's system, you will come to his same conclusions about the world."[9]

It is Baraka's view that the creation of a black value system, a new way of viewing the world, is essential if black people in the United States even expect to free themselves from internal colonialism. This is true, he believes, because once the mind is free, anything is possible. And he believes that the seven principles of the doctrine of *Kawaida* can serve as an ideology around which to unite Afro-Americans. In an effort to put these principles into practice, Baraka organized the African Free School within Spirit House. The school conducts classes on the elementary level, with the black value system at its core. For example, the children are taught the value system as they learn the alaphabet: "L" equals love, "O" equals one, "P" equals pride, "S" equals strength, "T" equals truth, "U" equals unity, and so on.

Because of the success of the methods used in the African Free School, an African Free School class was established in a public school in Newark in September 1970.[10] This experiment was financed by the federal Office of Education in an effort to determine whether these methods would improve the academic performance of so-called problem children and slow learners. The class consisted of 30 pupils, with a comparable group taught by conventional methods and using a traditional curriculum serving as a control group.

Each morning the school day began for those in the ungraded African Free School class with a pledge of allegiance to the red, black, and green flag of black liberation. The pledge they recited was "Red is for the blood of our forefathers which has not been shed in vain. Black is for the color of our faces and the job we must do. Green is for youth and new ideas." The classroom was decorated with drawings of African villages, and the only formal textbook for the students (grades five through eight) was *The Autobiography of Malcolm X*. Field trips to hear black speakers and see black performers were made regularly. The curriculum of the class consisted of Swahili, history, reading, mathematics, and health.

The teaching methods were unorthodox. There was one certified teacher, as required by state law, and four teacher aides. They all wore identical red, black, and green clothes, and when a question was asked the children responded in unison. Questions were prefaced by "please," and the teachers responded with "thank you" to their answers. When questioned about this method by a reporter, the teacher responded, "We call this method collective education. It teaches collectively, not individually." In explaining its purpose, she continued, "The students don't have to feel left out or in competition. Individualism is a white man's idea. We want to reduce the conflict that individualism and competition produces and achieve consensus."[11] Baraka has said, "We recognize personality, but not individuality."[12]

The principal of the school in which the African Free School class was established expressed the view that the experimental class was an important alternative to traditional education, which had failed these pupils. In an effort to compare the experimental class with the control group class, an outside agency, AFRAM Associates, was asked to evaluate the program. While the evaluation team reports that it made "no attempt to compare [the experimental class] with the control class," the final report did note positive changes in attitudes about school by the pupils; improvement in reading, writing, and oral communication; and positive changes in self-concept and social consciousness.[13] Furthermore, both pupils and their parents appeared to be pleased with the experiment.

The principle behind the African Free School approach is that black children frequently lag behind middle-class white children in academic achievement because of a lack of self-esteem. That is, they experience difficulty learning when they have been taught, directly and by example, that they are worthless. Public school teachers, black and white, expect them to perform poorly and hence do not teach them with the same degree of diligence that they do middle-class children. And since they are not expected to achieve according to middle-class standards, they indeed fail to do so. The African Free School approach, which has been adopted in several black alternative schools throughout the country, requires that teachers instill self-confidence in pupils and that their parents become involved in the educational process. The assumption is made that once the children are taught pride in themselves and in their heritage, they are better equipped to learn such conventional and necessary skills as reading, writing, and arithmetic.

The Pan-African party.   In addition to his many other activities, Baraka has emerged as a political leader on the international, national, and local levels. One of his most ambitious projects was the organization of the Congress of African Peoples which met in Atlanta, in September 1970. On the national level Baraka was one of the leaders of the first National Black Political Convention, held in Gary, Indiana, in March 1972. And on the lcoal level he was largely responsible for the transfer of political power from whites to blacks in Newark in the June 1970 election.

Baraka's black nationalism rejects repatriation to Africa, the formation of a separate nation–state within the United States, and instant revolution at the present time.[14] It is his view that at the present time black people are unwilling to move to Africa. He sees Pan-Africanism as creating a unified and strong Africa, capable of demanding respect for people of African descent wherever they are found. He rejects separation into an autonomous nation–state, because "separation must come *mentally* before *any* physical movement can begin." Finally, he rejects instant revolution, because "there is no revolution without the people." Before a political revolution can be accomplished, there must be a change in the consciousness of the people. Further, because of the technological might of the United States, a successful revolution by black people is impossible. Instead, Baraka proposes self-determination, self-efficiency, self-defense, and self-respect for blacks wherever they are found. It is his view that the cultural revolution, manifested in a new value system, must precede any potential political revolution. The creation of the Pan-African party, the political arm of the Congress of African Peoples, is seen as a first step in this process.

The first Congress of African Peoples attracted some 2,700 delegates from around the world, including Afro-American integrationists and separationists; peoples of African descent from the Caribbean and South America; Africans from independent nations and colonies; oppressed minorities from other continents, including Australian aborigines; and observers from the Mexican American, Puerto Rican, and Japanese communities.[15] The purpose of the Congress was the establishment of unity among peoples of African descent throughout the world and the development of political, economic, and social institutions to liberate blacks from oppression.

During its four-day session the delegates were divided into 11 workshops devoted to black technology, economics, education, communications, creativity, community organization, history, law and justice, political liberation, social organization, and religious systems. These workshops were designed to produce proposals for new institutions based on a value system beneficial to the African peoples of the world. As coordinator of the political liberation workshop, Baraka defined its function as the creation of a worldwide political party, the Pan-African Party, which would function to gain power through elected and appointed public offices and community organizations, establish alliances and coalitions with other Third World organizations, and engage in actual or threatened disruption. Such a party would operate wherever large numbers of black people are concentrated and engage in the following activities: voter registration; mobilization of the community by uniting it around specific issues; organizing the community to work for a common goal; politicizing members of the black community by teaching them how to gain, maintain, and use political power; running candidates for office; making alliances in order to develop operational unity; and maintaining close relations with other Third World peoples. In terms of organization, the party would operate on the local, regional, state, national, and international levels.[16] After four days of meetings the political liberation workshop passed resolutions in the areas of community organization, alliances and coalitions, and disruption.

At each of the 11 workshops specialists presented resource papers, and resoltuions were passed for the group. One of the striking features of the congress was its diversity. The leaders who addressed the delegates included such diverse positions as those of Whitney Young of the Urban League; a black dentist from Alabama who was a candidate for governor of that state; the ambassador from Guinea to the United States; and a national spokesman for the Nation of Islam. The delegates were equally diverse in their ideological positions. In addition, the Congress attracted professionals, lay people, community workers, and college students. They demonstrated that operational unity without clashing over ideological positions is possible among different black groups.

In 1971 the Congress of African Peoples held its eastern regional conference in Newark. The progress made in implementing the resolutions of the first Congress was reviewed, and it was announced that 10 new chapters had been established in major cities throughout the country. In addition, the Congress had played a major role in promoting the National Black Unity Conference in Washington, D.C., had held West coast and Midwest regional conferences, and had sponsored leadership conferences in several cities. The 11 workshops met in the four days of the conference, again drafting resolutions and reviewing progress on the implementation of past resolutions. A major concern of this regional meeting was the forthcoming 1972 political elections. The delegates agreed to support blacks seeking elective office, but the role of the Congress at the Democratic National Convention was left vague, except that it would attempt to organize a strong national black political force. However, the group agreed to play a major role in the National Black Political convention in March 1972.

One of the concrete proposals resulting from the eastern regional meeting was that calling for the establishment of teacher-training centers in which black teachers would be taught to "exemplify the African personality, whether they teach in independent black educational institutions, the public school, or in the home or community."[17] These centers would also develop curricula for institutions serving black children.

The second annual meeting of the Congress of African Peoples was convened in San Diego in September 1972. The unity which had characterized the first Congress was less evident, because the Congress devoted much of its time to the establishment of a separate black political party. Though representatives of several African political parties participated, the meeting was boycotted by the National Association for the Advancement of Colored People and members of the Congressional Black Caucus. The National Black Political Convention had been held in Gary, Indiana, in March, and the political agenda adopted there had been opposed by many groups and individuals.

In appealing for the establishment of an all-black political party, as opposed to working within the American party system, Baraka supported the former on the grounds that "both the Republican and Democratic parties have betrayed us when their interests have conflicted with ours, which is most of the time." He continued, "The American political system, like all other white institutions in this country, is designed to operate for the benefit of the white race. Both the Democratic and the Republican parties are guilty of racial arrogance."[18] All members of the Congressional Black Caucus are Democrats, some elected from predominately white constituencies, and therefore opposed the formation of an all-black political party.

Although the second annual meeting of the Congress of African Peoples did not evidence the operational unity that characterized the first meeting, it is clear that the Congress represents one of the strongest influences on national politics of any black nationalist organization to date. Unlike preceding nationalist movements, the Congress is composed of all strata of the black community, including intellectuals. The 220 organizations represented at the first Congress included professional groups such as black psychologists, engineers, social workers, college and university student groups, theater groups, and black-owned banks.[19] In addition, the Congress attracted groups throughout the country, from both large cities and small towns. At the Atlanta meeting groups from Aligruppa, Pennsylvania; Warrentown, North Carolina; Saginaw, Michigan; and Palo Alto, California, were present. This occupational and geographic diversity no doubt results from the spread of nationalist ideology among Afro-Americans in recent years.

A major problem for the Congress remains that of financing. Although Baraka has said that for such a movement to succeed, it needs resources, as well as ideology, organization, and communications, on the question of resources the Congress is vague. Money can come from several sources: from national parties interested in the black vote, from government agencies, and from fund-raising drives. The important factor here is that the money be controlled by the Congress.[20] And the economics workshop's finance subcommittee recommended several potential sources for financing the Congress, including membership fees, contributions from public and private corporations, the sale of publications, and the marketing of products. But these suggestions appear to be less clear-cut than most of the other resolutions and recommendations. For example, it was resolved in the political liberation workshop that the Congress "raise a substantial amount of dollars in American money to be given to the Tanzania–Zambia railroad project," but how such "substantial" funds were to be raised was not spelled out.[21] Judging from the organizations represented, the Congress was largely financed by white-controlled institutions and government agencies. It seems unlikely that such agencies will continue to finance an organization which is fundamentally opposed to a system which permitted them to amass these resources in the first place.

The National Black Political Convention. Although the first National Black Political Convention was organized by a coalition of black leaders, including the Congressional Black Caucus. Baraka, a member of the steering committee, emerged from the Convention as a national political leader. And he was largely credited with maintaining unity among the 2,776 delegates and 4,000 alternates from 43 states gathered at Gary, Indiana, in March 1972. Those in attendance represented elected public officials, national civil rights organizations committed to integration, national separatist organizations, the Black Panther party, local community groups with varying ideological positions, and businessmen.

According to its major document, *The National Black Political Agenda*, the Convention was called to establish an independent black political movement, because "the American system does not work for the masses of our people, and it cannot be made to work without radical, fundamental change."[22] Ideological differences were widespread at Gary, but the first black political convention in American history achieved a significant degree of operational unity. Baraka served as chairman of the general sessions and was active in setting up the meeting.

The Convention did not call for the creation of a separate black political party; rather, it adopted an agenda which would establish an independent black political assembly to strengthen black political power and bring blacks together in a political convention every four years, before the Democratic and Republican conventions. The resolutions adopted by the Convention totaled 88 in number and ranged anywhere from black control of institutions in the U.S. black community, to reparations for Afro-Americans and support for African liberation movements. Two controversial resolutions, one calling for the dismantling of the state of Israel, and the other opposing the bussing of black children to white schools, were later greatly amended. Opposition to these resolutions came primarily from civil rights groups and individuals representing organized labor.

The First National Black Political Convention was held amidst considerable confusion, much of which resulted from the role blacks would play in the forthcoming Democratic and Republican conventions. Many of the delegates had strong ties to the Democratic party, and at the time Representative Shirley Chisholm of Brooklyn, a member of the Congressional Black Caucus, was actively campaigning for the Democratic nomination for the Presidency. The question of support for her candidacy was discussed, but such a position was opposed by those who believed her candidacy was merely symbolic.

In spite of the confusion, there were several important results from the Convention. It was from the Convention that the National Black Political Agenda, with its resolutions and criteria for evaluating political candidates and social programs, emerged. At the suggestion of Baraka, the National Black Political Assembly, a national organization representing a cross-section of ideological views, was formed. The Assembly was designed to function similarly to a Congressional body and would serve to endorse candidates, conduct voter education and registration drives, assess black progress, and make recommendations to the national convention and to the black community. In essence, it would function in the same manner as a political party without officially being considered such an organization. This compromise move accommodated those opposed to the creation of an all-black political party. Finally, the Convention served notice to the Democratic and Republican parties that blacks are no longer willing to blindly follow the dictates of the two major parties.

Perhaps the greatest achievement of the Convention was the amazing degree of unity displayed, in spite of the diverse ideological views of its participants. To a great extent, Baraka is to be credited with creating and maintaining this extraordinary degree of unity.

Committee for a Unified NewArk. On the local level, Baraka's nationalism has achieved a measure of success in his native Newark. Under the auspices of the Committee for a Unified NewArk, significant strides toward implementing Baraka's conception of nationalism have been made. The Committee is a diverse organization of community groups which functions to secure black political power in Newark, a city with a predominately black population. In its organization the Committee consists of six basic units. These units include the Creators, or the creative part of the organization, who focus on the arts. The core of the Creators is the Spirit House Movers, a drama group. The Young Lions unit is composed of young males who train mentally and physically to develop themselves into the core of the task of nation building. An older group of males, the Lords, is charged with raising the political consciousness of the community and such organizational work as voter registration and education.

Women in the Committee form a separate group called the Good Spirits. Their functions include inspiring men, educating youth, and participating in community development. Another unit of the Committee is the Jihad Productions, the publishing arm which produces and distributes books, pamphlets, magazines, records, and films. Finally, the African Free School is organized in an effort to teach black children through the use of African concepts and images relevant to present-day life.

Perhaps the most important accomplishment of the Committee to date was its crucial role in the transfer of power in Newark from whites to blacks in June 1970. Newark, the largest city in New Jersey, had a population of approximately 380,000 at the time of the election. Its population was composed of 61 percent blacks and 11 percent Puerto Ricans. For years the city had been controlled by a coalition of corrupt white politicians and businessmen. When Kenneth Gibson, the city's first black mayor, assumed office, the city had already witnessed a major black rebellion in 1967, during which 26 persons were killed, more than 1,100 injured, and more than 1,600 jailed. The black community was occupied for several days by a force of 3,000 national guardsmen, 1,400 local police, and 500 state troopers.[23]

The rebellion erupted as a result of the plethora of problems plaguing the black community and the insensitivity of the political leaders to the needs of black people. For example, Gibson inherited a city with an overall unemployment rate of 14 percent, and an unemployment rate of 30 percent among blacks and Puerto Ricans. At least one-third of the residents were on public assistance. There were an estimated 20,000 drug addicts in its population, few of whom were being treated. Furthermore, Newark had the highest rates of several indicators of social disorganization of any city in the country: the highest crime rate, the highest percentage of substandard housing, and the highest rate of veneral disease, infant and maternal mortality, and tuberculosis.[24]

Given these circumstances, Baraka and the Committee set out to bring about representative government and political equity for Newark's blacks. Describing the work of the Committee during the election, Baraka said, "What the black people, the African people, are trying to achieve here is an old American concept—community control. All we want is our equitable share."[25] The Committee, through Baraka's leadership, is widely credited with solidifying support for Gibson. Since his election, the mayor has been criticized for cooperating with Baraka and the nationalists allied with him, but they have become an important part of his constituency, and without their assistance he would never have been elected. Furthermore, the main concern of the Committee is to insure that the city's leaders are responsible to Newark's black community, the majority of its population.

A city as steeped in social problems as Newark has been for

decades is unlikely to resolve them in a few years, regardless of who is elected mayor. And Gibson has been hampered in his efforts in the first term by a city council dominated by an antagonistic white majority, which frequently vetoes his appointments and sabotages his programs. Nevertheless, in his first two years in office Gibson has been credited by all segments of the community with restoring integrity to the office of the mayor, and with the cooperation of Baraka and the Committee, notable advances have been made.

One of the major achievements of Gibson's administration has been instilling pride in Newark's black population. And mainly through the organizational efforts of Baraka, Newark has become probably the most cohesive black nationalist community in the nation. The school board has a black and Puerto Rican majority for the first time, and there is some evidence that the schools are becoming more responsive to the needs of their client population. Because of these changes and the mayor's insistence upon honesty in government, some of the city's financial problems are being solved.

New housing is replacing the slums and the sections burned out in the 1967 rebellion. For example, Baraka and his supporters organized a corporation in October 1972 and received state support for the construction of a 16-story low- and moderate-income housing project, which cost $6.4 million.[26] In addition, the increasing nationalism in Newark is reflected in the election of officers for the United Community Corporation, a $6 million antipoverty fund. Baraka's supporters effectively won control of this agency in a city-wide election. Baraka insists that these funds be utilized for the poor blacks of Newark. Furthermore, he insists that since blacks comprise a majority of the population, they should control the city council. He defines the relationship between the city council and the black community as one of neocolonialism and charges that the council is not concerned with the city's blacks. "This city does $3.5 billion worth of retail business every year, but our percentage is less than six-tenths of one percent... there will have to be black control of the City Council in 1974."[27]

On a more symbolic level, Newark's black nationalist community is responsible for other changes. Three schools have been renamed for blacks: Marcus Garvey, Martin Luther King, Jr., and Harriet Tubman. The birthdays of Malcolm X and Martin Luther King, Jr., are celebrated with ceremonies at City Hall. Because of the influence of Baraka, Newark's black population is being educated to the realities of life for Afro-Americans in the United

States, and in increasing numbers they appear to be responding affirmatively.

Although Baraka has become involved in politics at several levels, he continues his artistic pursuits, mainly through the medium of the theater. He finds no conflict between the two, because he sees art as politics and politics as art.[28] He believes that the theater is an important means of raising the consciousness of Afro-Americans, because it reaches a wider public in the black community than does literature. For him cultural nationalism is important in that "it's the only way to keep a people committed against their enemies." Although it is important for cultural revolution to precede armed struggle, Baraka believes it is important for the black playwright to have a revolutionary commitment. Those who are not attempting to transform the present-day reality of black people, according to Baraka, are "enemies of the people."

Other cultural nationalists

Although he has not received much national publicity as a leader when compared with Baraka, Maulana Ron Karenga was one of the founders of the contemporary cultural nationalist movement in the United States. He established the US Organization in Los Angeles in 1965 and is the originator of the doctrine of *Kawaida*, from which the seven principles of the black value system stem. Furthermore, Karenga played an active role in organizing the three black power conferences held between 1966 and 1968. An articulate spokesman, he is perhaps best known as a theoretician and synthesizer of the thoughts of other black leaders. Unlike Baraka, Karenga's published works have not received wide distribution. He has, however, published one book and several articles setting forth his ideas.[29]

The essence of Karenga's thought is the doctrine of *Kawaida*, an ideology which sets forth a completely new value system as a means of understanding the history of Afro-American people and as a blueprint for raising political consciousness through the restructuring of their value system. Nationalism is viewed as a precondition for revolution, and culture is seen as the major vehicle for achieving national awareness and commitment. Therefore, before a people can seriously consider political revolution, a cultural revolution is necessary. "When we talk about a cultural revolution," he writes, "we're talking essentially about cultural reconversion, the conscious and programmatic restructuring of attitudes and relationships that aid us in our aspiration for national liberation."[30] Consequently, the major focus of the black struggle must be geared toward winning the hearts and minds of black people.

Culture is important, because it gives a people "identity, purpose and direction." Realizing that after centuries of oppression black people in the United States have assimilated various aspects of the dominant white culture, the first step in the struggle for liberation is the creation of a new set of values. According to the doctrine of *Kawaida*, one method of accomplishing this goal is for Afro-Americans to internalize the seven-point system of values. They must "Think Black, Talk Black, Act Black, Create Black, Buy Black, Vote Black, and Live Black."[31] This cultural reconversion encompasses mythology, history, social organization, economic organization, political organization, creativity, and ethos. Further, culture provides a moral dimension to the struggle for liberation. It "establishes rules and systems of association and behavior as well as resolving contradiction among its people and harmonizing diverse yet interdependent interests."[32] Cultural reconversion begins on the individual level, because the first step toward national unity is individual unity. Individual reconversion then leads to group solidarity in which Afro-Americans put forth unified responses to oppression.

Realizing the present diversity among Afro-Americans, Karenga has been a strong advocate of operational unity, or unity without uniformity. Since the problems that confront black people are so diverse, he believes that many organizations are needed to deal with them. Given the present status of black people in the United States, complete unity must be a long-term goal. However, Karenga maintains that it is essential for all groups to support each other in the defense of black people and in the attempt for black people to develop their potential.

Though Karenga maintains that the cultural reconversion of Afro-Americans is essential and that a variety of approaches is necessary, it is his view that the black community must achieve autonomy from the larger white society if unity is to lead to liberation. However, in a speech at Yale University in 1968, he outlined what he perceives as the supporting roles whites should play in the struggle for black liberation.[33] These consist of three functions: nonintervention, foreign aid, and civilizing committees. By nonintervention he means that sympathetic whites have no direct role to play in the black community, that they should not impose their authority and value system on the black community.

Since the black community is essentially a colony of white

America, Karenga maintains that whites can provide "foreign aid" in the form of financial aid and technical assistance. Financial aid should be given, without strings attached, in the form of reparations for past injustices. Technical aid, he suggests, could take the form of research geared toward improving the quality of life for black people. He also suggests that once research data are collected, they should not be interpreted by whites, but turned over to blacks, so that blacks might use them to their own advantage.

The establishment of civilizing committees among whites is seen by Karenga as the most important task whites, especially university students and teachers, can play in the black liberation struggle. This task involves attempts to instill humanitarian values throughout the larger society by communicating a new ideology to the masses. Since his audience was made up of university students and teachers, he suggested that they take the lead in the effort to spread humanitarian values.

A major theoretician of cultural nationalism, Karenga has been the target of much abuse in recent years. He has been maligned by blacks and whites, especially those blacks who consider themselves revolutionary nationalists and who consider cultural nationalism to be reactionary. In his most recent writing Karenga accepts blame for contributing to the heated and divisive debate between the cultural nationalists and the revolutionary nationalists.[34] He admits that the US Organization has never issued a clear statement on the meaning and objectives of cultural nationalism, thereby permitting the concept to be misinterpreted and manipulated. He feels that the division between cultural nationalism and revolutionary nationalism is false, because nationalism is a precondition for revolution, and culture is the primary means of achieving national awareness.

Although Karenga has never achieved the status of a popular national leader, his impact on the contemporary black nationalist movement has been widespread. The principles of the doctrine of *Kawaida* are integral components of the work of the Congress of African Peoples and were repeatedly proclaimed by various speakers at the Black Political Convention in Gary. Furthermore, black leaders and spokesmen freely quote them from public platforms whenever the occasion arises. At the same time, Karenga's influence on the black community in Los Angeles has been minimal when compared with that of Baraka in Newark. The size and racial composition of Los Angeles have no doubt been partly responsible for the lack of impact of the US Organization on the black community, but the organization and its founder must share responsibility for its apparent demise. Though some of the charges made against the US Organization (e.g., collaboration with the Central Intelligence Agency and the Los Angeles Police Department) were probably invented by its critics, others (e.g., warfare with the Black Panthers resulting in at least two Panther deaths) appear to have some degree of plausibility. As a theoretician of cultural nationalism, Karenga's contribution is notable, but as a community organizer his abilities appear to lag behind those of Baraka. In short, he has experienced difficulties translating his theories into viable programs for the black community.

In June 1971, Karenga was sentenced to one to ten years in prison for "assault with intent to do great bodily harm."[35] He was tried for the "torture" of two "innocent young black women." After two years he had not been released from prison, and there is every likelihood that his case represents still another in the long series of black leaders being imprisoned for their political views. During his trial, testimony against him was provided by two undercover agents and by one of the women who was allegedly tortured. As a reward for her testimony, charges of grand theft pending against her were dropped. Karenga is continuing his writing from prison, and he appears to have clarified and extended his views on the role of cultural nationalism in the struggle for black liberation.

Imamu Amiri Baraka and Maulana Ron Karenga are the persons most often identified with the contemporary cultural nationalist movement. However, a sizeable proportion of the Afro-American population probably subscribes to the central notion of cultural nationalist ideology; namely, that it is through culture that national awareness is achieved and that nationalism is essential for black liberation. This is especially true of students who form a strategic element in the black community. Indeed, the demands of black college and university students for Afro-American studies programs might rightfully be considered part of the general cultural nationalist movement. Furthermore, elements of cultural nationalism are found in the ideology of all who consider themselves black nationalists.

On the organizational level, Barbara Ann Teer, founder and director of the National Black Theater, has attempted to create an alternative system of values in the black community through the medium of the theater. In an interview she discussed the role of the National Black Theater in the black liberation struggle, emphasizing its aim to liberate and regain spiritual freedom through it performances and to convey this freedom to the audience.[36] Performancesat the theater are called "rituals," to which she attributes a revitalizing function. Performers in the National Black Theater are called "liberators," and during the rituals they move freely among the members of the audience, attempting to "convert" them, as is characteristic of black fundamentalist churches. It is from these churches, as well as bars, barbershops, beauty parlors, and street corners, that the National Black Theater collects material for its performances. According to Barbara Ann Teer, "Our technique is all about the strengthening of the mind. We start with the premise that the Western system is a very surface system, dealing with the surface as opposed to the essence of things, the center, the spirit of people." She continued, "A spiritual journey is the opening of new avenues of thought redirecting the whole concept of who we are and how we must function."

The National Black Theater attempts to establish a theatrical concept based on the black life-style, using the black church as its model. For Barbara Ann Teer, blackness is a "spiritual value." And the aim of the Theater is "to create an alternative system of values to the Western concept. The Western concepts are so surface they cannot fulfill the spiritual needs of our people." Like Baraka and Karenga, she believes that for Afro-Americans to make progress toward liberation, they must engage in a variety of activities, including politics, economics, and culture.

One of the outstanding cultural nationalists at the present time is Harold Cruse, writer and teacher. His *The Crisis of the Negro Intellectual* is perhaps the clearest statement extant on the use of culture as an ideological weapon. In addition, he has elaborated on his position in subsequent writings.[37] In *The Crisis of the Negro Intellectual*, Cruse had this to say: "As long as the Negro's cultural identity is in question, or open to self-doubts, then there can be no positive identification with the real demands of his political and economic existence." Later in the same work he writes: *"Thus it is only through a cultural analysis of the Negro approach to group 'politics' that the errors, weaknesses and goal-failures can cogently be analyzed and positively worked out."*[38] He ends the volume with the following:

The farther the Negro gets from his historical antecedents in time, the more tenuous become his conceptual ties, the emptier his social conceptions, the more superficial his visions. His one great and present hope is to know and understand his Afro-American history in the United States more profoundly. Failing that, and failing to create a new synthesis and a social theory of action, he will suffer the historical fate described by the philosopher who warned that "Those who cannot remember the past are condemned to repeat it."[39]

Throughout this and other works Cruse has repeatedly championed the cause of black cultural nationalism, although taking a different approach from other cultural nationalists at times.

The essence of Cruse's cultural nationalism is that in the United States cultural imperialism by the larger society, aided and abetted by black assimilationists, has served to maintain the oppression of Afro-Americans by precluding the creation of black values; it is the responsibility of black intellectuals to resist this cultural imperialism, to preserve the black cultural heritage, and to demonstrate that American artistic originality is founded on elements of the black esthetic. He maintains that the only real political role for the black creative intellectual is the politics of culture. He writes that "the path to more knowledge for the Negro intellectual is through cultural nationalism–an ideology that has made Jewish intellectuals into a social force to be reckoned with in America."[40] Cruse demonstrates that in the black community there has always existed a strain of thought that contains the elements of nationality, and that those espousing this ideology have been overshadowed by those committed to assimilation. Since the assimilationist intellectuals have historically been accorded greater prominence in the media, they must share responsibility for the cultural imperialism imposed on Afro-Americans. In an address at Yale University in 1968, Cruse said, "Black cultural nationalism has to be seen as an attempt, a necessary historical attempt, to deal with another kind of cultural nationalism that is implied in our society, namely, the cultural nationalism of the dominant white group." He continued, "I think we find that an ideology exists which *has* to deny the validity of other kinds of cultural values that might compete with its own standards–whether in the social sciences, the arts, literature, or economic activity.[41] Cruse believes that Afro-American studies programs should be geared to the development of black institutions–political, economic, cultural, and social–and that they must begin with an analysis of the historical problems of Afro-Americans. In response to a question posed at the 1968 Yale conference on Afro-American studies, he defined cultural nationalism as "nothing but the attempt of a group or nation or minority to express what is indigenous to its own historical background in order to enhance its public image–social image–in the eyes of the world."[42]

In addition to Afro-American studies being a major vehicle for the spread of black cultural nationalism, Cruse envisions the theater as playing a major role. It is through the theater that blacks in the United States have made many notable cultural contributions, but prior to the advent of the black nationalist movement, the theater was not utilized as a vehicle for promoting black culture. Black playwrights most often adhered to the dictates of various elements in the white community, which were primarily concerned with the advancement of special interests at variance with those of the black community. In this regard, his position parallels that of Imamu Baraka, Barbara Ann Teer, and other black artists–namely, that the black theater should serve as a political force in the black liberation movement.

While advocating the spread of cultural nationalist ideology within the black community, Cruse also calls for a radical restructuring of the entire American cultural apparatus. Here he differs from other cultural nationalists in that he extends the concept to include what he calls a cultural revolution, which he believes "affords the intellectual means, the conceptual framework, the theoretical link that ties together all the disparate, conflicting, and contending trends within the Negro movement as a whole in order to transform the movement from a mere rebellion into a revolutionary movement that can 'shape actions to ideas, to fit the world into a theoretic frame.' "[43] It is his view that such a cultural revolution should transform all American instruments of cultural communication and place it under public control. Black intellectuals are the logical people to initiate this task, because Afro-Americans are the only peole in the United States with the need, motivation, and historical prerogative to demand such changes. In addition, Cruse feels that racial equality cannot be achieved until and unless Afro-Americans force certain fundamental structural changes in the larger society.

Although Cruse's concept of a black-led cultural revolution in the United States extends the notion of cultural nationalism beyond that of some other cultural nationalists, it is difficult to perceive his programmatic approach as a viable one in a society in which racism is so deeply ingrained in the psyches of its citizens. The question that remains is: How does a powerless people assume control of a cultural revolution in a society intent on maintaining its oppression? One of the essential elements of powerlessness is lack of control by a group over the decisions affecting the lives of its members. Power is rarely shared voluntarily; it is usually gained through forcing concessions from the dominant group. It seems unlikely that Afro-Americans can gain control over the cultural apparatus of the United States short of a social revolution, and Cruse does not envision such an eventuality in the near future.

On revolutionary nationalism

The cultural nationalists differ from the revolutionary nationalists on both ideological and tactical grounds. Writing in the *New York Times*, Baraka was severe in his criticism of revolutionary nationalism in general and of the Black Panther party in particular. "We 'support' the white revolution of dope and nakedness, because it weakens the hand that holds the chain that binds Black people. But we must not confuse the cry of young white boys to be in charge of the pseudo destruction of America (with a leisure made possible by the same colonialism) with our own necessity."[44] He charged that the Panthers had "turned left on Nationalism, and turned left on Black people." Referring specifically to Eldridge Cleaver, he wrote, "And the love of Beverly Axelrod has left terrible Marx on the dirty Lenin Black people have been given by some dudes with some dead 1930s white ideology as a freedom suit." He dismissed the Panthers as "violent integrationists."

It is the position of the cultural nationalists that a cultural revolution among black people is necessary before a radical political change can come about. They reject the revolutionary ideology of Marxism–Leninism. Karenga was specific on this point when he wrote, "We must free ourselves culturally before we can succeed politically."[45] He continues, "A lot of brothers play revolutionary; they read a little Fanon, a little Mao, and a little Marx. Although this information is necessary, it is not sufficient, for we must develop a new plan of revolution for Black people here in America." Finally, Karenga sums up the ideological position of the cultural nationalists when he writes; "There must be a cultural revolution before the violent revolution. The cultural revolution gives identity, purpose, and direction."

Because of these differing ideological positions, the two branches of black nationalism adopt different strategies. Whereas the revolutionary nationalists are willing to form coalitions and alliances with white groups, the cultural nationalists reject such working relationships. Karenga set forth the role of whites in the black movement as nonintervention, foreign aid, and the formation of civilizing committees.[46] Though Baraka advocates alliances and coalitions with Third World groups, he rejects such working relationships with white groups, because he believes their interests are at odds with those of black people. In an effort to unify the black community, however, Baraka is willing to form coalitions with black integrationist groups. At the first meeting of the Congress of African Peoples, he said, "I would rather make a coalition with Roy Wilkins or Whitney Young—with any of the most back-wards upside down Negroes in the world—because they must be, in their jivist moment, committed to change. There are more black people involved with Roy Wilkins than are involved in the Congress of African Peoples."[47]

Unlike the revolutionary nationalists, the cultural nationalists do not advocate at the present time the use of revolutionary violence or even the stockpiling of arms. Karenga has written, "To play revolution is to get put down. . . . Violence in itself without consideration for time is as inadequate as nonviolence."[48] And Baraka sees the revolutionary nationalists as misguided. According to him, they think that when they say, " 'Pick up the gun' that the devil will wither up and die, or just by picking up that literal gun, without training, using the same sick value system of the degenerate slave master, the same dope, the same liquor, the same dying hippie mentality, they will liberate all the slave peoples of the world. NO."[49]

The differences between these two nationalist camps are real and understandable. Although they agree on a number of points, their disagreements overshadow them, thereby rendering any operational unity unlikely, at least at the present time. And though the Congress of African Peoples uses as its theme "Unity without uniformity," their meetings have never been attended by members of the Panthers or other revolutionary nationalist groups. Indeed, the 1970 meeting was held in Atlanta at the same time the Panthers were meeting in Philadelphia.

On the major point separating these two camps, that of ideology, it is true that most of the revolutionary nationalist groups rely on theories of revolution which have been developed in situations strikingly different from that of the contemporary United States. The conditions prevailing in U.S. society are hardly such that these ideologies can be implemented at the present time. On the other hand, "nation building" and the creation of a new value system in the black community hardly seem to be sufficient to achieve the liberation of black people. Though they might develop greater political awareness and solidarity, this is clearly a first step, and the cultural nationalists are usually vague beyond this point.

In recent years some degree of operational unity has developed between cultural nationalists and revolutionary nationalists. Bobby Seale was a major speaker at the Black Political Convention in 1972, at which Baraka presided. In addition, Karenga was imprisoned for a brief period at Vacaville prison in California, during which time he apparently maintained friendly relations with fellow prisoner David Hilliard, chief of staff for the Black Panther party. Perhaps most important, the continuing attacks and denunciations between spokesmen for the two camps have diminished in recent years. The Panthers have taken over the roles of community organizing and political participation in Oakland, in much the same way as Baraka has done in Newark.

Cultural nationalism is an important element in the struggle for black liberation. The attempt to unify the black community by those who consider themselves cultural nationalists is an essential first step. For a people who have been oppressed as long as Afro-Americans, this becomes an especially difficult task in a society ostensibly based on individualism. In spite of the difficulties involved in unifying the black community, the cultural nationalists have made significant inroads. The process is long, and short of total social revolution, which most observers believe is unlikely, the efforts of the cultural nationalists are essential in the struggle for black liberation.

Postscript to Chapter 7

Since this chapter was written, Imamu Amiri Baraka and the organization he heads–the Congress of African People– have shifted ideological positions and now embrace Marxism-Leninism-Mao Tse-Tung thought "as the most scientific means of analyzing the Black Liberation Struggle." According to the official newspaper of the Congress of African People, *Unity and Struggle* (October 1974, p. 1 ff), the development had been under discussion for some time. "And at each point, these theories only served to confirm the revolutionary experience of Marx, Engels, Lenin, Stalin, Mao, Ho, *et al.*, and closer reading of progressives like Nyerere, Toure, and the contemporary revolutionary Amilcar Cabral, only revealed that much of the thought of these comrades was based directly on Scientific Socialist theory, the founders of which were Marx and Engels." According to the article, Baraka's "espousal of reactionary nationalist theory" in the past may be traced to several factors, including the influence of the Nation of Islam; confusing "bourgeois nationalism" with the "national liberation struggle"; a misunderstanding of culture as applied to Afro-Americans; negative experiences with such groups as the Communist Party, U.S.A., and the Socialist Workers Party; and the failure to study Marxism-Lenism seriously.

The struggle of Third World people, the article continues, cannot be separated from the struggle against capitalism, but must be linked to the worldwide movement for socialist revolution (i.e., the struggle against imperialism and monopoly capitalism). "We must, everyday, with every ounce of our energy and consciousness struggle to gain ideological clarity, struggle to build revolutionary systems (organizations, parties, etc.) so that we can raise our struggle to the ultimate level of confrontation with the system of capitalism and its destruction." Finally, the Congress of African Peoples has dedicated itself to "reorganizing all our work along revolutionary lines and practicing ruthless self-criticism in order to unite our theory and practice, and contribute to the building of a socialist society."

Baraka now admits that the ideology of the Black Panther party, which is both anticapitalist and anti-imperialist, was perhaps its most important contribution to the struggle for black liberation in the 1960s. At the same time, he gives credit to Maulana Ron Karenga and the cultural nationalists for emphasizing the importance of the African heritage of black people in the United States, but he regards such emphasis as static and inappropriate in the 1970s, unless given a sound ideological underpinning. The current worldwide anti-imperialist struggle is broader than the movement to liberate Africa, for its focus must be the liberation of all the oppressed people of the world from imperialism.

The new ideological position adopted by Baraka and the Congress of African Peoples is an important development in the movement for black liberation, for it serves to unify divergent elements in the movement. There was more than an element of truth in the assertion by Huey P. Newton and others in the Black Panther Party that much of cultural nationalism was reactionary. The attendance by Baraka and other members of the Congress of African Peoples at the Pan-African Congress in Tanzania in June 1974 no doubt contributed to this new development, for the need for socialist revolution was one of the themes of the Congress. It is to the credit of Baraka and his associates that they are willing to admit what they consider to have been past mistakes and to move to rectify them.

8
Religious nationalism

Throughout their long and difficult history, Afro-Americans have maintained strong religious beliefs, and the black church has always been one of the most cohesive institutions in the black community. Prior to their forced migration from Africa, few of the slaves were Christians, but upon their arrival in North America, they were denied the right to practice what the slaveholders considered their "heathen" native religions. Christianity had made inroads into black Africa, but it had succeeded in converting few Africans, because the Africans soon realized that when the Europeans arrived with their Bibles, this was merely a gimmick to steal their land. Furthermore, although Christianity taught the brotherhood of man, Christian missionaries practiced racial superiority.

The first Africans to arrive in North America were initially denied the right to participate in white Christian religious observances, for it was difficult for religious leaders to reconcile their Christianity with the brutality of the institution of slavery. However, at the beginning of the eighteenth century Christian leaders resolved this dilemma by declaring that slaves were not persons in the same sense as whites, and therefore slavery was compatible with Christianity. Thereafter Christianity was to play a crucial role in the enslavement of black people; it provided a religious rationale for slavery. There was no contradiction in being a "good" Christian and owning slaves. Indeed, many slaveholders were themselves ministers. These ministers and those who were not slaveholders taught that it was "God's will" that blacks should be slaves, and they supported their views with quotes from the Bible.

During slavery the so-called free blacks were usually rebuffed when they attempted to worship in white Christian churches, and after emancipation blacks were excluded from participation in white religious observances. Most white churches maintained a rigid policy of racial segregation until the 1960s, and desegregated

151

only after other institutions had been forced to do so by law. This segregation was maintained because Christian ministers and their congregations supported the policy of white supremacy. In short, Christianity supported the colonization of Africa (and other parts of the world), rationalized the institution of slavery, and has subsequently sustained the oppression of Afro-Americans.

The responses of blacks to these circumstances have differed, depending upon circumstances. The first separate black churches were established in response to the humiliation blacks encountered when worshiping with whites. Although the black church historically played a passive role in the struggle for black liberation, concentrating on otherworldly matters rather than temporal problems, several of the major slave revolts were led by black ministers: Gabriel Prosser, Nat Turner, and Denmark Vesey. Throughout much of its history the black community has turned to the church for leadership, and often the most militant leadership came from the clergy. A few notable examples are Henry Highland Garnet, a Presbyterian minister to a white congregation, who urged slaves to kill any slaveholder who refused to release them; Henry M. Turner, the militant bishop of the African Methodist Episcopal church, who championed the cause of black repatriation to Africa and who was the first to teach that "God is a Negro"; George Alexander McGuire, who left the Episcopal church to head Marcus Garvey's African Orthodox church; Adam Clayton Powell, the long-term congressman from New York's Harlem and the convener of the first black power conference in 1966. The list includes others: Martin Luther King, Jr., the respected leader of the civil rights movement in the 1950s and 1960s; Albert B. Cleage, Jr., the founder of the Shrine of the Black Madonna and a leader in the movement for a black theology; Jesse Jackson, formerly of the Southern Christian Leadership Conference's Operation Breadbasket, and more recently founder of People United to Save Humanity. These clergymen were (are) not all black nationalists, but they were (are) firmly committed to the cause of black liberation.

During the height of the civil rights movement, Martin Luther King, Jr., was jailed in Birmingham, Alabama, when he attempted to change the rigid system of racial segregation in that city through the use of nonviolent direct action. Violence flared during this campaign, but it was initiated by city officials and white citizens. While King was in jail a published statement appeared, signed by eight high-ranking white clergymen in Alabama, addressed to King. They called his activities "unwise and untimely" and attacked his action on several grounds, including what they called outside agitation, fomenting violence, disturbing the peace, and defiance of the law. King responded with his lengthy "Letter from Birmingham Jail–April 16, 1963, " in which he answered each of the charges made against him. Among other things he wrote:

I must make two honest confessions to you, my Christian and Jewish brothers. First, I must confess that over the past few years I have been gravely disappointed with the white moderate. I have almost reached the regrettable conclusion that the Negro's great stumbling block in his stride toward freedom is not the White Citizen's Counciler or the Ku Klux Klanner, but the white moderate, who is more devoted to "order" than to justice; who prefers a negative peace which is the absence of tension to a positive peace which is the presence of justice; who constantly says: "I agree with you in the goal you seek, but I cannot agree with your methods of direct action"; who paternalistically believes he can set the timetable for another man's freedom; who lives by a mythical concept of time and who constantly advises the Negro to wait for a "more convenient season." Shallow understanding from people of good will is more frustrating than absolute misunderstanding from people of ill will. Lukewarm acceptance is much more bewildering than outright rejection.[1]

King's response to the eight clergymen came at an especially appropriate time, because of all the groups that ultimately participated in the movement for greater civil rights for blacks, the clergy was among the last when they might logically have been expected to be among the first. White Christian clergymen are among the most conservative forces in American society; they not only were among the last to join the civil rights movement, but they were also among the last to condemn America's genocidal war of aggression in Indochina.

In general, the white clergy responded angrily to the National Black Economic Development Conference's Black Manifesto, which James Foreman interrupted the services at New York's Riverside Church to read on May 4, 1969. The Black Manifesto read in part:

We are therefore demanding of white Christian churches and Jewish synagogues which are part and parcel of the system of capitalism, that they begin to pay reparations to black people in this country. We are demanding $500,000,000 from Christian white churches and the Jewish synagogues. This total comes to 15 dollars per nigger. This is a low estimate, for we maintain there are probably more than 30,000,000 black people in this country. Fifteen dollars a nigger is not a large sum of money, and we know that the churches and synagogues have a tremendous wealth and its membership, white America, has profited and still exploits black people.... This demand for $500,000,000 is not an idle resolution or empty words. . . . We are no longer afraid to demand our full rights as a people in this decadent society.[2]

The manifesto declared that the $500 million was "a beginning of the reparations due us as a people who have been exploited and degraded, brutalized, killed, and persecuted." The money, the manifesto declared, would be used to form a southern land bank for blacks who have been forced off their land; to establish four major publishing houses and printing industries for the black community; to create a training center to teach community organizing; to support the work of the National Welfare Rights Organization; to establish a National Black Labor Strike Fund; and to set up an International Black Appeal.

On May 10 the senior minister of the Riverside Church responded to the Black Manifesto over the radio station owned by the church. At first he announced that the disruption of the church services was a serious act and that the church had received a civil restraining order to place anyone interfering with the services in contempt of court. On the question of reparations he said that the church, through its board of deacons, had decided to make a fixed percentage of its annual budget available to improve the lot of all disadvantaged Americans.[3] The Synagogue Council of America and the National Jewish Community Relations Advisory Council adopted a joint statement on May 12. Although admitting to past and present injustices against Afro-Americans, it was their view that the demands contained in the Black Manifesto were not an answer to the injustices of the society. In addition, these groups, which represent all the major Jewish religious and social agencies in the country, deplored the tactics used by Foreman.[4] The Roman Catholic Archdiocese of New York responded on May 21 by reporting that it did not endorse the Black Manifesto or its demands.[5] The National Committee of Black Churchmen, an all-black organization made up of black caucuses in Protestant denominations and the Roman Catholic Church, strongly supported the Black Manifesto. In a statement to the National Council of Churches on June 26, the National Committee of Black Churchmen wrote, "Unmistakably, our position is one of recognition of and support for NBEDC [National Black Economic Development Conference.]"[6]

The long history of oppression and the complicity by white religious groups in the United States has served to radicalize black religion. In recent years black nationalist ideology has made significant inroads in black religion. Religious nationalism has taken three forms. There has been widespread rejection of Christianity in the black community and a concurrent movement to Islam. Within traditional Protestant denominations and Catholic churches, all-black groups have developed. Finally, there has been an attempt to create a black Christian theology, emphasizing the blackness of God. Each of these developments will be discussed, and though black churches which parallel white churches frequently espouse black nationalist ideology, the discussion of them is minimal, because they are less nationalistic than the religious groups described above.

The rejection of Christianity: the Nation of Islam

Several black non-Christian religious groups exist in the United States and embrace a variety of religious beliefs, but the one which has attracted greatest attention and probably the largest membership is the Nation of Islam, also known popularly as the Black Muslims. The official name of the organization is the Lost-Found Nation of Islam in the Wilderness of North America. Since the early 1960s several books and articles have been written about the Nation of Islam by members of the organization and by outsiders.[7] However, many of the recent activities of the organization are not available in print.

Development.   As an organization, the Nation of Islam is primarily religious in its orientation, but like Marcus Garvey's Universal Negro Improvement Association, it embraces several aspects of black nationalism, including economic and educational nationalism. The undisputed leader of the Nation of Islam was Elijah Muhammed, who considered himself Allah's last prophet. He was one of the country's leading black nationalists and proponent of racial separation. Born on a tenant farm in Sandersville, Georgia, as Elijah Poole in 1897, he was the son of a Baptist minister and one of twelve children. In 1923 he migrated with his wife and two children to Detroit, where he worked in an automobile factory for six years, followed by periods of unemployment. For a brief time he was a Baptist minister. He later became an assistant minister to W.D. Fard, who had assumed leadership of the Moorish movement in the United States.

The Moorish movement had been founded in the United States by Noble Drew Ali, who established the Moorish-American Science Temple in 1913.[8] This movement, under Drew Ali's leadership, spread to cities throughout the country. He taught that Islam was the only instrument through which Afro-Americans could unify themselves in preparation for liberation. Furthermore, he taught that American blacks were really descendents of the Moors who had inhabited Morocco before Africans were enslaved in North America. Drew Ali, in addition to his religious teachings, established several business enterprises in Chicago, then headquarters of the Moorish movement. His leadership was contested in 1929 by Sheik Claude Greene, which contest ended with Greene's death. Drew Ali was arrested in 1929 and spent several weeks in jail. Shortly after his release on bond, he died under mysterious circumstances.

After the death of Drew Ali, W.D. Fard claimed that he was Drew Ali reincarnated. Some of Drew Ali's followers accepted Fard's claim of reincarnation, but others did not. Those who did not founded the Moorish Science Temple, and those who did now constitute what developed into the Nation of Islam. Fard formed a temple in Detroit in 1930, the year Elijah Muhammad first met him, and declared that his mission was to secure freedom, justice, and equality for America's blacks. Fard succeeded in recruiting many blacks to his Detroit temple in the early 1930s, including Elijah Muhammad.

Muhammad said that he recognized that Fard was Allah the first time he met him. Fard conceded this identity, but asked Muhammad not to tell others until he could teach Muhammad to replace him. Again an internal dispute erupted in the Detroit temple, and a Chicago branch was established in 1933. According to Muhammad, Fard disappeared as mysteriously as he had appeared, on March 19, 1934. Some of his followers claimed that he had returned to the holy city of Mecca, but he was never heard from again. With his disappearance, Muhammad became the spiritual leader of the Nation of Islam and settled in Chicago. Those who opposed him as a replacement for Fard are alleged to have followed him to Chicago, forcing him to flee to Washington, D.C.

Between 1935 and 1941, Muhammad remained in Washington. With the advent of World War II, he was drafted but refused to be inducted and was sent to prison. He claimed that at 45 he was too old for military service and that his refusal to serve was an excuse for jailing him. Following his release from prison in 1946, he returned to Chicago, where he assumed firm control of the Nation of Islam and its vast business empire, both of which spread rapidly throughout the country.

Theology. The theological doctrine of the Nation of Islam, as put forth by Elijah Muhammad, differs in significant regards from orthodox Islam as taught in Africa and Asia. One of its most controversial aspects pertains to the origin of mankind.[9] Muhammed taught that there was a massive explosion which split the earth from the moon some 66 trillion years ago. The black man's origin is said to have coincided with this explosion; therefore, the black man was the original man. Blacks in the United States are the chosen Black Nation and are good by nature. Whites, on the other hand, have inhabited the earth for only 6000 years, and they were created by a black man, Yakub, an evil scientist who was determined not only to defy Allah but also to destroy fellow blacks. Yakub discovered that the black man could be broken down into two germs, one black and one brown. After mating the lighter strains he created the brown race. He then created the yellow and red races. This hybridization continued for 600 years, during which time Yakub filtered all the pigmentation out of his guinea pigs, thereby creating the white race. Yakub's creations not only lacked skin pigmentation, but humanity as well. According to Muhammad, whites were initially called Caucasion, which he says means "one whose evil effects is not confined to one's self alone, but affects others." The white race is physically and mentally inferior to other races and is incapable of such normal human emotions as love, honesty, and compassion.

Other apsects of the theology of the Nation of Islam have been set forth by Muhammad and are printed in each issue of the organization's weekly newspaper, *Muhammad Speaks*, in a column entitled "What the Muslims Believe." They include the following:

1 *We Believe in the One God Whose proper Name is Allah.*

2 *We Believe in the Holy Qur-an and in the Scriptures of all the Prophets of God.*

3 *We Believe in the truth of the Bible, but we believe that it has been tampered with and must be reinterpreted. . . .*

4 *We Believe in Allah's Prophets and the Scriptures they brought to the people.*

5 *We Believe in the resurrection of the dead—not in physical resurrection—but in mental resurrection. We believe that the so-called Negroes are most in need of mental resurrection; therefore they will be resurrected first.*

6 *We Believe in the judgement; we believe this first judgement will take place as God revealed, in America.*

7 *We Believe this is the time in history for the separation of so-called Negroes and the so-called white Americans.*

8 *We Believe in justice for all, whether in God or not; we believe as others, that we are due equal justice as human beings.*

9 *We Believe that the offer of integration is hypocritical and is made by*

*those who are trying to deceive black peoples into believing that their
400-year-old open enemies of freedom, justice, and equality are, all of
a sudden, their "friends."*

10 *We Believe that we who declared ourselves to be righteous Muslims
should not participate in wars which take the life of humans.*

11 *We Believe our women should be respected and protected as the
women of other nationalities are respected and protected.*

12 *We Believe that Allah (God) appeared in the Person of Master W. Fard
Muhammad, July, 1930; the long-awaited "Messiah" of the Christians
and the "Mahdi" of the Muslims.*

The complete content of the theology of the nation of Islam was
set forth by Muhammad in his *Message to the Blackman in
America* and in other works.[10] Muhammad taught that Afro-
Americans are the "chosen people," but that they have been kept
in mental slavery by the white man. They are guilty of loving their
enemies, which he terms a sickness. The white man, on the other
hand, is sicker than the black man and is fatally doomed because
he is responsible for the plight of the black man. The black man
remains sacred to Allah, who has promised to rescue him from his
oppressors. Afro-Americans must be willing to rise up against their
oppressors and must be willing to die for freedom, justice, and
equality, for Allah will protect them. They must never initiate
aggression, but if attacked they must, by Divine Law, protect
themselves.

Muhammad taught that Allah will reappear and that America is
the place where He will make Himself felt. Allah is the supreme
black man, and his reappearance will signal the beginning of
justice for Afro-Americans. It is necessary for the black man to give
up his slave name and refrain from the evil practices of the white
man if he is to be saved. If this should happen, the destruction of
the world, which is imminent, will mean only the destruction of
the devils (whites) and the Christian religion. Muhammad taught
that the day of judgement will occur sometime before the year
2000, but the exact date is known only to Allah. When this
happens, a new world will be created on earth, and the "chosen"
will inherit the power of the earth. This will signal the beginning
of the Black Nation, which will rule the earth under the guidance
of Allah.

Members of the Nation of Islam believe that no white man can
accept the religion of Islam as taught by Muhammad, because the
white man is by nature the devil. Therefore, Muhammad taught
absolute separation of the races. The Muslim program, "What We
Want," which is also printed in each issue of *Muhammad Speaks,*

addresses itself to racial separation on two of its ten points. Point four declares that "We want our people in America whose parents or grandparents were descendents from slaves, to be allowed to establish a separate state or territory of their own–either on this continent or elsewhere." Furthermore, this program calls for white Americans not only to provide such land, but also to provide financial support (reparations) for Afro-Americans in this separate territory for twenty to twenty-five years. Point 10 addresses itself to the question of racial purity. It reads: "We believe that intermarriage or race mixing should be prohibited."

It is on three specific points that the teachings of Elijah Muhammad are at odds with those of Orthodox Islam: his insistence that the black man must separate from the white man, his belief that the black nation will inherit the earth, and his teaching that he is a messenger of Allah. Orthodox Islam teaches the universal brotherhood of man which transcends racial boundaries, and that Mohammad was the last prophet of Allah. In spite of these differences, Elijah Muhammad has been recognized as an important leader in several Moslem countries, and according to C. Eric Lincoln, while on a visit to Cairo in 1959, Elijah Muhammad was permitted to make the traditional Moslem pilgrimage to Mecca.[11] More recently, in 1972, the government of Libya made an interest free loan of $3 million to the Nation of Islam for the purchase of a church to be used as a mosque in Chicago. It is reported that the request for a second loan of the same amount was denied by Colonel Muammar el-Qaddafi, the leader of Libya, who has been known for supporting revolutionary groups and guerrilla movements around the world, because of opposition from other Arab countries and from orthodox Moslem groups in the United States.[12] The refusal to grant the loan is also said to have resulted from the questionable religious beliefs and teachings of the Nation of Islam.

Muslim membership and morality. Although individuals do not conceal their membership in the Nation of Islam, the total membership in the organization has been kept a secret. *Ebony* magazine estimated the membership at 100,000 in 1970. The *Yearbook of American Churches* estimated the membership at 250,000 in 1969. Whatever the official membership, it is clear that the influence of the organization has been and is widespread among Afro-Americans. Some idea of the influence of the movement can be seen in the increasing number of temples springing up throughout the country. Whereas *Ebony* estimated that there were 40 Muslim temples in the United States in 1970, *Muhammad Speaks* (March 30, 1973) lists 64 temples and carries a notation, "For addresses of other temples in your area, see your phone directory." The likelihood is that the estimates of both membership and the number of temples fall short. Furthermore, the influence is far greater than the membership implies; for example, *Muhammad Speaks* has a weekly circulation of 600,000, the largest of any black-owned newspaper in the United States.

The most comprehensive study of the characteristics of members of the Nation of Islam is that which resulted from Lincoln's study in the late 1950s.[13] Though the membership has no doubt increased significantly since that time, it is likely that the Nation of Islam continues to attract the same type of members. Based on his experiences, Lincoln concluded that the membership was predominately (up to 80 percent) male, with the typical congregation ranging in age from 17 to 35. The ministry reflects the membership on both age and sex composition. The Nation attracts young members because of its activist orientation, and its theological teachings represent a shift in thought which is too radical for older people.

The membership is said to be predominately male, with men assuming the dominant role in the affairs of the temples. Women are honored and are assigned specific roles, but their roles are secondary to those of men. They work along with men but are given minor responsibility. Furthermore, membership is said to consist mainly of working-class Afro-Americans, though it has managed to recruit some intellectuals and college students. Many of the members are recruited from prisons and several temples exist in prisons around the country. Others are recruited from drug addicts, alcoholics, pimps, and prostitutes. The Nation of Islam has a remarkable record of achievement in rehabilitating such persons, as their record of full employment attests. Recruitment is carried out in slum neighborhoods, and Muslim temples and business enterprises are also located in these neighborhoods.

Unlike the Garvey movement, the Muslims concentrate their efforts on recruiting blacks who were born in the United States, as opposed to West Indian immigrants. Lincoln believes that this is a strategic move to avoid some of the conflicts based on skin color which plagued Garvey's Universal Negro Improvement Association. In addition, most of the members are ex-Christians or those whose families were members of Protestant denominations. Since the membership is predominately young, many of them have had little or no direct involvement in Christianity.

Members of the Nation of Islam are required to adhere to a strict code of morality, which is rigidly enforced.[14] They are required to pray five times daily and to attend temple services twice weekly. Male members must also spend time attempting to enlist new converts. Cleanliness is essential, for both the individual's body and his surroundings. Certain foods are forbidden, many of which are common to rural southern blacks. Foods that are permitted must be fresh and eaten in proper quantity. Elijah Muhammad published two books on proper eating habits.[15] Muslims may not drink alcoholic beverages, and all forms of tobacco are forbidden.

Courtship and marriage outside the group are not encouraged, and if a Muslim man should marry a non-Muslim woman, she is expected to join the Nation of Islam. Although men are required to live according to a rigid code of behavior, that demanded of a woman is even stricter, for "a Muslim can rise no higher than his woman." Women are forbidden to wear provocative or revealing clothing. They may not enter a room with a man to whom they are not married. They are expected to cook, sew, clean the living quarters, and care for their husbands and children. In order to insure that these duties are properly performed, Muslim women attend "general civilization" courses offered at temples in the evening.

Finally, Muslims are required to uphold the laws of the society, even when these laws are considered corrupt. Men are expected to work hard and deal fairly and honestly with all people. Above all, members are expected to be self-reliant and of mutual assistance to fellow Muslims in case of need. It is no doubt because of such teachings as these that unemployment is virtually non-existent, even though membership is drawn from the lower classes of the black community.

Economic nationalism. Within a reasonably short period of time the Nation of Islam has established an economic empire of considerable proportions. According to *The New York Times*, its holdings were estimated to be approximately $70 million in 1973.[16] Virtually all its economic enterprises are operated by blacks, but if it is impossible to find qualified blacks for positions, they will employ whites until blacks can be properly trained. Their policy is one of separating religion from business. The business empire of the Nation consists of many enterprises. There are many restaurants, snack bars, and carry-out food shops in virtually every large city. Giant supermarkets, called "Your" Supermarkets, market

Muslim-produced merchandise under "Your" label. In order to stock these supermarkets, the Nation operates canning factories, where such vegetables as green beans, squash, okra, tomatoes, and corn are processed. Several large orchards produce apples. The Nation owns the farms from which the products come. By 1972 they owned land totaling 20,000 acres in Michigan, Georgia, and Alabama. In addition to vegetables, these farms raise thousands of heads of cattle and sheep. The Nation owns slaughterhouses for processing these meats, as well as dairies for processing milk and chicken breeding plants for eggs and poultry. The wheat grown on the farms is stored in Muslim-owned grain storage silos and is ultimately converted into bread and pastries in Muslim bakeries.

Muslim business enterprises include factories to manufacture clothing and retail stores to sell the finished products. The Nation owns jewelry stores, dry-cleaning plants, and import shops. They also own several apartment houses in major cities to house Muslim and non-Muslim families, because it was Elijah Muhammad's belief that every black family should "enjoy a home in which they can have love, peace, and happiness."[17]

One of the largest of all the business enterprises owned by the Nation of Islam is that of printing. Elijah Muhammad's books, as well as textbooks for the schools and the weekly newspaper, *Muhammad Speaks*, are printed by Muslim-owned presses. The newspaper contains news about the activities of the Nation, about Afro-Americans in general, and about the Third World. It takes a consistent stand against American imperialism and regularly reports on revolutionary struggles in the world, especially those in the Middle East and Africa. Frequently it contains a special section to report the progress of the Nation's economic enterprises.

Elijah Muhammad promised his followers that by 1980, the Nation's empire would include many more important business enterprises.[18] These are to include a 200-bed hospital, a 2,000-seat mosque (which has already been purchased), a modern bank with 36 teller windows, radio and television stations, a fleet of jet cargo airplanes, ocean liners, new schools, additional farm land, and a new University of Islam, estimated to cost at least $30 million.

These economic enterprises are a combination of black capitalism and socialism. They are mainly profit-making ventures, but the profits are used for the welfare of the Nation's members. The aim of the Nation of Islam is to create a separate black economy within the United States. It is projected that the farms, food-processing plants, and supermarkets will ultimately supply the needs of most Afro-Americans.

Educational nationalism. Elijah Muhammad has insisted that black children be taught by black teachers. In an effort to implement this goal, the Nation of Islam has established elementary schools in major cities. Though the Muslims claim to operate two universities, one in Chicago and the other in Detroit, these are in reality secondary schools.[19] They were among the first to teach black history and deliberately attempt to instill positive identification in the students. There are indications that those pupils attending Muslim schools perform at a higher level than their counterparts in public schools.

In addition to black history and black pride, Muslim schools are required to teach a regular complement of such traditional subjects as reading, spelling, languages, mathematics, art, and physical and biological sciences. These subjects are necessary if the schools are to meet the educational requirements established by the various states within which they operate. Similarly, Muslim teachers must be licensed by the state in which they teach. Students are evaluated in several areas other than academic performance; for example, they are graded for attendance, conduct, cooperation, effort, and reliability.

Boys and girls are taught in the same buildings, but in separate classrooms, except those in kindergarten and first grade, who may attend the same classes. This is part of the strict moral code characteristic of the Nation of Islam. Furthermore, a high premium is placed on the education of girls, as well as Muslim wives and mothers. As is true in most other parochial schools, children attending Muslim schools are required to wear special uniforms. For girls the length of their dresses is prescribed, depending upon age. Requirements for the length of the sleeves and the height of neck bands for blouses are well-defined, as are shoes and socks. For boys, suits are prescribed, and they must be blue, brown, or gray. Matching caps are required, and boys must wear black or brown shoes.

In Muslim schools Arabic is taught, beginning in the third grade, but the main emphasis of these schools is on black history and the contributions of people of African descent to world culture. Elijah Muhammad has written, "First, my people must be taught the knowledge of self. Then and only then will they be able to understand others and that which surrounds them.... The lack of knowledge of self is a prevailing condition among my people here in America. Gaining the knowledge of self makes us unite into a great unity."[20] Although no concrete comparative evaluations between Muslim schools and public schools have been undertaken, most observers of both systems agree that children in Muslim schools exceed public school pupils in academic performance.

There is some speculation among outsiders that the Nation of Islam is experiencing financial difficulties and that it is on the decline. At the same time, it is said that greater numbers of well-educated Afro-Americans are being attracted to its ranks and that membership in general is increasing. It is impossible for outsiders to assess accurately the current status of the Nation. However, in the past two decades, it has established itself as a major nationalist organization in the United States, encompassing a wider range of nationalist activities than any organization since Marcus Garvey's Universal Negro Improvement Association.

Black unity within traditional Christianity

Although a vast majority of Afro-American church members attend all-black Christian congregations that operate as parallel organizations to white churches, increasing numbers of middle-class blacks are members of predominately white churches. Of the nearly 12 million black church members, approximately 1 million are members of predominately white churches. With the spread of black nationalist sentiment in recent years, blacks who are members of predominately white churches have organized themselves into black caucuses and other comparable organizations. At the same time, the Afro-American Christians who are members of the all-black Baptist and Methodist denominations have become increasingly militant.

Since the advent of the civil rights movement in the 1950s, those Afro-Americans who are members of predominately white churches have been demanding and receiving a greater degree of decision-making authority in these churches. Furthermore, research conducted in 1964, during the height of the civil rights movement, demonstrated that those blacks who were members of predominately white churches were more militant about civil rights than those who were members of all-black churches.[21] Blacks who were members of the more fundamentalist groups tended to be oriented more toward otherworldly than temporal matters.

Within Protestantism all of the major predominately white

denominations with enough black members to form a separate black group have done so. The objectives of these groups vary, but they are all oriented toward black unity, and most of them are attempting to make Christianity serve the cause of black liberation through the empowerment of black members. Among the first of these groups to organize was the National Committee of Black Churchmen, formed in 1966. This committee is a nationwide ecumenical organization of black clergy and laymen, formed for the purpose of aiding the black community in its struggle for liberation. Its members emphasize economic, social, and political issues affecting Afro-Americans. Though its membership includes ministers and laymen from all-black churches, many are members of predominately white denominations, and one of their functions is to coordinate the activities of the 10 national black caucuses existing in predominately white denominations.

The activities of this committee have often met strong opposition from white clergy. In addition to the support which the group expressed for the Black Manifesto, they have taken stands which have been considered controversial. For example, in the summer of 1966 the National Committee of Black (then "Negro") Churchmen published a statement in *The New York Times* entitled "Black Power."[22] This action was taken during the height of the debate on black power, only weeks after Stokely Carmichael had introduced this controversial concept into the civil rights movement. The committee introduced its statement with the following: "We, an informal group of Negro churchmen in America, are deeply disturbed about the crisis brought upon our country by historic distortions of important human realities in the controversy about 'black power.' What we see, shining through the variety of rhetoric, is not anything new but the same old problem of power and race which has faced our beloved country since 1619." The statment continued:

The fundamental distortion facing us in the controversy about "black power" is rooted in a gross imbalance of power and conscience between Negroes and white Americans. It is this distortion, mainly, which is responsible for the widespread, though often inarticulate, assumption that white people are justified in getting what they want through the use of power, but that Negro Americans must, either by nature or by circumstances, make their appeal only through conscience. As a result, the power of white men and the conscience of black men have both been corrupted.... Powerlessness breeds a race of beggers. We are faced now with a situation where conscience-less power meets powerless conscience, threatening the very foundations of our nation.

The statement then addressed itself to four groups of Americans: the leaders of America, white churchmen, black citizens, and those who control the mass media.

The leaders of America were charged with failing to use their power to create equal opportunity for blacks in practice as well as in principle. "When American leaders decide to serve the real welfare of people instead of war and destruction; when American leaders are forced to make the rebuilding of our cities first priority on the nation's agenda; when American leaders are forced by the American people to quit misusing and abusing American power; then will the cry for 'black power' become inaudible, for the framework in which all power in America operates would include the power and experience of black men as well as those of white men." White churchmen were criticized for their emotional rejection of the concept of black power and were charged with refusing to permit blacks to share power in the church. They were warned that "so long as white churchmen continue to moralize and misinterpret Christian love, so long will justice continue to be subverted in this land."

The bulk of the statement was addressed to black citizens, who were told that they had historically been oppressed as a group, not as individuals, and that it was necessary for them to wield group power to end their oppression. "We must first be reconciled to ourselves lest we fail to recognize the resources we already have and upon which we can build. We must be reconciled to ourselves as persons and to ourselves as an historical group. This means we must find our way to a new self-image in which we can feel a normal sense of pride in self, including our variety of skin color and the manifold textures of our hair."

The mass media was praised for the accuracy of its coverage of the civil rights demonstrations in the South. At the same time, however, the media was urged to provide the same type of coverage to the problems faced by blacks in urban areas outside the South.

In June 1969, in Atlanta, the Committee on Theological Perspectives of the National Committee issued a statement on black theology.[23] In the view of the National Committee, black theology is a theology of black liberation. It is through black theology that Afro-Americans have managed to survive the brutalities inflicted on them throughout American history, and it is through black theology that Afro-Americans will achieve liberation, through whatever means necessary. And at their third annual convocation in November 1969, the National Committee issued a statement from Oakland, California.[24] This statement was addressed to the churches of America. In it the National Committee rejected the racism of white Christianity and vowed to establish a new vocation compatible with the experience of black people. The message described the new vocation:

This new vocation to which we are called is *political* in the sense that it seeks radically to change, by whatever means necessary, the racist structures which dominate our lives; *cultural* in the sense that it seeks to identify, re-create, unify, and authenticate whatever traditions, values, and styles of life are indigenous or distinctive to the black community; and *theological* in the sense that we believe it is God–however He chooses to reveal Himself today to oppressed peoples in America and in the Third World–who has chosen black humanity as a vanguard to resist the demonic powers of racism, capitalism, and imperialism, and to so reform the structures of this world that they will more perfectly minister to the peace and power of all people as children of God and brothers of one another.

White churches were called upon to reject racism, imperialism, and economic selfishness. They were called upon to take a revolutionary position, one that would force the transfer of power to the oppressed. In addition, they were urged to use their great wealth for technical assistance for the poor of the world.

In July 1970, on the eve of Independence Day, the National Committee of Black Churchmen issued a "Black Declaration of Independence" on behalf of the black community.[25] This declaration began as follows:

When in the course of Human Events, it becomes necessary for a people who were stolen from the lands of their Fathers, transported under the most ruthless and brutal circumstances 5,000 miles to a strange land, sold into dehumanizing slavery, emasculated, subjugated, exploited, and discriminated against for 351 years, to call with finality, a halt to such indignities and genocidal practices–by virtue of the Laws of Nature and of Nature's God, a decent respect to the Opinions of Mankind requires that they should declare their just grievances and the urgent and necessary redress thereof.

The declaration further enumerated the injustices to which Afro-Americans have been subjected historically, including the isolation of blacks in the most dilapidated section of cities, the maintenance of armed forces in these communities without the consent of the people, the imposition of taxes on blacks without protection of constitutional rights, the forcing of black men to kill fellow Third World people in wars of aggression, the imprisonment of black people without just cause, and the indiscriminate killing of blacks by police and other law enforcement officials. It declared that the United States is unfit to receive the respect of free people. Finally, it ended with the following:

We, therefore, the Black People of the United States of America, in all parts of this Nation, appealing to the Supreme Judge of the World for Rectitude of our Intentions, do, in the Name of our good People and our own Black Heroes–Richard Allen, James Varick, Absalom Jones, Nat Turner, Frederick Douglass, Marcus Garvey, Malcolm X, Martin Luther King, Jr., and all Black People, past and present, great and small– Solemnly Publish and Declare, that we shall be, and of Right ought to be, FREE AND INDEPENDENT FROM THE INJUSTICE, EXPLOITA- TIVE CONTROL, INSTITUTIONALIZED VIOLENCE AND RACISM OF WHITE AMERICA, that unless we receive full Redress and Relief from these Inhumanities we will move to renounce all Allegiance to this Nation, and will refuse in every way, to cooperate with the Evil which is Perpetrated upon ourselves and our Communities.

Though the Black Declaration of Independence received wide circulation, it met silence from the white community. Blacks, who have always looked to the black clergy for leadership and direc- tion, were enthusiastic. At a Black Solidarity Day meeting in New York in November 1970, the declaration was ratified by some 6,000 Afro-Americans representing a diversity of ideological posi- tions.

The National Committee of Black Churchmen has not limited itself to issuing statements through the press. Among other things, it has formed working coalitions with other groups, such as the Black Economic Development Conference and the National Wel- fare Rights Organization. And through its efforts black churchmen have achieved greater power in such organizations as the National Council of Churches, as well as the various denominations of which it is composed. On the international level, the National Committee's Commission on African Relations has supported lib- eration movements in South Africa, Rhodesia, Southwest Africa, Angola, and Mozambique. Through its Pan-African Skills Project, interaction between American blacks and independent African nations has been established.

In addition to the National Committee of Black Churchmen, all major predominately white religious groups in the United States contain black caucuses. The major function these caucuses serve is to share power among blacks, thereby forcing their churches to consider the needs and aspirations of the black community. To some extent they have been successful. For example, religious groups are among the wealthiest organizations in the United

States, and because of black pressure, the Interreligious Foundation for Community Organization, an ecumenical organization established in 1967 for the purpose of channeling funds from churches to organizations of poor people, has been quite active. In recent years such funds have been used to finance low-income housing in urban areas. The Interreligious Foundation initially convened the National Black Economic Development Conference in 1968, and the conference presented its Black Manifesto the following year. The Interreligious Foundation could hardly denounce the manifesto, and this prompted some major groups, principally the American Jewish Committee, to withdraw from the foundation. Because of pressure from black members, and as a means of circumventing the demands of the manifesto, the United Presbyterian Church, the American Baptist Convention, the United Methodist Church, the Unitarian-Universalist Association, and the Lutheran Church of America, among others, contributed millions of dollars to assist blacks and other poor people in the United States.

The Roman Catholic Church, the largest single group of Christians in the United States, has not escaped the spread of black nationalist sentiment in recent years. It is estimated that there are only 800,000 Afro-Americans among the nation's nearly 50 million Catholics.[26] Of these, some 900 are nuns, approximately 160 are priests, and one is an auxialiary bishop. Black Catholics consequently have been somewhat isolated from the mainstream of the church and the black community as well. Nevertheless, they have recently organized several all-black organizations within the church. These include the National Office of Black Catholics, the National Black Sisters' Conference, the National Black Catholic Clergy Caucus, and the National Black Catholic Lay Caucus.

The National Black Sisters' Conference held its third annual meeting at the University of Notre Dame in 1970, during which the nuns expressed anger at what they called the irrelevance of the Catholic Church to the black community and discussed ways in which they could contribute to the liberation of Afro-Americans. Some of the comments expressed at this meeting illustrate the growing black awareness among Afro-American nuns: "Entering an order meant ceasing to be black and looking on what you grew up with as uncouth," said a young sister, referring to her isolation from the black community. "You could do the Irish jig, but anything African was taboo." Another said, "After the assassination of Martin Luther King, I told my superiors that I could no longer work in a white school." A sister from New Orleans declared, "The church is a racist institution, and no one knows this better than young black Catholics." Still another said, "Christianity has been the arm of oppression since early times, and that is the way blacks have experienced it. But the Word of God can also be used as a force for liberation."[27]

Perhaps the new role of blacks in the Catholic Church was best articulated in a recent article by the president of the National Black Sisters' Conference. "The church, by her very nature, is meant to be the revolutionary agent in all times." After commenting on the paucity of blacks in the Catholic Church, she wrote, "Black Catholics have finally begun to demand black self-determination and leadership within their ecclesiastical system, the fullest use of Catholic resources for the liberation of black people, and the survival of the Catholic Church in the black community." The demand for self-determination was put forth because "life for black people in the Catholic kingdom has generally been submission and dependence, limitation and control, obligation and subtle coercion, paralysis of fear and the dehumanization of oppression." She calls for unity among all black Christians, so that Catholics and other religious groups can join in the struggle for black liberation.[28]

Because of the lack of response to their demands by the Catholic hierarchy in the United States, a delegation of black Catholics presented their grievances to the Vatican in 1971. There they held a meeting with the Vatican's Deputy Secretary of State. They sought a black archbishop for Washington, D.C., a special black rite comparable to that used in Oriental churches, and Afro-American representation in the Vatican's central administration. While there these representatives accused the American Catholic Church of presenting false information to the Vatican about the status of blacks in the church in the United States.[29]

Several individual black clergymen have advocated what is generally called a black theology of liberation. Prominent among these is James A. Cone, who teaches theology at Union Theological Seminary in New York. Cone contends that Christianity is a religion of liberation, and for Christian theology to fulfill its true mission consistent with the teachings of Jesus Christ, it must become black theology, because Afro-Americans are oppressed because they are black.[30] He maintains that any theology not oriented toward the liberation of the oppressed is not Christin theology. Like Henry M. Turner and Marcus Garvey before him, Cone maintains that God must be viewed as black, because "either God is identified with the oppressed to the point that their experience becomes His or He is a God of racism."[31] He argues that "knowing God means being on the side of the oppressed, becoming *one* with them and participating in their goal of liberation." Further, Cone maintains that in a racist society "God is never color blind," and to argue that he is, is to say that he is blind to injustice and evil.

Cone maintains that black theology is a survival theology for Afro-Americans in that it addresses itself to the conditions facing them in the United States.[32] In the first place, Afro-American existence is such that physical survival amounts to constant tension between life and death. White society has yet to regard black people as human beings and has refused to permit Afro-Americans to affirm their blackness. When they assert their humanity as black people, they are often killed. Black theology links God to the plight of Afro-Americans and guides them toward liberation. Furthermore, black theology assists Afro-Americans in resolving their identity crises. At first blacks were considered to be nonhuman and were constantly brutalized. Later, attempts were made to assimilate them into the larger society by stripping them of their identity. Through black theology Afro-Americans are able to destroy white America's definition of blackness and sustain themselves in their struggle for black identity by identifying with revolutionary teachings of Jesus Christ. Finally, black theology enables Afro-Americans to cope with white social and political power. In this regard, it teaches the black community to focus on self-determination and to do whatever is necessary to preserve its existence. The black community must define its way of life, regardless of the consequences to white society.

According to Cone, black theology for whites means "becoming black with God," for God reveals himself in America through the oppressed, the Afro-Americans, and to "receive his revelation is to become black with him by joining him in his work of liberation."[33] That is, to know God is to identify with oppressed blacks. Cone, unlike some other contemporary black theologians, is less concerned about the literal black Christ than about Christ the revolutionary leader of the oppressed, but he does not dismiss the notion that Christ was a black Jew. It is his position that black theology is more concerned with present-day injustices than with otherworldly matters.

The black Christ

Unlike James Cone, Albert Cleage, another leading proponent of black theology, maintains that historical evidence proves that Jesus Christ was the "nonwhite leader of a nonwhite people struggling for national liberation against the rule of a white nation, Rome."[34] He was a revolutionary black leader, and blacks are the "chosen people." It is Cleage's position that for nearly 500 years the illusion has been created that Jesus was white, simply because Europeans dominated the world. Simply stated, Cleage contends that "there never was a white Jesus. Now if you're white, you can accept him if you want to, and you can go through psychological gymnastics and pretend that he was white, but he was black. If you're such a white racist that you've got to believe he was white, then you're going to distort history to preserve his whiteness."[35] He bases his position on the racial composition of the people in the area at the time of Christ and on the racial amalgamation of Mediterranean and African people.

Cleage sees the black church in the United States in the forefront of the creation of a *"Nation within a Nation,* uniting Black people in such a way that we have the basic beliefs of nationhood in the interim while we prepare for the liberation of our homeland, Africa."[36] His program for black nationhood centers on black self-determination, by which he means the complete control of the black community by its inhabitants. In pursuit of self-determination he maintains that black people must be willing to sacrifice, even to the point of death, for the black Messiah was willing to die so that black people might achieve freedom from oppression. And the black Messiah's interest was in building an independent black nation.

Cleage's theology is predicated on the assumption that unity is the essential ingredient in nation building. He writes, "Today our basic task consists of bringing together a Nation, bringing together black men, women, and children with courage, who believe in themselves and who love each other.... We must realize that our strength, our power, our hope, everything we dream of, lies in our coming together."[37] As he analyzes the contemporary situation of Afro-Americans, the black church must serve as the focal point in the emerging black nation, for historically it has served a special function for the black community, specifically providing strength in the midst of persecution. And for Cleage the promised land is not to be found in the afterlife, but in life on earth.

In his most recent book, *Black Christian Nationalism*, Cleage begins with the Black Christian Nationalist Creed, which reads, in part, as follows:

I Believe that Jesus, the Black Messiah, was a revolutionary leader, sent by God to rebuild the Black Nation, Israel and to liberate Black people from powerlessness and from the oppression, brutality, and exploitation of the white gentile world. I believe that the revolutionary spirit of God, embodied in the Black Messiah, is born anew in each generation and that Black Christian Nationalists constitute the living remnant of God's Chosen People in this day, and are charged by Him with responsibility for the Liberation of Black People.[38]

Cleage goes on to project the role of the black church in the movement for black liberation. It is his contention that black theology must emphasize communalism over individualism and life on earth rather than the afterlife. Black people and white people can coexist peacefully in the United States, he feels, only through the acquisition of economic and political power by Afro-Americans, power sufficient to create a black nation.

The essential function of black Christian nationalism is the restructuring of society to bring about black liberation. Cleage sees the black church serving a variety of activities leading toward that goal.[39] These include creating a new theology based on the revolutionary teachings of Jesus Christ; developing educational programs to be taken to the people; training community organizers and communication experts to mobilize the black masses; supporting existing organizations in the black community; and mobilizing black people for action. He sees the black church as essential in the liberation struggle, because it is controlled by Afro-Americans.

Black Christian nationalism as advanced by Cleage envisions seven steps to black liberation:

1 *Seeking integration, a period characterized by self-hatred;*

2 *Crying out in protest, an era characterized by protest demonstrations demanding integration;*

3 *Striking out in violent rage, manifested by ceasing to identify with the oppressor and by developing black consciousness;*

4 *Analyzing the nature of oppression and its insititutional basis, characterized by the emergence of the new black theology;*

5 *Developing an educational process in order to disseminate information in the black community, manifested by black Christian nationalist educational research and training programs;*

6 *Restructuring the black church in order to achieve a power base among Afro-Americans; and*

7 *Attacking the institutional basis of oppression and building black counter institutions.*[40]

In other words, Cleage sees the black church as being in the forefront of the black liberation movement. The ultimate society would be based on the seven principles of the doctrine of *Kawaida* (see Chapter 7).

Black nationalist ideology has made an impact on religious institutions in the United States. Although the vast majority of black churches no doubt continue to remain aloof from the black liberation movement, focusing instead on otherwordly matters, increasing numbers of theologians and rank-and-file members have embraced the thrust of black nationalism. They have forced white religious institutions to reevaluate their roles in relationship to black oppression. This is not a new development, for black religious leaders were organizing slave revolts as early as 1800. One of the major differences between the early black religious radicals and those of today lies in the amount of support they receive from the black community. Black nationalist sentiment has had its greatest impact on the black community in the 1960s, and religion, like other areas of life, has not been spared. Consequently, black nationalist religious leaders have found more sympathetic audiences.

The hypocrisy of religious institutions inevitably made them logical targets for attack, and they are being attacked from various segments of the black religious community. For example, in addition to the groups and organizations discussed above, black students at schools of theology throughout the country have become increasingly militant. At the University of Chicago's Divinity School, Afro-American students organized a black caucus and presented their demands in 1971. They demanded that "each black student admitted to, or enrolled in the Divinity School... be guaranteed the minimum of full tuition scholarship and the current basic housing subsidy, as long as he maintains an overall academic record of 'B' or better." Their letter accompanying this and other nonnegotiable demands, included the following paragraphs;

We confront you today, not as 18 individuals with 18 different personalities and 18 different sets of problems and economic needs; we confront you today as one corporate body with one purpose, one problem, and the overriding concern and need for justice. We confront you today as representatives of the black community of the University of Chicago, the black community of the city of Chicago, and the black community of this hell called America–land of the free whites and home of the brave blacks. We confront you today to speak on behalf of that personality which you have ignored up till now, but which, we assure you, will be ignored no longer.

We confront you today representing those invisible black people who view with awe from the squalor and poverty of their existence this multimillion dollar complex (in the heart of *their* community) with its Divinity School which doesn't know or do anything about the Christ who said clothe the naked, cure the sick, and feed the hungry. We confront you today representing those invisible black people who don't know anything about epistemology, methodology, hermeneutics or phenomenology, but who *do* know Jesus and wish that somebody in this Divinity School would get to know Him too.

It is not surprising that black clergymen and black religious worshippers should be in the forefront of the black liberation struggle. Christianity in the United States has always been racist in practice, although less overtly so in recent years. Afro-Americans have always known that when Christian ministers taught that one should love his enemies or that violence would never solve anything, such teachings were meant to be applied only to black people. White Christian ministers gave their blessings to American servicemen who destroyed millions in wars of aggression. The church, through millions of dollars in investments, supports racist regimes in southern Africa. Black children were killed in church by those who profess Christian beliefs. In short, Christianity in American has generally supported the status quo (i.e., black oppression) and impeded revolutionary movements among the oppressed both at home and abroad. Because the teachings of Christianity in the United States have been so perverted by whites, it is not unlikely that American-style Christianity has served to foster the growth of black nationalism among Afro-Americans. And the black church, still the major institution in the black community to provide a place in which worshippers can feel a sense of worth, dignity, and independence in response to white hypocrisy, is playing a leading role in the development of black nationalist ideology.

The Nation of Islam, the black organizations within predominately white Christian groups, the advocates of a black theology of liberation, and the proponents of black Christian nationalism differ on many points, but all are concerned with advancing the cause of black self-determination as a means of achieving black liberation. Because of the conservative role religion has played in society, many younger Afro-Americans have completely rejected it. Therefore, although Cleage's black Christian nationalism, like the Nation of Islam, appears to be gaining adherents throughout the country, it is unlikely that any such group will attract substantial numbers of young black militants. But black people have always been a religious people, and through these movements their loyalty to traditional Christian values and norms is being shaken. Increasingly, black nationalism among black clergy and rank-and-file members is an important step toward black liberation. Some of the groups are building coalitions with nonreligious black nationalist organizations, a vital step toward unity, without which black liberation can never be achieved.

9

Educational nationalism

It is quite likely that the oppression of Afro-Americans could not have succeeded to the extent it has in the United States if the educational system had not operated to promote and sustain black subordination. For a people who have been forced into a caste-colonial situation, control of the education of their youth is crucial for the oppressor if the system is to be maintained. Therefore, the demands by black students for Afro-American studies programs and courses at all levels of the educational system may be seen as a necessary component of the black liberation struggle. At the same time, the resistance they faced from the administrators of white-controlled schools may be seen as an attempt to preserve their subordinate status in the society, or at the very least to remain aloof from the struggle for black liberation.

Since the second half of the 1960s, the number of Afro-American studies programs and courses in the United States has multiplied, mainly as a result of the insistence of the students themselves. The introduction of such programs and courses has paralleled the spread of black nationalist ideology among Afro-Americans. Historically American colleges and universities have offered few courses concerned with the experience of Afro-Americans, and those few courses that did exist usually presented a biased and distorted view. Even fewer courses were offered on the secondary level.

When such courses were first introduced, concern about their validity was expressed by educational administrators throughout the country. Yet the more than 25 million Afro-Americans have a special history, a series of peculiar problems, and many elements of a separate culture. This culture stems not only from the survival of elements of their original African cultures, but also from the peculiar circumstances of their existence in North America. Still the introduction of such courses was resisted, for Afro-Americans were never taken seriously except when there was dirty work to be

177

done for white people, or wars to be fought in the interest of white people, or during what has come to be known as "civil disorders." American colleges and universities have historically offered courses in such areas as Celtic poetry and Croatian literature, yet the poetry and literature of Afro-Americans were not considered legitimate areas of study.

The content of Afro-American studies programs and courses continues to be a source of controversy among black students and teachers, as well as among white administrators and teachers. Because of the climate out of which they developed, the major concern of white administrators initially seemed to be that the courses and programs would prove to be training grounds for cadres of blacks eager to overthrow the American system. Some black students and educators, by their actions and statements, contributed to these fears. But a vast majority appeared to be seriously concerned with correcting the inadequacies which had characterized the treatment of blacks in American scholarship. They recognized that colleges and universities were unwilling to sponsor courses and programs geared to the destruction of the society which has depended on the colleges and universities for its continued existence. Consequently, in some schools black students withdrew and established alternative institutions in which they could control the content and administration of their education. The concern here is with Afro-American studies programs as they exist both in traditional educational settings and in alternative educational programs.

Afro-American studies

Although Afro-American studies courses have been introduced into public school systems throughout the country,[1] it is such courses and programs on the college and university levels that are of interest here. A body of literature on the subject has developed in recent years, especially since these programs have gained a measure of acceptance.[2] It is perhaps too early to evaluate these programs, for the debate still rages over what constitutes an Afro-American studies curriculum. Some programs stress the decolonization of the minds of the students; others emphasize professional training in an effort to prepare students to teach in such programs; still others focus on preparing students to confront the oppressive forces in American society; and yet others attempt to reexamine old theories and develop new materials on the experience of Afro-Americans.

Many questions have been raised about Afro-American studies, by both supporters and critics. These include such questions as: What is the purpose of such programs? Should these programs be autonomous from their host colleges and universities? Who should enroll in such courses? Who should teach? Should Afro-American studies be in the curricula of all colleges and universities or should there be regional centers? What about the question of standards? Are such programs basically anti-intellectual? In addition to these questions, a series of charges have been made against these programs, mainly by individuals (black and white) who oppose at least some facet of them. It has been charged that prestigious white colleges and universities are deliberately rejecting qualified middle-class black students in favor of "authentic ghetto types." Some claim that these schools apply different (and lower) standards of evaluating black students enrolled in these programs than are used for white students. Others have charged that Afro-American studies programs are administered by "hustlers" who are more concerned with self-advancement than with the education of students.

The contemporary revolt of black students probably had its genesis in the early stages of the civil rights movement, when Afro-American students initiated sit-ins at all-white lunch counters in stores in the South in February 1960, but these actions were not specifically geared to the establishment of Afro-American studies programs. It was only after the black rebellions in American cities from 1964 through 1969 that demands for such programs were made. Furthermore, these activities originated on predominately white college and university campuses outside the South, and only later did they surface at both predominately white and predominately black schools in the South.

Many colleges and universities have offered courses on aspects of black history for decades, and on the secondary school level "Negro History Week" has become something of a long-standing tradition. The first Afro-American studies program was established at San Francisco State College in 1967. This program initially consisted of 11 courses, and the following year a sociologist, Nathan Hare, became its coordinator. The program gained departmental status, and a full complement of 26 courses was offered in 1968. The organization of black students on campus, the Black Students' Union, demanded that the department be limited to black students and faculty and that it be granted autonomy from the administration of the college. Because of resistance to these demands, the Black Students' Union initiated a strike which,

together with a faculty strike called by the teacher's union, succeeded in closing the college. The strike at San Francisco State
College ultimately became one of the most violent incidents on
any college campus. The president left the college, and when S.I.
Hayakawa, a long-time supporter of "law and order," assumed the
post, he dismissed the coordinator of the Afro-American studies
program.

The events at San Francisco State College were to be repeated
at several colleges and universities around the country. Following
the assassination of Martin Luther King, Jr., in April 1968, most of
the major colleges and universities agreed, as a result of pressure
from black students, to establish Afro-American studies programs.
Furthermore, for the first time these schools actively recruited
black students, many of whom were veterans of the black rebellions around the country. It was a widely held view that these
recruiting efforts were part of a campaign to forestall future rebellions by removing young militant blacks from the streets. What
happened, however, is that the anger and frustrations of the
students were simply transferred from the streets to the campuses.

At Antioch, long known as one of the more progressive liberal
arts colleges, an Afro-American Institute was established in 1969.
Both white teachers and students were excluded from the program
at the insistence of the black students. In addition, black students
at Antioch demanded and were given separate living quarters. The
separation demanded by black students became a major controversy, and the admissions policies of the Afro-American Institute were alleged to have excluded middle-class black students,
concentrating instead on "high risk" students who failed to meet
the normal entrance requirements.[3] The Antioch controversy
caused its black member of the Board of Directors, Kenneth B.
Clark, to resign in protest. In his letter of resignation, Clark
indicated that he objected to the college's "black separatist policy,"
because "I continue to believe...that racial prejudice, discrimination, and segregation are damaging to the human personality,
without regard to the racial rationalizations or excuses offered to
support such practices."[4]

As the number of Afro-American studies programs increased,
greater and greater controversy accompanied them. This was especially true at the Ivy League schools and other prestigious colleges
and universities around the country. Many widely publicized
incidents occurred at Columbia, Cornell, Harvard, Yale, and virtually every other major college and university in the country. The
demands by black students for the establishment of Afro-American

studies coincided with the general student revolt against the basic assumptions of American higher education. These circumstances forced several schools to cease operations for long periods of time.

Perhaps the most controversial, and certainly the most highly publicized of these events occurred at Cornell University. In the spring of 1969 a confrontation erupted which paralyzed the university. Cornell had attracted few black students prior to the mid-1960s; the number of American-born blacks enrolled in the university had traditionally been lower than the number of students from African countries, for example. Prior to the decade of the 1960s, one rarely found as many as a dozen black undergraduates among the more than 10,000 students enrolled. By 1968 more than 250 blacks were enrolled at the university, the result of special recruiting efforts. The increased black enrollment combined with the growing demands for an Afro-American studies program created major problems for the university.

The various accounts of the events which rocked Cornell's campus differ, but there is general agreement in several of them.[5] Like black students elsewhere, those at Cornell demanded an autonomous Afro-American studies program, administered and controlled by the students and faculty in the program. Furthermore, after several incidents of friction between black and white students in dormitories, black students demanded separate living facilities on campus. These demands were eventually met, but only after several confrontations on campus. At one of the black residence halls, a co-op for women, a burning cross was thrown into the building. The culminating event of a year-long series of confrontations occured in April 1969, when several blacks seized the student union building in the early morning hours during traditional Parents' Weekend. After several attempts by white students to evict them from the building, the black students somehow acquired guns for their protection and for the protection of black female students. When the students were finally persuaded to leave the building, they left in military formation, complete with weapons. Scores of news photographers were present, and pictures of the armed black students marching out of the building found their way onto the front pages of most major newspapers. The university was in a state of turmoil; several faculty members and the president resigned, and although there was no loss of life during the revolt, several students sustained injuries.

The tensions that gripped the students, faculty, and administrators at Cornell occurred on other campuses throughout the country. The brief descriptions of difficulties presented above are not meant to be exhaustive; rather they attempt to provide background for a discussion of the questions raised earlier.

The demands for Afro-American studies programs and courses, coming as they did after the demise of the civil rights movement and the advent of the black power movement, may be seen as part of the broader movement for black liberation and the spread of nationalist sentiment, especially among black youth. Never having been full participating members of American society, black students, more than their white counterparts (with a few exceptions), were able to see the relationship between higher education and other social institutions. Higher education in the United States reflected and reinforced the institutions in the society as they existed, including the racism so endemic to its structure. Yet college and university administrators claimed objectivity about the neutrality from the larger society, but at the same time they supported the privileged few and remained oblivious to the plight of the underprivileged, especially blacks, who often precariously shared the same geographical area. Rather than attempt to utilize their resources to eradicated the glaring inequalities of the society, colleges and universities chose to support the positions of the rich and powerful at home and American imperialism at home and abroad.

As Edwards has pointed out, several factors accounted for decisions by black students to enroll in predominately white schools.[6] These students recognized that if they were to play a role in the liberation of their community, it became necessary for them to acquire the skills required to control the community. Upon entering these schools, the students quickly learned that like all the other institutions in the society, education was both racist and oppressive. In addition, black students felt that from their privileged positions they must assume leadership roles in the black liberation struggle. This included support of the political activities of those waging the struggle in the black community by exposing the societal injustices on college and university campuses. Furthermore, many black students were unwilling to continue to confront the police, national guardsmen, and state troopers in the streets, for it was necessary to prepare themselves through education for leadership positions in the community.

Once large numbers of black students arrived on predominately white campuses, demands for establishing Afro-American studies programs and courses naturally followed. The historical struggle for knowledge by Afro-Americans has been well documented, most recently by Ballard.[7] Predominately white schools have simply refused to address themselves to the questions facing black people in the United States and elsewhere. The traditional curriculum was one that could lead to the quasi-assimilation of a few middle class-oriented blacks, but it was insufficient to prepare them for collective liberation. Perhaps most important, most of American higher education has perpetuated American racism. Although racism has seldom been explicitly taught in recent years, through various means–textbooks, teacher bias, course content, etc.–colleges and universities have supported the oppression of Afro-Americans. In virtually every academic discipline black people were either deprecated or ignored. Given these circumstances, there is little doubt that black students were justified in demanding courses that would assist them in dealing with a basically hostile white society. It should be added here that in 1968–1969, the apex of demands for Afro-American studies programs, white students were also insisting upon a general restructuring of American higher education. The brutal war of aggression waged by the United States against the people of Indochina and the support of educational institutions in this grotesquely imperialist and racist venture forced students to question the nature of American education. For many, especially those in organizations like the Students for a Democratic Society, the connection between internal and external imperialism was obvious, and the major difference was one of distance.

The fear the Afro-American studies programs would serve as centers for the propagation of black revolutionary ideology was intensified when students demanded that such programs be given autonomy from host schools. On some campuses this demand was met, but on others it was rejected. It is important to understand why such a demand was put forth in the first place. The black students knew that opposition to Afro-American studies was strong among white faculty members and administrators. Given this situation, they were determined to see that the staffing, course offerings, and financing of these programs would not be impeded by the inevitable delaying tactics of divisional and college committees, composed of persons who questioned the validity of such programs in the first place. Anyone familiar with the petty politics and in-fighting of the countless committees throughout most college and university structures can readily understand the demand by black students for autonomy for Afro-American studies. It frequently requires years to introduce a new course, for there is always some departmental chairman who insists that such a course is already adequately covered in his or her department. Since the demand for Afro-American studies originiated in a climate of strong opposition, it was to be expected that every delaying tactic available would be utilized by the opposition. Although some black students no doubt pressed the demand for autonomy as a means of avoiding a rigorous college experience, it is unfair, as Sowell maintains, to charge that this demand was largely a cover-up on the part of "underprepared" black students and "hustlers."[8]

Closely related to the demand for autonomy were questions about who should enroll and teach in such programs. Coming at a time in which black separatism (as opposed to segregation) was at its peak in the black movement, many black students opposed both white teachers and students in Afro-American studies. Some black educators, most notably Kenneth Clark, maintain that "it is whites who need a black studies program most of all."[9] This is essentially the integrationist point of view, and it is a romantic one which holds that the more white students learn about black people, the more likely they are to accept them as equals. Though it is true that generations of white students have been propagandized by a racist ideology which holds that blacks are innately inferior to whites, prejudices are more easily learned than unlearned. However, the demands for Afro-American studies were originated by black students within the broader context of black liberation. Their demands rarely included the exclusion of white students from the programs, but if such programs are to serve the interests of the black community, it should be expected that they would attract mainly black students. One recent study indicated that more than half (55 percent) of schools offering some Afro-American studies courses reported that whites were enrolled in such courses, and more than half of these said that white students were in a majority of students enrolled in Afro-American studies.[10]

Furthermore, many black students felt that classroom discussions with white students would ultimately develop into encounter groups, a situation which would impede the discussion of serious problems facing the black community. Though this fear may have been largely unjustified, it is true that in courses about Afro-Americans the interests of white students often differ sharply from those of blacks. It must be added, however, that many black students often enter such courses with the attitude that having been black all their lives, there is little for them to learn. Such an attitude is often more naive than the questions asked by their white counterparts.

The demands by black students for separate housing and eating facilities, while puzzling to some blacks and whites, are understandable within the context of the times. It was first and foremost an initial step on their part toward achieving self-determination, the building of a united front with which to confront the oppressor. Since most schools involved were predominately white, one might wonder why the black separatist students did not attend predominately black schools. Edwards has suggested several reasons for this development. Predominately white schools are better equipped in terms of facilities and teachers than black schools. Although often uncooperative, white administrators are more likely to tolerate political activities than black administrators who must be concerned about financing from conservative state legislatures and boards of trustees. In addition, at predominately white schools black students can assert their nationalist feelings with greater ease than at the conservative black colleges. And, finally, attendance at a predominately white school is for most black students a more realistic experience than that of a black school.[11] It is likely that most black students will be surrounded by whites throughout most of their lives, which means that their educational experience at predominately white schools will prepare them for life after graduation.

From their inception, the question of staffing Afro-American studies programs has been one of the most controversial. Many black students have insisted that only black teachers are capable of teaching such courses objectively, but large numbers of educators, black and white, have maintained that the racial background of the teacher is unimportant. The likelihood is that most black students in Afro-American studies prefer black teachers, although many such programs have employed white teachers. Arguments in favor of and those opposed to white teachers are complex, but given the nature of American scholarship, it is possible to make a strong case in favor of the exclusion of most, if not all, white teachers from Afro-American studies programs. This is not to imply that any black scholar is better qualified for such a task than any white scholar. But white American scholars have in many cases supported the racist norms of the society, and in some cases it has been these very academicians who have provided the rationale for the oppression of black people. As Ballard has pointed out this has taken three general forms: outright defense of white supremacy; neglect of the problems faced by blacks, especially in textbooks; and unnecessary and unfair intervention in matters relevant to the black community.[12] These scholars have come from various disciplines, but the social sciences have contributed a significant proportion of racist white scholars.[13]

Of all the academics sociologists have contributed most to the oppression of black people. Many white scholars have built national reputations through their research and writings on the black community, and they have frequently served as consultants to governmental agencies concerned with the problems of black people. Far too often they have presented a biased and distorted view of black people, and even so-called liberal white sociologists have engaged in research designed to maintain the oppression of Afro-Americans. For example, they have often focused on social control in the black community rather than on the creative use of conflict as a means of facilitating black liberation. The black community has most often been presented as a pathological entity, a conglomeration of crime and delinquency, bizarre religious cults, matriarchal families, emasculated males, children born out of wedlock, drug addicts, hustlers, and prostitutes. Rarely has the black community been pictured as one which has been able to achieve and maintain stable social institutions in spite of the overwhelming odds of white racist oppression. And there has been a tendency to engage in the age-old American form of deception: blaming the victim rather than the criminal. Black people are often blamed for their oppression, when it is a function of the social structure.

This is not to imply that all white scholars or even all white social scientists have lacked objectivity in research and writing about black people. However, a significant portion of the positions in sociology and urban studies in major universities have been occupied by whites insensitive to the needs and aspirations of Afro-Americans. With the advent of Afro-American studies several white scholars who had concentrated their research and writing on Afro-Americans and who were sympathetic to the civil rights movement, but unable to adjust to and accept the black nationalist thrust of many contemporary black students, have felt that they have been unfairly forced to abandon an area in which they have great investments of both emotional commitment and time.[14] Such feelings are understandable, and it should be noted that many Afro-American studies programs include white scholars who have demonstrated their objectivity in the field. Most black students appear to accept this arrangement, at least temporarily. But their demands for qualified black scholars are legitimate, given the biases of many white scholars.

The clamor for Afro-American studies accelerated at a rapid pace, and many schools experienced great difficulty in locating black scholars to staff such programs. Two-year technical colleges as well as major universities initiated massive searches for black teachers who possessed the requisite academic training and who were acceptable to militant black students. Frequently a black scholar found himself in the position of commuting between schools to offer courses. And often teachers who were acceptable to administrators were not "black" enough for the students. Many black scholars, trained in the same schools as white scholars, share the same ideological positions about Afro-Americans. They maintain that they are scholars first and black people second, a position which is hardly tenable in the United States. In some cases students selected teachers who did not meet conventional academic criteria insofar as training was concerned, and not infrequently these persons were rejected by administrators. Prior to the decade of the 1960s most blacks receiving the Ph.D. degree were forced to accept positions in black schools where conventional academic requirements such as research and scholarly publications did not hold. Furthermore, throughout American history there has been a dearth of black doctorates awarded. For example, A Ford Foundation study showed that during the five-year period between 1964 and 1968, less than one percent of all doctorates awarded were earned by blacks.[15] In short, the number of black scholars available to staff Afro-American studies programs remains inadequate to meet the need.

The large number of schools offering Afro-American studies, coupled with the shortage of competent black scholars, raises questions about whether every school should attempt to meet the demands of students for these programs. Whatever the reasons for agreeing to offer Afro-American studies, and they are no doubt varied, it appeared that by 1969 hundreds of colleges (including junior colleges) and universities decided to initiate such programs. A recent study of all four-year colleges in the United States reports that 64 percent of the 1,734 schools polled responded to a questionnaire about Afro-American studies. Of these schools 18 percent have Afro-American studies programs, some 46 percent offer courses in the area, and another 2 percent offer African studies, ethnic studies, or lecture series in the field.[16] It therefore appears that by 1970 (when the data were collected) some two-thirds of the four-year colleges in the United States offered courses which could roughly be classified as Afro-American studies.

The proliferation of these courses and programs has presented severe strains on available teachers. Consequently, it has been suggested that rather than having programs in each school where students have demanded them, regional centers be established until adequate numbers of teachers have been trained.[17] Such an arrangement would no doubt improve the quality of instruction in

Afro-American studies and train the requisite teachers to staff increasing numbers of programs. This would mean that few schools could offer the full complement of courses for several years, but it would also mean that once given, the quality of the courses would be greatly enhanced. There is no rational reason that every college and university in California should offer Afro-American studies. Perhaps one center could be located in Los Angeles, and another in Berkeley. By the same token, not every school in the Boston area or the metropolitan New York region need have such programs, when the resources of the many colleges could be pooled in order to make programs more effective. Such a suggestion might not initially meet the approval of black students in schools without programs, but ultimately they would understand that regional centers might be in the best interest of Afro-American studies.

A great deal of discussion has centered on educational standards prevailing in Afro-American studies. In many cases students exercise greater control in such programs than in conventional departments, and charges have been made by critics that scholarly standards in these programs are lower than in others.[18] In some cases black students have demanded that no black student be dismissed for academic reasons for a period of two years. Because public schools in urban areas have largely failed to prepare many black students for college-level work, such a situation would mean that many black students admitted to colleges are underprepared by conventional standards, whether they major in Afro-American studies or in some other discipline. The failure of high schools to prepare students for college work is not the fault of the students, but rather the fault of the schools. With adequate remedial work, which would perhaps add an additional year to their college study, most of the students could not doubt successfully pursue regular college work equivalent to that of students who are admitted under regular procedures. Should it develop that some students fail to measure up to standard (as is likely), they would then be dismissed from the school. The demand for a two-year trial period for black students has not usually been accompanied by a comparable demand for remedial education, but if such programs are to succeed, it is essential that the students receive adequate basic education before they move on to more advanced courses.

Several schools have attempted to cope with the problems by requiring students to enroll in haphazard remedial programs for several weeks during the summer preceding their enrollment. These programs are inadequate in both coverage and time. It is possible that the entire first year might have to be devoted to rigorous remedial education. The question should not be whether the quality of educational training should be lowered to accommodate students lacking in conventional academic preparation, but rather how intensive remedial programs can be developed to prepare these students for quality educational work.

Finally, some critics of Afro-American studies have maintained that such programs and courses are anti-intellectual. Such a view is more a reflection of the biases of critics than an objective appraisal of Afro-American studies. Clearly, it is legitimate area of scholarship and one which has been neglected and distorted for far too long. As is no doubt true of other academic disciplines, some programs maintain higher standards than others. And in the mad rush to get these programs underway for political reasons, many were hastily conceived, poorly staffed, and underfinanced. Several programs were discontinued shortly after their inception for a variety of reasons. But such acts do not discredit those programs that were well planned and properly financed. Some critics of these programs have charged that they are not geared toward serious intellectual effort. These judgements are made as hastily as some of the Afro-American studies programs were created.

The black students, who are largely responsible for the creation of Afro-American studies, were often naive about higher education, since most of them were the first members of their families to attend college. Once in attendance, however, they quickly gained knowledge of the politics of higher education in the United States. And in those cases where serious programs were established in response to their demands, they settled down to serious scholarship and insisted upon seriousness on the part of those teaching in such programs. It is virtually impossible to create quality educational programs on a crash basis. Even in major universities known for quality education, many years are often required before viable departments can be developed. Therefore, since the debate on the legitimacy of Afro-American studies has subsided, it is perhaps too early to appraise fully the quality of their intellectual content. The Faculty Committee on African and Afro-American Studies established at Harvard University declared, "It can hardly be doubted that the study of the black men in America is a legitimate and urgent academic endeavor."[19] It also can hardly be doubted that many such programs will develop the same degree of intellectual rigor as the more traditional fields of study, given time, resources, and the support of those who recognize their validity. Furthermore, given the history of American higher education and its complicity with the oppressive forces in the larger society and the world, Afro-American studies could develop greater intellectual honesty and humaneness than has been true of conventional academic disciplines. If this should be the case, people the world over will owe an enormous debt of gratitude to the courage of black students, inspired by the spread of black nationalist ideology, who are largely responsible for the introduction of Afro-American studies.

Alternative Afro-American education programs

In their frustration over the failure of the civil rights movement to significantly alter the status of black people relative to that of white people in the United States, black students, especially the veterans of the rebellions of the 1960s, frequently conveyed the impression that Afro-American studies would become ideological training grounds through which they could develop the body of doctrine and skills to eradicate racial oppression in America. But as Nathan Hare has pointed out, "We must understand that no educational program or institution can serve two cultural and political masters, two contradictory courses, whether freedom and oppression or racism and black liberation."[20] Furthermore, higher education in America has always functioned to maintain the status quo, to socialize students into the structure of the society as it exists. Endemic to that structure is the oppression of Afro-Americans and other Third World peoples. Afro-American studies programs, then, cannot be expected to radically alter the structure of the larger society, which colleges and universities support in the main. Recognizing the limitations of such programs, a movement arose among some Afro-American students to develop alternative educational institutions for the exclusive education of black people. These schools are totally controlled by black people, and their total support comes from the black community.

Within some urban areas, most notably Chicago and New York, predominately black colleges that are ostensibly black nationalist or Third World in orientation have been established to meet the demands of the more militant students. In both of these cases the schools are supported by public funds and are therefore not autonomous. Furthermore, both are component parts of large educational systems that include several colleges. In New York Medgar Evers College, a branch of the City University of New York, was created in 1971 to serve a predominately black student enrollment. Since this school is so recent in its origin, little can be said about it. However, Chicago's Malcolm X College, a branch of the City Colleges of Chicago, is a junior college with a history dating back to 1954, but it was renamed in 1969 in honor of Malcolm X. Its present campus was opened in 1971. For one week, during which the new campus was dedicated, the college sponsored a series of programs, "Focus on Black." Throughout the week workshops in a variety of areas were conducted. A sampling of the workshop topics gives some of the flavor of these cere- monies: "The Function of Black Education," "How the School Destroys the Black Child," "A Black Perspective in Higher Education," "Narcotics as a Tool of Oppression," "Plantation Men- tality in the Black Community," "Black Ritual Art," and "Blacks and Capitalism."

In his introduction to the booklet containing the activities of "Focus on Black" week, the president of the college wrote, "Many pressing issues are upon us at this crucial time in our existence. Not least among these is the need to deal with such questions as the need for a black value system and a black philosophy to guide us in all dimensions of our lives." The week of activities was initiated on Sunday, May 16, 1971, during which time the presi- dent included in his dedication address the seven principles of the doctrine of *Kawaida*. The guests of honor included Betty Shabazz, the widow of Malcolm X, and Benjamin Davis, the father of Angela Davis, who was imprisoned at the time. But perhaps the most memorable event of the series was the flag-raising ceremony, during which time the red, black, and green flag of black liberation was raised, to the accompaniment of the singing of the Black National Anthem by Harry Belafonte and the audience. This marked the first time that the black liberation flag had been raised over a public building in the United States. The significance of this event has no doubt been exaggerated, for the important question is whether Malcolm X College is playing a meaningful role in the quest for black liberation.

While the college is forbidden by law to discriminate on the basis of race, Malcolm X College is admittedly a black school, "one in which the educational services are designed to serve in a unique way the goals of black people." A brochure issued by the school declares that it offers "a black-oriented curriculum and philosophy" and "where necessary, the college serves as a catalytic agent to synthesize the varied components of the community into a viable force for liberation." The college proposes to educate black students for "freedom, individuality, and services." Freedom is defined as liberty from external constraint; individuality is viewed as "built-in capacities (not necessarily apparent) for good which are inseparable from the good of the community and ultimately of all mankind;" and service denotes that "learning is combined with an understanding of social injustice and a commitment to correcting it." At Malcolm X College power is shared equally by administrators, faculty, and students.

Although the college has developed two-year career study programs in such areas as health services, business and secretarial skills, and data processing, an examination of the catalog for the academic year 1971–1972 reveals a relatively extensive program in Afro-American studies. With a core of 15 courses in humanities and social sciences, a total of some 35 courses are offered in Afro-American studies. Whether these course offerings will ultimately succeed in training students to serve the needs of the black community in its quest for liberation remains to be demonstrated. It appears, however, that in this regard schools like Malcolm X College fall somewhere between traditional colleges and the alternative schools which have developed in recent years.

Several alternative schools exist today, although they differ greatly in outlook, facilities, and financing. One is Nairobi College in East Palo Alto (Nairobi), Claifornia. Founded in a San Mateo country suburban community with 20,000 residents of whom 80 percent are black, Nairobi College commenced operation in September 1969. By September 1971 it had enrolled some 200 students, assembled a faculty of 16, and an administrative staff of 8.[21] In addition to the permanent faculty, the instructional staff was supplemented by graduate students from nearby universities. Nairobi College includes among its aims and objectives the changing of value systems "to create positive self-concepts and confidence in our students together with the skills and technical expertise necessary to plan, organize, develop, and maintain viable communities for peoples of color." The primary objective is to develop and train leaders for the black community. Unlike traditional colleges, Nairobi accepts students without previous academic training, provided they accept the philosophy of the college and assume responsibility for community work and self-development.

Service to community is an integral part of the program of Nairobi College, and each full-time student is required to work on community projects four hours daily. Such projects include developing new agencies, serving as teacher aides in elementary schools, working on the Municipal Council, assisting in the community health center, and serving as counselors for legal aid. These projects are central to the college, for it is a "community" college, although it operates on a four-year basis. The community in which it exists serves as its campus. Courses are held in various community facilities—churches, public schools, recreation centers, social service agencies, and faculty homes. Plans are underway for the construction of several buildings, but these buildings will serve the community as well as the school.

Instruction at Nairobi College differs from that of traditional colleges. There are no lectures, because it is felt that the objectives of the college are best served if students and faculty interact with each other directly. For students who plan to transfer to other institutions and who feel the need for lecture courses, an arrangement has been developed between Nairobi College and Stanford University to allow students to enroll in courses at Stanford free of charge. A core curriculum in the sciences, communications, and humanities is required for all full-time students. Instruction is provided largely from a black perspective, and the college provides a variety of other services, including counseling, child-care, legal assistance, job development and placement, and a talent search program which includes counseling and recruitment of high school students and dropouts.

Student participation in the operation of Nairobi College is perhaps the most far-reaching in existence. Students, to a great degree, run the college. They are well represented on the board of trustees and have full voting power in all college committees. Through the student-dominated central committee, students control the decision-making process in the college, because the committee is the governing organization of the college and all other committees come under its jurisdiction. In addition, students control the employment of teachers and administrators.

As in all such ventures, financial support poses problems. Full-time students pay an annual fee of $500, but this is waived for those who are unable to pay, and funds for their tuition come from federally funded grants and loans. Each member of the college planning committee contributes part of his or her salary each month, as do faculty members employed elsewhere. Additional financial support is contributed by individuals and foundations. Such sources accounted for $500,000 in one school year. Interested individuals in the community donate their time to the college; for example, the volumes in the college library, which were accumulated through a student-run book drive, were catalogued by a volunteer staff of 15 librarians. Also, the college sponsors an annual Black Music Festival, the proceeds from which are used to support its programs. But the college depends heavily on federal funds, usually in the form of grants and loans to students.

Since federal funds were crucial in the first years of its operation, charges have been made that Nairobi College has proceeded with extreme caution. For example, the trustees of the college established the largely Chicano Venceremos College in nearby Redwood City, but in 1971 they voted to discontinue support of the college, because much of its activity included organizing political demonstrations which led to confrontations with the police. Such activity, officials of Nairobi College charged, hampered their ability to raise funds.[22] Officials at Venceremos College charged that Nairobi College is too dependent on federal funds to engage in activities critical of the government.

It is perhaps too early to determine whether or not Nairobi College is a viable alternative to traditional higher education for Afro-Americans. However, it is an important experiment which has achieved some degree of success in its short history. If the college is able to develop a permanent base of support within the black community, a formidable task, it will be well on the road to becoming an educational institution geared to training the leaders necessary for black self-determination.

One of the closest approximations to an independent black alternative college was Malcolm X Liberation University, founded in Durham, North Carolina, in 1969. The school had its origins on the campus of Duke University, where a dispute arose over the proposed Afro-American studies program.[23] Many of the black students withdrew from the school in protest over a compromise curriculum which they found unacceptable. The main branch of the university moved to Greensboro, North Carolina, the place of origin of the sit-in demonstrations, and Durham became a branch.

Malcolm X Liberation University attracted blacks who were disenchanted with the conventional educational system and who were willing to create a school "within which black education can become relevant to the needs of the black community and the struggle for black liberation." The original director of the school defined it as "a nation-building school, a school for people who want to build an independent African nation some day and who want to be doing the right things right now."[24] According to a brochure issued by the university, its curriculum focused on physical and land development, ideological seminars, and the development of such technical skills as teaching, engineering, biomedicine, and communications. Students were expected to study in Africa while enrolled, and after completing the program, they were expected to work in African and Afro-American communities as food scientists, tailors, architects, engineers, community organizers, teachers, medical technicians, artists and linguists. As might be expected, financial support posed a problem for a school such as Malcolm X Liberation University. The original operating funds were provided by a grant from the Episcopal Church and from individual contributions. Students paid tuition if they were able, according to their ability. Initially the annual tuition fee was $300. One means was devised to meet the financial needs of the university when a consortium of six independent alternative Afro-American schools formed the Federation of Pan-African Educational Institutions in July 1970. These schools pooled financial resources as a means of minimizing expenses. Each school in the federation had as its focus "the development of educational institutions focused around Pan-Africanism and the acquisition of technical skills." The other schools in the federation were the Center for Black Education in Washington, the Pan-African Work Center in Atlanta, Our School in New York City, the Chad School in Newark, and the Clifford McKissick Community School in Milwaukee. Except for Malcolm X Liberation University, most of these schools offered no courses on the college level, but together they were equipped to offer students education for liberation from preschool age through adulthood.

In general, Malcolm X Liberation University attempted to provide both the technical skills and the ideological training for Afro-American youth as an alternative to conventional Afro-American studies programs. Such a school was important because the students and teachers were not obliged to enter into disputes with white administrators and teachers regarding the teaching the black nationalist ideology. Writing about the prospects of Malcolm X Liberation University, Ballard noted that "It is uncertain whether the university will fail or succeed in its mission, but the very attempt to provide a structured and well-conceived alternative to traditional education is worthy of great praise and suggestive of similar efforts that could be mounted in large urban areas."[25] Unfortunately, Malcolm X Liberation University has permanently closed because of inadequate funding.

One of the most important alternative educational institutions in recent years, although not a university, is the Institute of the Black World in Atlanta.[26] The institute is "an independent research center whose work is based upon the conviction that black people must move to control the definition of our past and our present if we are to become masters of our future." The basic purpose of the institute "is to bring together a community of black scholars, artists, and organizers who are committed to use the skills of research and analysis to forward the struggles of the black community towards self-understanding, self-determination, and ultimate liberation."[27]

Originally a component of the Martin Luther King, Jr., Memorial Center, the institute is now an autonomous operation based in the former home of W. E. B. DuBois in Atlanta. The severance of organizational ties from the center resulted in part from a disagreement with the center's board of directors. The disagreement focused on the institute's refusal to give priority to nonviolence and to include white people on its staff. The institute attracted a research staff which includes a group of distinguished young scholars from several academic disciplines, especially the social sciences. Because of inadequate funding, these scholars made financial sacrifices to get the work of the institute underway. In addition to the research staff, there is an administrative staff, a governing board of distinguished educators, and a network of scholars throughout the country who serve as associates. The associates assist the Institute as "collaborators in research, evaluation [of black studies programs] and writing." In addition, they aid in the institute's fund raising efforts.

The Institute of the Black World, at its inception, announced a 10-point program which would guide its work:

1 *Defining and refining of the field of black studies;*

2 *Developing of a new consortium for black education;*

3 *Encouraging basic research on peoples of African descent;*

4 *Encouraging and providing support for black artists;*

5 *Developing new materials and methods of teaching black children;*

6 *Establishing a Black Policy Studies Center for the continuing analysis of the black community;*

7 *Creating a dialogue with black scholars, artists, and organizers in other areas of the black world;*

8 *Training a cadre of teachers for the black community;*

9 *Sponsoring seminars, workshops, and conferences;*

10 *Developing a publishing program.*

During its first year of operation, important activity occurred in each of these areas. Perhaps the most impressive output has been a series of papers and books on peoples of African descent. These include books on the black woman, Marcus Garvey, and black poetry. Some two dozen papers appeared in both scholarly and popular journals, and several chapters were prepared for books edited by others.

The importance of the work of the institute's staff and associates extends beyond these publications. A seminar was sponsored for directors of Afro-American studies programs in predominately white universities. A consortium arrangement was effected with Fisk and Howard universities, and cooperative relationships have also been established with Brooklyn and Dartmouth colleges, and Cornell and Wesleyan universities. Through these arrangements members of the institute staff lecture at these schools, and black students attend courses at the institute, for which they receive credit and for which their schools pay the fees. Members of the institute staff have traveled to Africa to establish ties with institutions and individuals. Exchange scholars between the institute and universities in countries in the Caribbean are commonplace, and Institute staff members serve as consultants to many Afro-American studies programs throughout the country. One of the institute's chief functions is to appraise critically existing Afro-American studies programs.

The institute's "Monthly Report," which is mailed to some 4,500 readers, provides a summary of its activities and an analysis of important news events relating to black people. These analyses are also published in several black newspapers. Among the events to which these analyses have been addressed are the controversial African trip by the Vice-President of the United States; the massacre of prisoners at Attica prison; the deaths of Ralph Bunche, Kwame Nkrumah, and Amilcar Cabral; the National Black Political Convention; and the murder of black students at Southern University. The institute also makes appeals on behalf of black political prisoners in both the United States and Africa. When the 30 inmates and 9 guards were slaughtered by law enforcement officials at Attica in September 1971, staff members of the institute sponsored a "Peoples' Indictment" and accompanying petition in which the black community and its elected officials were asked to call upon "the legislature of the State of New York to form a court of impeachment and indictment in order to remove from office and criminally prosecute those responsible for the murders at Attica."

Members of the institute's staff view education as basically political; therefore they believe education should provide students with the tools for restructuring society. Thus the institute has continued to face financial problems. Each year funds are raised by staff members through appeals to individuals, organizations, and foundations. Some financing comes from the sale of publications and lecture and consultation fees, but the "Monthly Report" usually contains appeals for contributions from readers. The institute's staff members believe that if their independent work is to continue, funding must come from the black community.

Finally, in its endeavor to create a program designed to lead to a definition of the black experience (past, present, and future) from a black perspective, the institute works closely with alternative educational institutions. Close association is also maintained with organizations like the National Committee of Black Churchmen, the African Heritage Studies Association, the Congress of African Peoples, and the Organization of Black and Urban Studies Directors.

The Institute of the Black World is clearly a major educational force in the black liberation movement. Its staff and associates are among the most able minds available, and they are firmly dedicated to the cause of black selfdetermination as a step toward black liberation. Because of the quality of its scholarship, it has been suggested that the institute might become the accrediting agency for Afro-American studies programs.[28] Of all the agencies in existence, the institute is the logical choice to insure high-quality programs.

A note on the blackening of Howard University

The brief discussion of Afro-American studies programs in predominately white colleges and universities and black alternative educational programs has dealt with a few such programs, the proliferation of which accompanied the ascendency of nationalist consciousness of Afro-Americans, and some of the problems they continue to encounter. It has not attempted to be exhaustive and has no doubt raised more questions than it has answered. Although Afro-American studies programs exist in the predominately black colleges and universities, no mention has been made of them, because they did not generally receive the publicity that accompanied their introduction in white schools. Furthermore, the impetus for black studies arose on the campuses of predominately white schools.

The black colleges in the United States, especially those which are publicly supported, are struggling for existence. Historically they have made important contributions to the black community. They have provided higher education for generations of southern blacks who otherwise would have been financially unable to pursue a college education. In addition, black colleges have provided employment and refuge for some of the best-known black scholars, for until recently white schools refused to employ black scholars.

However, black colleges have not provided their students with the type of education that a growing number of black students believe is necessary to liberate the black community.

The best-known of the predominately black colleges, Howard University, was founded by an act of Congress in 1867 and has traditionally been the gathering place for the largest collection of black scholars in the world. Throughout most of its history Howard could hardly be considered a "black" university, for it was patterned after its white counterparts. Furthermore, it had been insensitive to the needs of the black community, focusing instead on traditional European-oriented education and providing a haven for the children of the black bourgeoisie, preferably those with light skin and straight hair. Social activities, especially events sponsored by exclusive fraternities and sororities, appeared to assume a place of equal standing with academic endeavors. Faculty members were often more concerned with academic trivia than scholarship, a situation which prompted a former faculty member to write, "When I taught at Howard University... there were an average of ten mandatory academic (or cap and gown) processionals yearly."[29] In short, Howard University, throughout most of its history, represented little more than a caricature of white universities, although its list of distinguised black faculty members and alumni is impressive by any standards.

Howard University did not escape the movement by militant black students for radical structural change in the 1960s. The transformation of Howard from a "Negro" to a "black" university commenced in 1965, when a few students demonstrated for student rights, and against the compulsory Reserve Officer's Training Corps for men.[30] The president of the university responded by saying that the demonstration was inspired by communists. Two years later, when the director of the Selective Service System attempted to speak on campus, he was forbidden to do so by a group of students who shouted "America is the black man's battlefield." This demonstration led to both student and faculty dismissals, but compulsory ROTC was abolished. After the dismissals a group of students demanded that the administration cease its repressive policies and establish a black curriculum. Several months were given for these demands to be considered, but the president of the university simply ignored them. During the university's 101st Charter Day ceremonies in March 1968, a group of students, angered by the administration's silence disrupted the ceremonies. The demonstration escalated when hundreds of students seized the administration building, virtually bringing the activities of the university to a halt. Sympathetic persons and restaurant owners expressed support for the students by supplying the demonstrators with food.

The demonstration ended when charges against the rebellious students were dropped and the administration agreed to negotiate with them. The president was replaced in September 1969 by an educator sympathetic to student demands that the university be restructured and developed into a major black center of learning. The new president was quoted as saying, "It is in the national interest that there be institutions of higher learning that are recognized as being black, that are clearly identified with the black community, and that are using the resourses that knowledge can provide to resolve issues and problems that relate to the condition of black America." He continued, "I see an institution like Howard having as an important part of its mission the affirmation and celebration of the black presence in higher education."[31] In an effort to transform Howard into a black university, the president reorganized its administrative staff, and a vice-president was employed to recruit distinguished black scholars. By 1972 these efforts had succeeded in attracting to Howard hundreds of the most talented black scholars in the country.

Many changes have been introduced at Howard. Although the buildings remain, many have been redecorated with murals depicting various aspects of black life to convey visually the new thrust of the university. Black art, rather than European art, now predominates in the art department. Jazz and other black music have been incorporated into the curriculum through the Institute of Jazz Studies. Dramatic productions depicting facets of the black experience and written by black playwrights now dominate the presentations at the Ira Aldridge Theater. There is now an Afro-American studies department and an African studies program, which offers a graduate program leading to the doctorate degree. It is planned that the Afro-American studies department will become superfluous as the curriculum of each department incorporates relevant courses. The School of Communications was created to train black students for employment in the mass media, and the School of Business not only trains students, but also assists black businessmen with the problems they encounter. Since American cities are becoming black enclaves, the School of Engineering has launched a program dealing with the transportation, health, and ecological problems of cities. The School of Law, long noted for its civil rights program, recently assisted in such projects as the defense of Angela Davis and the defense of inmates at Attica.

Such social science departments as economics, political science, and sociology are developing graduate curricula from a black perspective.

In previous years homecoming week at Howard University was a major social event, complete with lavish balls and parades. This, too, has changed. During the 1972–1973 academic year most of the week's events were held at Cramton Auditorium and featured a long list of militant black speakers, including Julian Bond, Imamu Baraka, Stokely Carmichael, Dick Gregory, and Fanny Lou Hamer. Later in the year the School of Law sponsored a lecture by Angela Davis.

Howard is the only major university in the country to receive most of its operating budget (59.4 percent in 1971–1972) from the federal government. Many of the predominately white universities receive larger appropriations in federal funds, but no one relies on the federal government for most of its operating budget. This situation means that Howard is not completely autonomous. Members of Congressional committees concerned with appropriating funds for education are likely to be cautious about how the money is spent, but the administrators of the university maintain that federal appropriations have increased since the new thrust began at Howard. Since so much of the budget comes from federal funds, Howard operates on a nondiscrimatory basis, with a 10 percent white enrollment, mainly in the graduate and professional schools. Similarly, although the university recruits mainly black scholars, its faculty is interracial.

Not everyone is happy with the transformation of Howard into a black university. One of its more severe critics, even before the new thrust began, is the economist Thomas Sowell, who spent his first two years as an undergraduate at Howard in the early 1950s but later transferred to Harvard, from which he was graduated. In 1963 he returned to Howard to teach economics for a year. As a student he was unhappy with Howard, because of the lack of stimulation. He was later to write, "I encountered a number of very bright individuals among the students and faculty at Howard, but it was painfully obvious that there was no intellectual atmosphere there—not even to the extent found in New York City high schools. It was not a question of 'cultural deprivation' or the usual academic deficiencies. They were not *serious* about intellectual work." He continues, "At Howard everyone seemed to be playing a role, from the most naive freshman to the most cynical dean."[32] Sowell found teaching at Howard a distressing experience in many ways. He writes, "Most distressing of all, was to learn that cheating on exams was rampant. I had known about many isolated instances of cheating as a student at Howard, but only now did I realize how blatant, organized, and pervasive it was."[33] He contends that such practices characterized other employees of the university, including typists and secretaries who either leaked or sold examinations to students. It is his position that the students cheated because they were simply unwilling to exert themselves, not that they were incapable of serious scholarly work. Sowell believes that when black colleges replaced their overwhelmingly white faculties and administrators for "under-qualified" blacks in the last decades of the nineteenth century and the early decades of the twentieth, they exchanged the "skills of white teachers" for the "symbolism of black representation."[33]

It should be added that Sowell is critical of students, faculty, and administrators at predominately white colleges where he has taught, including Cornell University, where he taught during the period of turmoil surrounding the establishment of an Afro-American studies program. Indeed, he resigned from the faculty of that university in a widely publicized news release in which he charged the university with "paternalism" in its concessions to the demands of black students. He asserted that Cornell had been "interested in its image–anything to keep the black students happy."[35] Sowell, a product of the slums, has achieved a distinguished academic record, as both a student and a professional, having attended three of the most prestigious predominately white universities in the country. As a result of these experiences, he maintains an elitist and conventional view of higher education and is vehement in his concern for what he considers high standards.

More recently Howard University has been the target of attacks from those who believe that its transformation has deemphasized basic education in favor of "black relevancy."[36] Critics charge that the university is failing to prepare its students adequately to advance themselves after graduation, and that its undergraduates are not prepared for graduate study at major universities. In general, they believe that Howard has downgraded traditional academic studies. To these charges the university's president responded, "I'm just totally opposed to blackness as an academic cop-out. If being black is anything, it has to be excellence, not sloppy thinking, and that [a charge made by one critic] is sloppy thinking." He continued, "Nobody raises a question about the 'Jewishness' of Brandeis or Yeshiva, or about the 'Catholic-ness' of Georgetown or Notre Dame, or the 'Wasp-ishness' of Harvard or Yale. But somehow, there's something wrong with exploring blackness at Howard."

The president's position was supported by the chairman of the university's political science department. He maintains that the attacks on the university's new thrust come mainly from the "black right wing" and that Howard's undergraduates are not permitted to earn more than one-fifth of their total academic credits in courses that are specifically black-related.

The newspaper article, "The Big Debate at Howard U.," came as a surprise to many students and teachers, both black and white, who were generally sympathetic to the administration's position. Specific charges were made allegedly by past and present faculty members and alumni, all of whom insisted upon strict anonymity. They included discrimination against Africans and whites by "superblacks" on the faculty; political "rap sessions" in place of conventional courses; and greater concern expressed by the president in preventing student protest than in the welfare of the faculty. Such charges are unfair to the university and its new emphasis on black scholarship. One has only to read the catalog to see that the university maintains strong departments of astronomy and physics, classics, English, geology, German, philosophy, and romance languages, along with other traditional disciplines. In addition, Howard's critics fail to note that in the past few years the university has attracted hundreds of distinguished black scholars to its staff, many of whom left major white universities because of their serious scholarly interest in black education.

Since 1969, Howard University has made major strides in performing the function it should have assumed throughout its long history, namely that of combining quality traditional education with quality black-related scholarship. Like other universities which have experienced fundamental changes in the past few years, mistakes have no doubt been made, and it is impossible to predict the outcome of its experiment. However, as the major black university in the country, there can be little doubt that the goal of providing black students with the skills necessary to liberate Afro-Americans from racism, poverty, and low self-esteem should be its major function. The history of black education has proved that this cannot be accomplished if Howard simply imitates the educational programs of American white universities.

In their struggle for liberation, Afro-Americans are forging ahead on many fronts. Clearly one of the most important areas of activity is that of education. This chapter has focused primarily on some aspects of the struggle in higher education, although it is being fought on all educational levels. The efforts of black parents to control the schools in their community is part of the larger demand for self-determination, as are the alternative primary and secondary school experiments springing up throughout the country. But the major battle has been led by black students at predominately white colleges and universities. The impetus for the changes they demand stems largely from the increasing influence of black nationalist ideology in the black community. Though the outcome of these efforts remains uncertain, it is clear that traditional education has failed Afro-Americans.

In addition, the demands made by courageous black students have already had a significant impact on American higher education. Following the initiative of Afro-Americans, many other oppressed groups in the society have demanded the inclusion of courses and departments relevant to their particular problems. Since the struggle for Afro-American studies commenced, schools throughout the country have been forced to introduce courses and departments in Asian, Chicano, Chinese, Jewish, Native American (Indian), Puerto Rican, and women's studies. These studies will no doubt require time to become established, and some will fail in the process, but they have already had the positive impact of expanding and humanizing American higher education.

10

Black nationalism and liberation

Up to this point an attempt has been made to trace the historical development of black nationalism in the United States, to gauge its impact on the contemporary black community, and to assess developments in four specific areas of the nationalist movement–revolutionary, cultural, religious, and educational nationalism. In each case, with few exceptions, the discussion has been general in nature, and omissions abound. One such omission is the dearth of material relating to Pan-Africanism, and especially the role of W.E.B. DuBois, the father of the concept and clearly one of the most distinguished educators and thinkers in American history.

As a young child DuBois learned about Africa from his great-grandmother, who sang what he was later to call a "sorrow song" to him.[1] His grandfather's grandmother had been seized by a Dutch trader and brought from Africa to the Americas. The song was sung to the children of the family through the generations. DuBois's African heritage was ever present in his mind. As previously quoted, he wrote of the conflict he felt: "One ever feels his two-ness–an American, a Negro; two souls, two thoughts, two unreconciled strivings; two warring ideals in one dark body, whose dogged strength alone keeps it from being torn asunder."[2] Throughout his long and productive life (1868–1963), DuBois remained dedicated to the liberation of Africa and peoples of African descent throughout the world.

Although he was not the organizer of the First Pan-African Conference, held in London July 23–25, 1900, he traveled to the conference as a participant from his teaching post at Atlanta University. The purpose of the conference was to "bring into closer touch with each other the peoples of African descent throughout the world." Present at the conference were delegates from Ethiopia, Ghana (then, Gold Coast), Liberia, Sierra Leone, the United States, and the Caribbean. When the conference convened, DuBois was named chairman of the committee on the address to the nations of the world. His address ended with a call to action: "Let the Nations of the world respect the integrity and independence of the free Negro states of Abyssinia, Liberia, Hayti, etc. and let the inhabitants of these states, the independent tribes of Africa, the Negroes (people of African descent) of the West Indies and America, and the black subjects of all Nations take courage, strive ceaselessly, and fight bravely, that they may prove to the world their incontestable right to be counted among the great brotherhood of mankind."[3] Between 1900 and 1945 there were six Pan-African congresses, and DuBois either organized or played a leading role in each, thereby earning the designation of "father" of Pan-Africanism.[4]

The Second Pan-African Conference was organized by DuBois and held in Paris February 19–21, 1919. Some 57 delegates from 15 countries attended. The delegates at the conference asked that German colonies in Africa be turned over to an international organization and that a code of laws for the protection of Africans be established. DuBois called the Third Pan-African Congress in 1921. Delegates met in London, Brussels, and Paris in late summer. The congress sent a committee headed by DuBois to consult with officials of the League of Nations. A petition on behalf of African colonies was presented to this international organization. Two years later, in 1923, the Fourth Pan-African Congress met in Paris and Lisbon, and a set of eight demands was issued. In sum, these demands asked for equality of treatment for black people throughout the world.

New York was the site selected for the Fifth Pan-African Conference, held in 1927. The major resolution adopted by the more than 200 delegates stressed "the development of Africa for the Africans and not merely for the profit of Europeans." In addition, the delegates demanded national independence for China, Egypt, and India. The sixth and final Pan-African conference convened in Manchester, England, in October 1945. DuBois was selected to preside over the conference and was unanimously elected international president of the Pan-African Congress. This congress was attended by delegates and observers from Africa, Europe, the United States, the Caribbean, Cyprus, Ceylon, and India. By this time the mood of the delegates was considerably more militant. For example, the declaration on colonial peoples stated, "We affirm the right of all colonial peoples to control their own destiny. All colonies must be free from foreign imperialist control, whether political or economic. The peoples of the colonies must have the right to elect their own Governments, without restrictions from foreign powers. We say to the peoples of these colonies that they must fight for these ends by all means at their disposal." In their declaration to colonial powers, the delegates demanded independence for black Africa and condemned "the monopoly of capital and the rule of private wealth and industry for private profit alone. We welcome economic democracy as the only real democracy."[5] DuBois was delegated to present to the newly organized United Nations a memorandum demanding that the Universal Declaration of Human Rights apply to African as well as other peoples.

The Pan-African conference led directly to the Afro-Asian Bandung (Indonesia) Declaration of 1955 and ultimately to the First Conference of Independent African States held in Accra, Ghana, in 1958. Several subsequent All African Peoples conferences were held in various African countries, and finally in 1963 the Organization of African Unity was created. Because of his efforts, DuBois is rightly considered the principal figure in the movement for political independence in Africa.

While Afro-American support for African independence has had a long history, it has only been in recent years that such support has mushroomed in the black community. Each year thousands of Afro-Americans in cities throughout the country observe African Liberation Day, expressing support for the struggles of Africans and Afro-Americans, especially the oppressed Africans in Angola, Mozambique, and South Africa. Furthermore, many black Americans with technical skills have traveled to African countries to aid in economic development. For example, the Congress of Racial Equality has arranged for hundreds of Afro-American technicians to replace Asians expelled from Uganda.[6] In the years since the death of DuBois in Ghana, important strides have been made toward accomplishing one of his life-long dreams: the liberation of Africa from European colonial rule. And within the United States, the movement toward liberation has accelerated.

(The first Pan-African Congress to meet since the death of DuBois was held in Dar-es-Salaam, Tanzania, in June 1974. Since much of Africa became politically independent between 1945 and 1974, a major emphasis of this congress was on neocolonialism, imperialism, and the necessity for class struggle as well as the struggle for national liberation in those countries not yet freed from direct colonialism. This congress was the largest to date, including representatives from 26 African states and 7 African liberation organizations and delegates from Brazil, England, the United States, Canada, the nations of the Caribbean, and other liberation movements from around the world. Approximately 1400 people, including heads of state, were in attendance. For reports on this Pan-African congress, see *The Black Scholar*, July–August 1974.)

On black liberation

The liberation of Afro-Americans from their caste-colonial status in the United States is the most pressing problem facing them. There appears to be a consensus on the desirability of this goal, but differences on how to achieve liberation continue to plague the black community. Perhaps the greatest division among Afro-Americans in this regard today is that between the integrationists and the nationalists. The integrationists view assimilation into American society as the only viable means toward achieving black liberation; the nationalists maintain that integration is not only unlikely but that it is also undesirable. They maintain that assimilation is unlikely because black people historically have attempted this route to liberation, but since racism is so endemic to the structure of U.S. society, they have been constantly rebuffed by white resistance. Although prejudice and discrimination against Afro-Americans declined in the decade of the 1960s, the racism which produced these phenomena is ever present and is likely to remain for the foreseeable future. As an economic system, capitalism makes use of and reinforces various forms of oppression, including racism. Though American racism was more a product than a cause of slavery, the early European settlers eagerly seized upon racial differences as a means of maintaining the oppression of Afro-Americans.[7] And since the end of legal slavery, racism has achieved a functional autonomy of its own and has served to maintain the positions of economic dominance of those in power. This is not meant to imply that the elimination of capitalism is sufficient to end racism, but it is a necessary first step. However, there is little likelihood that this first step will be taken in the United States in the near future, despite the growing opposition to capitalism in much of the world, especially among Third World peoples.

The nationalists consider the assimilation of Afro-Americans undesirable, because the very notion of assimilation as defined by white Americans is racist in that it demands that Afro-Americans relinquish whatever cultural characteristics they share and adopt middle-class white cultural standards. They see these standards as decadent and unworthy of adoption, for such standards result in complacency and meaninglessness. Having been denied access into the mainstream of American society, Afro-Americans are uniquely qualified to view the society and all of its shortcomings in a way that those who are integral parts of it are incapable of doing.

Indeed, Afro-Americans, because of their oppressed status, are in the forefront of the movement to transform the United States into a humane society. The Watergate scandal surrounding the 1972 Presidential election is ample evidence of the decadence and corruption so prevalent in the United States, though it is but one example. The brutal massacre of inmates at Attica prison in 1971 that resulted from the orders of the governor of New York state to recapture the prison, in spite of their humane actions toward racist guards, clearly shows that if the United States were a decent society, the inmates would be the leaders of the state, while those who ordered the mass murder would be imprisoned. Finally (although the list is almost limitless), the relative complacency of most Americans about their government's acts of genocide in Indochina has demonstrated to the world that most Americans condoned what must be recorded as one of the most barbaric and criminal acts in all of human history.

Recent empirical evidence indicates that as late as the 1960s most black people preferred assimilation to pluralism (or autonomy) as a means of achieving black liberation.[8] But, as has been demonstrated in the preceding chapters, nationalist ideology has made significant inroads in the black community since the demise of the civil rights movement. Those black people who still cling to assimilation as the means for achieving black liberation are mainly older blacks and those who are either middle class or candidates for that status. The younger blacks and the mass of poor blacks appear to have reached the conclusion that assimilation for Afro-Americans has failed. Given the nature of power in American society, it seems unlikely that black Americans will achieve their liberation through assimilation at the present time. Therefore, some degree of separation (autonomy), leading to black control of the institutions in the black community, is a necessary prerequisite for liberation. Though comparisons between black and white ethnic groups are invidious, some form of pluralism has been the characteristic American pattern through which these groups, such as the Irish and Jews, have achieved their liberation. Whether such an approach will prove successful for Afro-Americans remains to be seen, but it appears unlikely that black liberation will be achieved without ethnic solidarity.

Liberation means different things to different people, and in regard to black–white relations in the United States, the concept presents complex problems. As the Black Panthers have apparently realized, a revolution to transform the society from capitalism to socialism is not on the horizon. And as the members of the Republic of New Africa have discovered, partition of the United States into two separate societies, one for blacks and one for whites, is equally remote. Also, few, if any, contemporary nationalists view repatriation to Africa as a viable alternative. Therefore, some type of rapprochement must be achieved within the context of American society as it is presently structured or minor changes must be made in institutions and practices while the basic structure remains.

Gibson Winter sees liberation as "the process of becoming a whole person who can rejoice in nature, respond to beauty, share in poetic visions, and participate in intimate human communities." He recognizes that liberation also requires that all persons share in the "goods and capacities" of the technological society that the United States has become, for to be a member of the society without having a voice in its operation is the opposite of liberation. He comments further that "the liberation of peoples means they must have the power to express their own identities in a pluralistic world."[9]

Within the context of the contemporary United States, where black people continue to struggle for mere survival, such processes as rejoicing in nature, responding to beauty, and sharing poetic visions are remote dreams, and significant changes in the society are required before these projections can begin to be of concern to Afro-Americans. Black Americans must first gain the necessary power which will allow them to take their place in the pluralistic society. Such power can only come through increasing black unity, for those in power in the United States have maintained the oppression of Afro-Americans by keeping them divided. Afro-American unity at the present time requires some degree of autonomy for the black community.

Given the complex nature of American society, it seems likely that black liberation must involve the achievement of parity between Afro-Americans and other groups. That is, they must gain the power sufficient to command a proportionate share of the social reward in the United States. They must share equally in economic, political, and social institutions. Such an exegesis will appear to some as advocating that Afro-Americans climb aboard a sinking ship, but repression is rampant in the United States, and in order for Afro-Americans to survive, they must rely on the strength which comes through unity, which in turn requires some degree of autonomy. A highly visible minority of approximately 11 percent of the population can hardly expect to seize the governing machinery of the most powerful nation in human history. But as the urban rebellions of the 1960s have clearly demonstrated, this minority can create problems that local and state officials are incapable of controlling without the assistance of federal troops. Furthermore, most Afro-Americans at present seem more interested in entering the mainstream of American society than in destroying it.

After robbing the Native Americans (Indians) of their land in North America, European settlers created in the United States what they consider to be the best of all possible worlds. Any threat to domestic tranquility (real or imagined) brings forth the forces of repression, and frequently minor concessions are made to those who are seen as responsible for what have come to be known as "civil disorders." For example, after the urban rebellions of the last half of the 1960s, those in positions of power responded by making higher education available to ever greater numbers of young Afro-Americans. In 1965 there were some 210,000 blacks between the ages of 18 and 24 enrolled in colleges and universities. This was approximately 10 percent of all Afro-Americans in this age category. By 1970 this number had increased to 416,000, or 16 percent of those in this age category. Though college enrollment in general increased during this period, the comparable increase for whites in the same age category was only one percent.[10] These data indicate that concessions to Afro-Americans are more likely to result from threats to the security of white Americans than from altruism.

It is often maintained that since the United States is a nation of many ethnic minorities, black liberation is likely to be accelerated if Afro-Americans form coalitions with other ethnic minorities, both Third World and white. Most black nationalists reject this notion, for as Carmichael and Hamilton have pointed out, coalitions between those with economic and political power and those without are unworkable.[11] Such coalitions are not likely to prove effective because of the lack of common interests. This means that meaningful coalitions between Afro-Americans and white ethnic groups are virtually impossible. If one considers that some white ethnic groups maintain the strongest racial prejudice in the society, then such coalitions are clearly impossible.

There is a greater possibility of effective coalitions between Afro-Americans and other Third World groups, but many of them have adopted the antiblack prejudice of the larger society, thereby complicating the problem. There is some evidence that meaningful coalitions can be effected between Afro-Americans and Puerto

Ricans. Puerto Ricans are the most recent large group of Third World people to enter the mainland of the United States. Coming from a society where they have lived under colonial domination by the United States for nearly a century, they understand American imperialism, both internal and external. Furthermore, Puerto Ricans come from a land largely devoid of antiblack racism. Upon reaching the mainland, they quickly learn that whatever their racial heritage, they are socially defined as nonwhite and are subjected to the same oppression as Afro-Americans.

In New York, where most Puerto Ricans on the mainland reside, there have been some indications that Afro-Americans can form coalitions with them. The cooperation between these two groups in such efforts as the school decentralization controversy, the struggle for open admissions in the City University of New York, attempts to elect municipal officials sensitive to the needs of the neighborhoods these groups are often forced to share, and the community action programs of the Office of Economic Opportunity, provide some evidence that such coalitions are possible. The cooperation between blacks and Puerto Ricans in Newark was responsible for the transfer of power from whites to these groups in 1970. Although these few isolated examples do not prove the viability of workable coalitions between Afro-Americans and Puerto Ricans (most of whom contain some African ancestry), they demonstrate that the possibility exists. And where the two groups have not cooperated, the Puerto Ricans have not hesitated to adopt black protest tactics.

If blacks are to achieve parity with whites in the United States, a variety of approaches must be attempted. In a capitalist society economics is perhaps the central problem in liberation. The differential in income between blacks and whites is a function of discrimination, and though slight progress has been made in this regard in recent years, the remaining gap is a wide one which is likely to require at least a century to bridge at the present rate. The economic plight of Afro-Americans in the richest country in history is nothing short of disgraceful. Though the leaders of the country have been willing to spend $1,000 billion between 1946 and 1969 for what was euphemistically called "defense," but in actuality meant aggressive warfare, they were loath to spend even minor sums for social welfare programs for the oppressed.

Some black nationalists call for reparations to be paid to Afro-Americans for past injustices, especially for the era of slavery, when the unpaid labor of their ancestors contributed heavily to the economic development of the country. These proposals, when taken seriously, are quickly dismissed. However, one legal scholar, Boris Bittker, has convincingly presented the case for reparations based on damages inflicted through the deprivation of Afro-Americans' constitutional rights since slavery. Bittker bases his case on Section 1983 of Title 42 of the United States Code, which provides that "Every person who, under color of any statute . . . of any State or Territory, subjects . . . any citizen of the United States . . . to the deprivation of any rights . . . secured by the Constitution and laws, shall be liable to the party injured in an action at law, suit, or equity, or other proper proceeding for redress."[12] Between 1896 and 1954, racial segregation in the United States was legally sanctioned by the Supreme Court. The *Plessy* v. *Ferguson* case of 1896 held that states could require the segregation of blacks in railroad cars. However, the *Brown* v. *Board of Education* decision of 1954 held that the legally imposed segregation of black children in schools violated the equal protection clause of the Fourteenth Amendment.

It becomes clear then that for nearly six decades black school children were deprived of their constitutional rights by forced segregation. Indeed, the *Brown* decision ruled that segregated education for Afro-American children "generates a feeling of inferiority as to their status in the community that may affect their hearts and minds in a way unlikely ever to be undone." In short, Bittker feels that "governmental misconduct" during this period invaded the constitutional rights of Afro-Americans, and that this is grounds for compensation. As he notes, "There are many shortcomings in our treatment of losers in our society, but none matches this record of institutionalized deprivation of a group's constitutional rights. In this respect, the case for black reparations is even stronger than the case for compensating the victims of poverty or miscarriages of criminal justice."[13]

The payment of reparations for past injustices is not without precedent in the United States and elsewhere in the world. In 1946, Congress attempted to make amends for the past treatment of American Indians by creating the Indian Claims Commission to adjudicate their claims. And after World War II, Germany initiated a program of reparations for the victims (mainly Jews) of Nazi persecution.

It is impossible either to correct or compensate all of the injustices of history, but the case put forth by Bittker is one which deserves serious consideration. Though such a program would present difficulties, it is hoped that this concept will stimulate lawsuits and national debate, because these payments could assist in the much needed economic development of the black community. This is not to imply that massive compensation in the form of reparations would liberate Afro-Americans from their oppression, but it is one of many approaches to deal with serious and pressing problems.

The present state of black unity

The major thesis of this work is that the ascendency of nationalist ideology in the black community in the past decade has resulted in greater unity among Afro-Americans than existed in any previous period of history, and that black liberation, however defined, depends on such unity. It therefore seems appropriate to assess the degree of unity attained among Afro-Americans. Anyone familiar with the black community can attest to the widespread lack of unity in many areas, and it might be worthwhile to delineate some of these differences.

Black leaders, especially the nationalists and the assimilationists, are constantly at odds with each other over goals. All too often assimilationists view integration as an end in itself, and for the nationalists, nationalism is seen as an end. Neither group is correct, because the goal to which both presumably aspire is black liberation. Integration and nationalism are mere means toward achieving the goal of liberation. It is impossible to say with any degree of assurance which means is most likely to produce fruitful results, but there is some evidence that greater progress toward liberation has accompanied the spread of nationalist ideology than was achieved through the civil rights (integration) movement. Such an assertion by no means minimizes the value of the civil rights movement and its accomplishments, for they were many. Indeed, it might be argued that without the civil rights movement, the black nationalist movement might not have developed. And many of the contemporary leaders of the nationalist movement are veterans of the civil rights movement.

In addition to differences between integrationists and nationalists, there exists a lack of unity within each of these camps. One example from the integrationist camp is the split between leaders of the Southern Christian Leadership Conference and those of Operation Breadbasket, its chief economic arm. The leadership of Operation Breadbasket finally withdrew from the parent organization and formed an autonomous group–People United to Save Humanity. This action severely hampered the work of the SCLC, causing serious economic problems. Furthermore, a dispute subsequently developed between the SCLC and the Martin Luther King, Jr. Center for Social Change, forcing the resignation of the president of the SCLC, the civil rights organization founded by Martin Luther King, Jr. Another schism exists within the National Association for the Advancement of Colored People, in which the national leadership is at odds with the Atlanta chapter over the compromise school desegregation plan proposed by the latter. The Atlanta chapter, in defiance of instructions from the national office, approved a school desegregation plan which would permit about two-thirds of the city's public schools to remain segregated in exchange for allocation of 50 percent of the school system's administrative positions to Afro-Americans.

Deep splits exist within the nationalist movement as well. The cultural nationalists and the revolutionary nationalists are at odds with each other over ideological issues, and these differences have resulted in deaths, as in the case of the Black Panthers and the US Organization in Los Angeles. Even within the Black Panther party, the international section and the New York chapter joined forces in opposition to the national organization, a split which was allegedly responsible for at least one death.

One of the most glaring examples of the lack of unity in the black community can be observed in the high incidence of crime, including homicide, by blacks against blacks. Such acts are daily occurrences in the black community, and although some nationalists attribute these phenomena to what they call the "officially sanctioned prevalence" of hard drugs in the community, the fact is that intrablack brutality is widespread and such behavior militates against black unity. Closely related to these practices is the frequent infiltration of black undercover agents into militant black groups. Black policemen and other spies often infiltrate groups considered by local and national leaders as threatening to the structure of the society. The infiltrators report the group's activities for such meager rewards as minor occupational advancement. Such practices date back to the earliest days of slavery, when the "house" slaves spied on the "field" slaves on behalf of the slaveholders.

Black union officials frequently unite with their white counterparts in opposition to black workers. Black political candidates often oppose fellow blacks in elections, thereby splitting the black vote, a situation which frequently leads to the election of opposition white candidates. Afro-Americans who advocate black capitalism as a form of economic development strongly oppose the cooperative economic ventures supported by the nationalists, and vice versa. Finally (but not exhaustively), a lack of unity is often manifested in the realm of education, on both the secondary and college levels. On the secondary level black parents in the South are struggling for integrated schools, whereas outside the South the thrust is toward community control of schools. On the college level black educators are at odds with each other over the content of Afro-American studies programs, and in some cases the controversy centers on whether such programs should exist at all.

These examples might appear to contradict the major thesis put forth in this work, but such an interpretation would be in error. Since the acceleration of the nationalist movement in the mid-1960s, significant gains have been made in black unity, solidarity, pride, and self-esteem. It is to these accomplishments that attention is now turned, although they have been discussed elsewhere (see Chapter 5). Examples of increasing black unity abound. The Congress of African Peoples and the First National Political Convention were clear examples of "unity without uniformity." Although dissent was clearly evident, both meetings were notable for their unity and for bringing together individuals representing diverse ideological interests, a cross-section of economic groups, and representatives from all geographic regions.

In the realm of conventional politics, Afro-Americans demonstrated a remarkable degree of unity in the November 1972 elections. They overwhelmingly rejected the incumbent President, Richard Nixon, not only because they traditionally vote Democratic, but mainly because of his antiblack stand on virtually every issue of concern to the black community. According to the Joint Center for Political Studies, only 13 percent of all blacks voted for Richard Nixon for President, while 87 percent voted for George McGovern, his Democratic opponent.[14] This demonstration of unity in a national election is especially noteworthy in view of the parade of popular black entertainers, athletes, educators, and civil rights leaders who endorsed the Republican candidate (for reasons difficult for most Afro-Americans to accept). On the state level, fully 90 percent of Mississippi black voters cast their ballots for McGovern, and 76 percent crossed party lines to vote against the racist senatorial candidate, James Eastland. And on the local level, Chicago provides another example of black unity. In this traditionally Democratic city, some 92 percent of all blacks voted for McGovern, but a vast majority voted against Edward Hanrahan, the Democratic nominee for Cook County Sheriff, thereby causing his defeat. Hanrahan had ordered the 1969 attack on the Black Panthers which resulted in the deaths of Fred

Hampton and Mark Clark, and his rejection by black voters may be directly attributed to this incident. Other examples of black unity from the 1972 election could be cited, but these examples are sufficient to illustrate the point.

In the armed services a remarkable degree of unity has been displayed by black servicemen, especially those of lower ranks, both at home and abroad. These servicemen have rebelled against segregation and discrimination and have shown an amazing degree of unity in the face of the extremely authoritarian structures of the military services. Their activities have been paralleled in cities throughout the country by groups of Afro-American policemen.

Black solidarity has been increasingly manifested in recent years on many occasions. When Adam Clayton Powell was refused his seat in Congress, his constituents in Harlem repeatedly rejected the actions of his racist opponents by reelecting him, and support for his case was voiced by blacks throughout the country. The same solidarity was expressed for Julian Bond when he was denied his seat in the Georgia legislature for publicly denouncing the racist war in Indochina. And when Muhammad Ali was stripped of his heavyweight boxing title for refusing to be drafted into the army in protest against this same genocidal war, the black community rallied to his support.

The officially sanctioned "search and destroy" missions against the Black Panthers brought forth widespread opposition from all segments of the Afro-American community, as did the political frame-up of Angela Davis. The latter case is especially important because anticommunist hysteria pervades the United States, and Angela Davis did not conceal her membership in the Communist party. In spite of the hazards of supporting her case, even those blacks who disagreed with her ideological position were firm in their opposition to the official persecution to which she was subjected.

The rise in nationalist sentiment among Afro-Americans was accompanied by increased repression on the part of law enforcement officials. Though most Americans reject the notion that individuals are jailed in the United States for their political views, for they maintain that such behavior is characteristic of overtly fascist governments, many black militant leaders were arrested and jailed in the late 1960s and early 1970s. In each case criminal charges were brought against these individuals, but in reality it was their political views for which they were arrested and tried. This technique serves the same function as imprisoning people directly for their political views. Several outspoken blacks were

arrested on a series of bizarre charges, resulting in highly publicized trials. These included the trials of Huey P. Newton, of
Bobby Seale and Ericka Huggins in New Haven, Connecticut, of
the New York Panther Twenty-One, and of Angela Davis. In most
of these cases the charges were ultimately dropped, often after
several retrials, as in the Newton case. Perhaps the' single most
crucial factor in the dismissal of charges in most cases was the
presence of Afro-Americans and other Third World people on the
juries. That is, the blacks who were finally selected to serve on
these juries (and the general rule is for the prosecution lawyers to
challenge them off such juries because they are black) understood
the government's motivation and refused to permit the defendants
to be convicted on trumped-up charges. This might be considered
an act of solidarity stemming from increased nationalist sentiment
in the black community. Also it is doubtful that radical blacks
could receive a fair trial in the United States if tried before
all-white juries.

Another trial which received less public attention because it did
not involve political leaders, and which did not initially have
political connotations, was that of the Harlem Six (later the Harlem
Four) in New York. These young men were tried and convicted of
murdering a white shopkeeper in Harlem and given life sentences
in 1965. Their first conviction was reversed in 1968 by the Court of
Appeals on constitutional grounds. Throughout a period of eight
years, during which time they were held without bail, they were
tried two additional times. Both of these trials ended in hung
juries, the latter voting seven to five for acquittal. As in the cases
cited above, it is doubtful that these young men would have finally
been freed if the last two juries had not had Afro-American and
other Third World representation. In sum, the refusal of some
members of these juries to convict in these cases is another
indication of increased black solidarity.

Finally, and equally if not more importantly, within the past
decade there has been a significant increase in black pride and
self-esteem and a concomitant decrease in self-hatred among
Afro-Americans. This is especially noticeable in standards of physical beauty, particularly insofar as hair styles, and dress are concerned. One rarely encounters black men with processed hair, and
black women increasingly are rejecting hair straighteners. While it
is impossible to make any statement about one's racial awareness
or ideological position by simply observing, say, his hair style, it is
likely that those black men who continue to process their hair are
less conscious of their blackness than those who wear their hair

natural. This does not mean to imply that wearing one's hair natural indicates that he is a black nationalist, for as H. Rap Brown once observed, processed minds can often be found under natural hair styles. Rather, it is maintained that processing one's hair is a political statement, albeit a subconscious one.

Many studies conducted in the 1950s showed that in experimental situations black children invariably expressed a preference for white dolls over brown dolls. Among the first and most influential of these studies was that by Kenneth and Mamie Clark, whose findings were cited by the Supreme Court in its *Brown* v. *Board of Education* decision outlawing racial segregation in public education on the grounds that forced segregation has an adverse effect on the personality development of children.[15] This and subsequent studies showed that black male children were more likely to express a preference for white dolls than black female children, and that middle-class black children were more likely to express this preference than the poor black children. Although some of these studies contain methodological flaws, the conclusion is clear: Self-hatred was widespread in the black community, and it was learned in early childhood.

Recent studies, however, show that since the spread of nationalist ideology among Afro-Americans, anywhere from 70 to 82 percent of black children express a clear preference for brown dolls.[16] In addition, these studies show no significant sex or social class differences. The interpretation to be drawn from these studies is that the black children (as well as Afro-Americans in general) are experiencing an increase in self-pride and group pride as a result of the changed political and social climate. This change in attitude among black children cannot be minimized, for its significance is critical in the movement for black liberation.

The future of black nationalism

The pace of change in the status of Afro-Americans is understandably disappointing and frustrating for many of the younger blacks, especially those born after World War II. Young blacks often sound as if they expect that "the revolution" to liberate Afro-Americans will begin at any moment. They are no doubt accurate in their assessment of the necessity for a social revolution to alter Afro-Americans' caste-colonial status in the United States, but such radical social change is unlikely in the near future. It is difficult to build a united front among a people who have been oppressed for centuries, especially when large segments of this population have internalized the way of life of the oppressor. Blacks have probably made greater strides in developing the necessary unity within the past decade than in all previous centuries, but the struggle is far from over. It must continue on every front if a collective force is to be achieved and sustained. This is especially true in a society in which individualism is the ethos and personal greed is the norm. Though black liberation is not likely to be achieved in the near future, it remains a possibility, and in many ways, it is essential for domestic tranquility.

The major task facing the black community, in addition to mere physical survival, is the development of unity. Blacks in the United States have never developed a concrete theory or strategy for liberation around which the various segments of the black community can rally. The issues separating various black individuals and organizations are real, and they are likely to remain for some time. But there are serious problems facing the black community, many of which are free of ideology and around which it is possible to organize a united front. It was suggested earlier that since racism is endemic to the society, assimilation is not a viable possibility at the present time. White Americans appear to be less entrenched in their prejudiced attitudes at present than in previous years,[17] but attitudes do not always accurately reflect how they will behave in concrete situations.

The overwhelming victory of Richard Nixon in the November 1972 election is a case in point. Although appeals to white racism were couched in such code words and phrases as "busing," "welfare handouts," "job quotas," and "crime in the streets," the American voters understood these to be racist appeals and voted accordingly. There can be little doubt that race was the underlying issue of the campaign. For example, in a preelection survey *New York Times* interviewers asked the following question of white voters: "Do you feel that minority groups [meaning blacks] are receiving too much, too little, or just about the right amount of attention?" Just four years after the demise of the so-called Great Society programs, two-fifths of all those questioned answered "too much." Of those, fully 80 percent said they would vote for Richard Nixon.[18] These were not all party-line Republicans; many were life-long Democrats.

Consequently, assimilation through integration versus black nationalism through separation should cease to be a major issue, and the thrust should be toward operational unity, centering on issues around which those with different ideological positions can rally.[19] One of the major problems facing the black community is the proliferation of hard drugs. There are those who maintain, with some degree of validity, that public officials at all levels permit the black community to become saturated with drugs as a means of pacifying it and diverting its residents from pressing for liberation. Whatever position one takes on this issue, the excessive use of hard drugs by black youth keeps the black community in a state of terror and is a major factor in its high rates of crime. The use of hard drugs by blacks is an understandable response to oppression, but drug addicts are not liberation fighters. Furthermore, drug addiction robs the black community of many of its potential leaders. There seems to be no reason that all camps in the black community cannot unite around this issue.

Prison reform is another ideologically neutral issue of central concern to the black community. The conditions in U.S. prisons are among the worst in the industrialized world, and blacks are vastly overrepresented among those incarcerated. Indeed, if blacks were not so greatly overrepresented in prisons, the likelihood is that reforms would have been introduced long ago. Black males who do not go to college (the vast majority) can be virtually assured of prison sentences before they reach age 30. Though it is true that prisons have served as schools for political consciousness among some black males, for the few who return to the community to make their contributions, thousands are literally stripped of their humanity. And as was demonstrated at Attica, government officials are eager to slaughter black prisoners on the slightest provocation, real or imagined.

Except in times of total war, unemployment has always been a major problem in the black community. Even those who journey abroad to fight America's wars of aggression are unable to secure employment upon their return. Regardless of one's ideological position in a society which assumes little responsibility for the welfare of its citizens, it should be possible to agree that meaningful employment is essential for the creation of a viable community. A unified black community with an annual income of some $30 billion could force concessions from both the private and the public sectors of the society.

Related to the issue of employment is that of providing citizens with a guaranteed annual income commensurate with the society's standard of living. Although this issue does have ideological overtones, opposition to it comes from whites, not blacks. Faced with massive unemployment and underemployment, the black community could unite around the issue and press for a decent standard of living for the country's oppressed people.

Police brutality is yet another issue involving all black people and one devoid of ideological dispute. According to the report of the National Advisory Commission on Civil Disorders, police misconduct was cited as their major grievance by residents of black communities which had experienced black rebellions between 1963 and 1967.[20] Not only do blacks experience the milder forms of police brutality more frequently than do whites, they are also more likely to be killed by the police. For example, one study showed that from July 1970 through March 1971, an Afro-American in Chicago was more than six times as likely as a white person to be killed by the police.[21] Widely publicized cases of police killings of Afro-Americans have brought forth expressions of unity from the black community, but these are usually short-lived. Most Afro-Americans are aware that simply being black makes them liable to police brutality.

Adequate medical care is still another issue around which the black community could unify. Blacks continue to die at disproportionately high rates from diseases that are easily controlled by modern medicine. Yet the society does not permit Afro-Americans sufficiently high salaries to pay for adequate medical care, long considered to be a basic right in most industrialized countries. Reliance on public hospitals and clinics in most cities is tantamount to no medical care at all.

Other issues around which the different ideological segments of the black community should be able to unite are those of decent housing and opposition to economic exploitation and oppression of Africans by European nations and the United States. The slum housing in which most blacks are forced to live because of their poverty leads to other social problems which affect the entire black community. A unified black community could exert enough pressure on local, state, and national officials to force a reordering of priorities so that money spent on such adventures as wars and space exploration could be diverted to domestic needs. Strong pressure from a unified black community could force American multinational corporations to discontinue their support for racist oppression in Africa, and the U.S. government to cease providing financial and military support to European countries maintaining colonial possessions in Africa.

These issues facing the black community are clearly not revolutionary, and they are largely free of ideology. They can be seen as survival issues around which the various segments of the community can unite, an essential precondition for black liberation. A powerless minority in a ruthless country is not likely to change the total direction of the society, but on many issues the profit motive takes precedence over all other considerations. A community of more than 25 million Afro-Americans united and acting on issues could perhaps exert some influence. Without such unity the oppression will continue unabated.

It might be argued that with the death of Lyndon Johnson's Great Society programs, and the acts of the repressive and punitive administration of Richard Nixon, Afro-Americans are faced with problems not unlike those they encountered following the Reconstruction. Since 1972 there appears to have been some decline in nationalist activity in the black community. With the impetus generated in the late 1960s, however, the likelihood is that this is temporary. Once a people have become politically sensitized to the nature of their oppression, it is difficult to maintain them in this oppressed status. The failure of the civil rights movement to achieve justice *in practice* for Afro-Americans, although it did accomplish the goal of legal equality *in principle*, coupled with heightened political consciousness in the black community, means that the struggle for liberation will continue. Its outcome is, of course, unpredictable, but the continued fight is certain.

The demise of several nationalist organizations and the apparent decline in nationalist sentiment among Afro-Americans in general are no doubt the result of several factors. Of crucial importance in these developments has been the role of the federal government. The massive wave of repression that swept the country during the Nixon years is especially relevant here. By its own admission, the Federal Bureau of Investigation, under the direction of J. Edgar Hoover, ordered all of its field offices in 1971 to disrupt and neutralize protest organizations. The communication entitled "Counterintelligence Program, Internal Security, Disruption of the New Left" gave instructions for exposing, disrupting, and neutralizing these groups. "We must frustrate every effort of these groups and individuals to consolidate their forces or to recruit new and faithful adherents," the communication declared.[22] Instructions were specifically included for what the F.B.I. called "black extremists." To a significant degree the government achieved its goals, at least temporarily. Afro-American organizations were under constant attack from the F.B.I., and leaders of these groups were murdered, jailed, or otherwise harassed. Given the impetus the movement had attained, its demise can only be considered temporary.

One of the major differences between the contemporary

nationalist movement and its predecessors is the active participation by large segments of the black middle-class. Data on the proportion of the black population which may be objectively classified as middle class (on the basis of income, education, and occupation) vary depending upon their source, but since the urban rebellions of the 1960s, increasing numbers of blacks have received college educations and have been employed in positions traditionally reserved for whites. Whatever the proportion of blacks who may now be considered middle class, there is no doubt that increasing numbers in this category have become involved in the struggle for black liberation, for unlike previous generations of the black bourgeoisie, they have come to realize that no black person can be free in the United States until all black people are free. The recent issue of *Ebony* magazine (August 1973) devoted to the black middle class illustrates its growing racial awareness. Differences in points of view are widespread, but even in such elite summer resorts catering to Afro-Americans as Oak Bluffs in Martha's Vineyard, Sag Harbor in Long Island, and Arundel on the Maryland shore, the black residents have become as involved in the problems of urban blacks as they once were with yachts. This is a relatively new development, one which has accompanied the spread of nationalist ideology among Afro-Americans in the past decade.

The conclusion must be reached that Afro-Americans are becoming increasingly aware of the nature of their oppression in the United States and that they have achieved an unprecedented degree of unity. Because of these circumstances they are moving to rectify the situation. The rate of change in the realm of race relations is a slow and difficult one, but it will continue, and it is unlikely that a concerned black community will long permit its inhabitants to remain an oppressed colony within the United States.

Epilogue

This book is an attempt to describe and analyze the black nationalist movement in the United States, beginning with its earliest manifestations but concentrating primarily on the contemporary movement, especially during the period of its greatest impact on the black community in the decade of 1963–1973. As was noted in the Preface, it makes no attempt to be comprehensive; rather, emphasis is placed on the most consequential and noteworthy expressions, both collective and individual. It is difficult to write about a movement during its zenith, especially one involving black people in the United States, because circumstances often force changes in ideology and strategy. This has been the case with the black nationalist movement, and, as the manuscript goes to press in 1975, it is necessary to chronicle some of the most important events bearing on the movement, particularly those which have altered the character of what is written in the preceding chapters. Although these events do not necessarily invalidate what has been written or the conclusions drawn, it is necessary to record them in order to put the material into current perspective, and, to a lesser extent, to bring the record of the movement up to date. The black nationalist movement, although in a state of flux and apparent decline, continues to be a vital force for Afro-Americans.

In the summer of 1974 Amiri Baraka and the organization he formed, the Congress of African Peoples, announced a change in ideological position from cultural nationalism to Marxism-Leninism-Mao Tse-Tung thought as the most logical means for analyzing the black liberation struggle. This move from a major emphasis on race to one of class struggle signaled a radical change in the nationalist movement and generated controversy in the black community. According to Baraka, this change is not an abandonment of nationalism but a move from cultural nationalism to revolutionary nationalism, that he sees as "necessary for Black People, and other oppressed nationalities...the struggle against our national oppression is real, and one important aspect of the struggle against imperialism wherever it occurs."[1] Furthermore, he feels that the problems faced by Afro-Americans can only be solved by revolution. "The present system of profit for a few and poverty for the multitude (capitalism) will be replaced ultimately, and the nationalism that says the struggle is only against racism, and does not see that racism is a byproduct of capitalism, one of its oppressive weapons as well as an existent ideology in its superstructure...people who cannot see that it is the economic system that supports, reinforces, and continues racism are shortsighted...."[2] (See postscript to Chapter 7.)

Several officials of the Congress of African Peoples resigned from the organization to protest this changed ideological direction. Among the first to denounce this change was Haki R. Madhubuti (Don L. Lee), director of the Institute of Positive Education in Chicago, and editor and publisher of the Third World Press. He sees the move as adopting the position that the critical element in the struggle for black liberation is class rather than race, and he urges black people to purge themselves of European conditioning."[3] Madhubuti maintains that "European aggression against our culture has resulted in the systematic wiping out of all sources of positive selfness and cultural directives that give a people identity, purpose, and direction, the end product being the acceptance of foreign values and beliefs forced on black people by white people, values, and beliefs that work against black people for the benefit of white people."[4] Marxism-Leninism, he maintains, is antiblack, and the problems faced by black people are created by white people. White racism preceded capitalism and imperialism. "Both Marx and Engels belonged to nineteenth century Europe–the same Europe that had been dealing with black slaves for over four centuries," and both were proslavery. And he is skeptical of the ideology which they propagated. "As far as we are concerned communism and capitalism are the left and right arms in the same white body. *And the highest stage of white supremacy is imperialism whether it's communist or capitalist.*"[5]

Madhubuti is making a plea for the cultural nationalism advocated so strongly by Baraka before 1974 (see Chapter 7). His article, like the events which gave rise to it, generated widespread controversy in the black community, and supporters and critics eagerly expressed their views in the pages of *The Black Scholar.*[6] The debate over the relative importance of class and race in the movement for black liberation had reached its peak by 1975.

In addition to Baraka and many of his supporters, Maulana Ron Karenga, one of Baraka's closest associates in the late sixties and early seventies and a leading cultural nationalist, has rejected cultural nationalism in favor of socialism.[7] And in March 1975, Nathan Hare, founder and publisher of *The Black Scholar*, resigned from the influential journal, charging that there had been a "black Marxist" takeover of the publication. In his letter of resignation he accused the editorial board of adhering to "conventional Marxist interpretations and of ironclad intolerance for and resistance to opposing views." Robert Christman, the journal's editor, denied these charges and accused Hare of "old-fashioned redbaiting."

Thus, it appeared that by 1975 the black nationalist movement, in which cultural nationalism had played a dominant role for a decade emphasizing race over class in the struggle for black liberation, had lost ground to its chief competitor, revolutionary nationalism. Those who support revolutionary nationalism hold that the liberation of black people can only come about through class struggle geared toward the elimination of capitalism, and that the black stuggle in the United States must be linked to the worldwide struggle of the oppressed. The cultural nationalists, on the other hand, charge that the revolutionary nationalists misinterpret Marxism-Leninism and fail to understand the role of race in Afro-American oppression.

It is possible that we are witnessing a period of introspection and searching for new ideological perspectives after a long period of activism. While the lines appear to be sharply drawn, there are socialists among the cultural nationalists, and those who place heavy emphasis on the role of race in black oppression among the revolutionary nationalists. In other words, there are many similarities in the two camps.

One of the chief parties to the earlier debate between cultural and revolutionary nationalists was Huey P. Newton, a cofounder and chief theorist of the Black Panther Party. As a leading revolutionary nationalist, Newton was severe in his criticisms of cultural nationalist ideology (see Chapter 6). But he is not a party to the current debate because he was forced to go underground in the summer of 1974 and has since surfaced in Cuba.[8] His exile there resulted from a series of charges leveled against him by the Oakland Police Department and the Federal Bureau of Investigation. In mid-1974 he was accused of a series of crimes, including the murder of a young black woman. It is widely believed in the black community that these charges were flagrantly fabricated by the police as part of a continuing harassment of black radicals, with the officials of the Black Panther Party as their chief targets.

Because of the party's impressive showing in the 1973 Oakland mayoralty race, in which Bobby Seale ran second and forced a run-off, and that of Elaine Brown for City Council, the forces of repression went into operation utilizing the Federal Bureau of Investigation memorandum of March 4, 1968 to destroy the party. This memorandum instructs agents of the Bureau to undertake a long range program to "Prevent the RISE OF A 'MESSIAH' who could unify and electrify the militant black nationalist movement ...prevent black nationalist groups and leaders from RESPECT-ABILITY, by discrediting them to three separate segments of the community..., first the responsible Negro community; second ...to the White community, both the responsible community and the 'liberals' who have vestiges of sympathy for the militant black nationalists...; third...in the eyes of Negro radicals, the followers of the movement."[9]

Newton was driven into exile, fearful that if imprisoned again, after serving time in prison for allegedly killing a white policeman, he would himself be killed. The forces of repression have at least temporarily succeeded in silencing Newton, and the Black Panther Party is forced to continue its "survival programs" in the black community without his leadership and inspiring presence.

The ideological split in the nationalist movement and the forced exile of Huey P. Newton have had their effect on the movement for black liberation in recent years. Still another development deserves mention here. Elijah Muhammad, the spiritual leader of the Nation of Islam died on February 25, 1975. The Nation of Islam is one of the more successful nationalist groups, spanning a history of more than 40 years. The organization remained rigidly separationist throughout the life of Elijah Muhammad, for the Muslims believed that integration was designed to deceive black people and "that such deception is intended to prevent black people from realizing that the time in history has arrived for the separation from the whites of this nation." Furthermore, the Muslim program called for "complete separation [of blacks] in a state or territory of their own."

Upon the death of Elijah Muhammad the spiritual leadership of the Nation was assumed by his son, Wallace D. Muhammad. One of his first acts was to announce that the Nation was now prepared to accept white people as members. In a public address in New York on June 29, 1975, Wallace D. Muhammad urged blacks to respect whites, and said that when members of the Nation spoke of the need to destroy whites reference was not being made to the "physical body" but rather to their "mentality." He urged whites "to put down your high names and high powers to become a part of a work that is more glorious and promises more dignity than anything you could possibly be doing."[10] In an article in the Nation's newspaper *Muhammad Speaks*, entitled "Whites in the Nation," previous discrimination against whites was seen as a necessary, although unpopular, move. It was "developmentally necessary at certain growth periods" of the movement. "Our growth has already clarified for us that the real source of evil is in the mentality of the people and not in their flesh."[11] Thus, the changed position on white people by the Nation of Islam is seen as an evolutionary stage in which the Nation has reached a higher level of development.

According to Jamillah Muhammad, such a move is not contrary to the principles established by the late Elijah Muhammad but one which follows in his footsteps. "When a person follows in the footsteps of another he does not mark time in the same tracks, but continues and makes new tracks in a progressional movement forward." Finally, he writes, "We have been complaining for centuries of the evils of segregation and discrimination perpetrated on our people, and now that we have been favored to enter a higher and more comprehensive level of development, we should not fall victim to our own accusations."[12]

Whether the Nation of Islam will attract many white members remains to be seen; if the drive succeeds it will spell the demise or at least the retrenchment of the most viable black nationalist membership organization in the United States since Marcus Garvey's Universal Negro Improvement Association. Through the years the Nation has been criticized by the leaders of Moslem countries for its discriminatory policies against white people as contrary to the teachings of Islam. In any event, the Nation of Islam has had an important and positive impact on the black community, especially insofar as self- and group-pride, self-reliance, and pride in cultural heritage are concerned.

The revelations of the Federal Bureau of Investigation's infiltration and disruption of groups considered threats to the security of the United States, which reached a peak with the administration of Richard M. Nixon, brought the country to the brink of hard core fascism, and had the effect of curbing radicalism in general. The several assassinations and lengthy prison terms for leaders of radical groups precipitated a decline in radical activity in the black movement and in the white radical movement. Furthermore, the withdrawal of American troops from Indochina and the subsequent liberation of that region from American imperialism climaxed a long and bitter struggle, one that had been responsible for generating a climate of radicalism among large segments of the American population.

In addition, economic conditions in the United States, in particular the high rate of unemployment combined with inflation, have served to reduce the black struggle to one of survival. Black unemployment has historically been at least twice that experienced by white workers, but by the summer of 1975 unemployment among young black males varied anywhere from 40 to 60 percent in the major urban centers, greatly exceeding that of comparable white workers. These conditions had been expected to lead to major black rebellions around the country/but such predictions failed to materialize, largely because police departments were prepared for massive retaliation. The Law Enforcement Assistance Administration, which grew out of the Omnibus Crime Control and Safe Streets Act of 1968, was established in part to assist local law enforcement efforts. Armed with a budget that increased from $63 million in 1968 to $1.75 billion in 1973,[13] grants were made to state and local police departments mainly for the purchase of such devices as armored cars, tanks, and bazookas. Realizing that the police would not hesitate to use these weapons on them, black militants curtailed their activities. Furthermore, out of feelings of hopelessness brought about by economic conditions, many young blacks have now turned their aggression inward, engaging in self-destructive pursuits: alcoholism, narcotics addiction, and suicide.

At about the same time that black nationalist activity was on the decline, the movement for the independence of Puerto Rico from American colonialism intensified both in Puerto Rico and the United States. The strength of the movement was demonstrated to the American public when the Puerto Rican Solidarity Committee, a coalition of Puerto Rican, Afro-American, Asian-American, white radical, and women's groups sponsored a massive rally in New York's Madison Square Garden on October 24, 1974. Some 27,000 people from throughout the country and Puerto Rico gathered to demonstrate support for Puerto Rico's independence.

The case for Puerto Rico's independence was introduced in the United Nations Decolonization's Committee by the Cuban government, and was supported by other Third World countries. In March of 1975 some 79 delegates, representing 28 countries and 12 international organizations, met in Havana, Cuba to prepare for the convening of the International Conference of Solidarity with the Independence of Puerto Rico, to be held later in the year.

Under the leadership of the Puerto Rican Socialist Party, the independence movement, which is anticapitalist in its orientation, has gained widespread support among the people of the island, especially trade union groups, students, teachers, women's groups, and progressive politicians. In a few years the movement has gained the support of many governments and individuals throughout the world and its activities are on the increase.

Along with Puerto Ricans, many other oppressed groups in the United States, most notably Chicanos, Native Americans, and women are waging concerted drives for liberation from oppression. Most of these groups emulate the black nationalist movement and, like the revolutionary black nationalists, most are convinced that liberation is impossible within capitalist society.

There are those who maintain that the black nationalist movement is virtually extinct but this is hardly the case. Afro-Americans and other oppressed groups throughout history have struggled for liberation, for the members of no group are content to permit invidious distinctions to deprive them of their fair share of social rewards. At the same time the oppressors have struggled to maintain their positions of dominance through the use of any means necessary. That oppression has often existed for centuries is more a function of the power held by the oppressors than the complacency of the oppressed. As the heroic people of Indochina have demonstrated to the world, a people united can never be defeated.

Notes

Chapter 1

1. John Stuart Mill, *Representative Government*, in Louis L. Snyder (ed.), *The Dynamics of Nationalism*, Princeton, N.J.: Van Nostrand, 1964, pp. 2–4.
2. See, for example, Karl W. Deutsch, *Nationalism and Social Communication*, Cambridge, Mass.: M.I.T. Press, 1966; Karl W. Deutsch,*Nationalism and Its Alternatives*, New York: Knopf, 1969; Hans Kohn, *The Idea of Nationalism*, New York: Macmillan, 1944; Boyd C. Shaffer, *Nationalism: Myth and Reality*, New York: Harcourt, Brace, Jovanovich, 1955; Louis L. Snyder (ed.), *The Dynamics of Nationalism*, Princeton, N.J.: Van Nostrand, 1964.
3. *International Encyclopedia of the Social Sciences*, New York: Macmillan, 1968, Vol. 11, pp. 63–69.
4. E. U. Essien-Udom, *Black Nationalism: A Search for an Identity in America*, Chicago: University of Chicago Press, 1962, p. 6.
5. James Turner, "The Sociology of Black Nationalism," *The Black Scholar*, December 1969, pp. 26–27.
6. Eric Foner, "In Search of Black History," *The New York Review of Books*, October 22, 1970, p. 11.
7. John H. Bracey, August Meier, and Elliott Rudwick (eds.), *Black Nationalism in America*, Indianapolis and New York: Bobbs-Merrill, 1970, p. xxvi.
8. George Breitman, *The Last Year of Malcolm X*, New York: Shocken Books, 1967, pp. 55–56.
9. Edwin S. Redkey, *Black Exodus*, New Haven, Conn.: Yale University Press, 1969, p. 304.
10. *Two Speeches by Malcolm X*, New York: Merit Publishers, 1969, pp.4–5.
11. Malcolm X, *The Autobiography of Malcolm X*, New York: Grove Press, 1964, p. 381.
12. Imamu Amiri Baraka (LeRoi Jones), *Raise, Race, Rays, Raze*, New York: Random House, 1971, p. 89.
13. Stokely Carmichael, *Stokely Speaks*, New York: Random House, 1971, pp. 206–208.
14. Harold Cruse, *The Crisis of the Negro Intellectual*, New York: Morrow, 1967, pp. 4–7.

15. See Milton Gordon, *Assimilation in American Life*, New York: Oxford University Press, 1964.
16. Harold Cruse, "Revolutionary Nationalism and the Afro-American," *Studies on the Left*, 1962 p. 13; reprinted in Harold Cruse, *Rebellion or Revolution?* New York: Morrow, 1968, p. 76.
17. Martin R. Delany, *The Condition, Elevation, Emigration and Destiny of the Colored People of the United States*, New York: Arno Press, 1968, p. 209.
18. See Robert Blauner, "Internal Colonialism and Ghetto Revolt," *Social Problems*, Vol. 16, no. 4 (Spring 1969), pp. 393–408.
19. See, for example, Robert Allen, *Black Awakening in Capitalist America*, New York: Doubleday, 1969; Lerone Bennett, "System: Internal Colonialism Structures Black, White Relations in America," *Ebony* (April 1972), pp. 33–42; Stokely Carmichael and Charles Hamilton, *Black Power: The Politics of Liberation in America*, New York: Random House, 1967; Kenneth Clark, *Dark Ghetto*, New York: Harper & Row, 1965; Harold Cruse, *Rebellion or Revolution?* New York: Morrow, 1968; Albert Memmi, *The Colonizer and the Colonized*, Boston: Beacon Press, 1967; William K. Tabb, *The Political Economy of the Black Ghetto*, New York: Norton, 1970.
20. I. F. Stone, review of Talcott Parsons and Kenneth Clark (eds.), *The Negro American*, Boston: Houghton-Mifflin, 1966, in *The New York Review of Books*, August 18, 1966.

Chapter 2

1. Herbert Aptheker, *American Negro Slave Revolts*, New York: International Publishers, 1963, chap. 8.
2. Herbert Aptheker (ed.), *A Documentary History of the Negro People in the United States*, New York: Citadel Press, 1951, p. 8.
3. *Ibid.*, pp. 17–18.
4. Benjamin Quarles, *The Negro in the Making of America*, New York: Macmillan, 1964, p. 96.
5. Adelaide Hill and Martin Kilson (eds.), *Apropos of Africa*, New York: Doubleday, 1971, p. 184.
6. Aptheker, *A Documentary History*, pp. 30–44.
7. E. U. Essien-Udom, *Black Nationalism: A Search for an Identity in America*, Chicago: University of Chicago Press, 1962, pp. 24–26.
8. Cited in John Bracey, August Meier, and Elliott Rudwick (eds.), *Black Nationalism in America*, Indianapolis and New York: Bobbs-Merrill, 1970, pp. 11–13.
9. Theodore Draper, *The Rediscovery of Black Nationalism*, New York: Viking Press, 1970, p. 7.
10. William Alexander, *Memoir of Captain Paul Cuffee, A Man of Colour*, London: published by the author, 1811; Bracey, Meier, and Rudwick, pp. 38–46; Draper, pp. 16–17; Sheldon Harris, *Paul Cuffee: Black America and the African Return*, New York: Simon and Schuster, 1972; Hill and Kilson, pp. 12–24.

11. Hill and Kilson, pp. 17–21.
12. Bracey, Meier, and Rudwick, pp. 41–43.
13. See Edwin S. Redkey, *Black Exodus*, New Haven, Conn.: Yale University Press, 1969, pp. 18–21.
14. See Draper, pp. 7–10.
15. Aptheker, *A Documentary History*, pp. 114–119, 133–137, 141–146, 154–157, 159, 341–356; Essien-Udom, pp. 19–23.
16. Aptheker, *A Documentary History*, p. 116.
17. *Ibid.*, p. 159.
18. Essien-Udom, p. 20.
19. See Bracey, Meier, and Rudwick, pp. xxxvii, 77, 110, 160; Harold Cruse, *The Crisis of the Negro Intellectual*, New York: Morrow, 1967, pp. 5 ff.; Draper; Jessie Fauset, "Rank Imposes Obligations," *Crisis*, November 1926; Frank A. Rollin, *Life and Public Services of Martin R. Delany*, Boston: Lee and Shepard, 1868; Victor Ullman, *Martin R. Delany: The Beginnings of Black Nationalism*, Boston: Beacon Press, 1972. Two important works by Delany are *The Condition, Elevation, Emigration, and Destiny of the Colored People of the United States*, first published by the author in 1852, and reissued by Arno Press, 1968; and *The Niger Valley Exploration Party*, New York: Thomas Hamilton, 1861.
20. Draper, pp. 27–28.
21. Published in Philadelphia by Harper and Brothers, 1879.
22. Martin R. Delany, *The Condition, Elevation*, p. 203.
23. Quoted in Draper, p. 24.
24. Delany, *The Condition, Elevation*, p. 31.
25. Bracey, Meier, and Rudwick, pp. 89–90, *passim*.
26. *Ibid.*, p. 93.
27. For a discussion of his experiences in London, see Draper, pp. 28–31.
28. Rollin, pp. 166–199.
29. W. E. B. DuBois, *Black Reconstruction in America*, Cleveland: World, 1935, pp. 84–127.
30. For accounts of Turner's life and work, see Mungo M. Ponton, *The Life and Times of Henry M. Turner*, Atlanta, Ga.: A. B. Caldwell, Co., 1917; Edwin S. Redkey. Other relevant works include Aptheker, *A Documentary History*, pp. 568 ff.; Bracey, Meier, and Rudwick, pp. 172 ff.; Draper, pp. 43–47.
31. The details of Turner's early life are reported in Redkey, on which this account is based.
32. Aptheker, *A Documentary History*, pp. 569–571.
33. Cited in Redkey, p. 27, from the *Atlanta Constitution*, September 4, 1868.
34. Redkey, p. 41.
35. *Ibid.*, pp. 47–72.
36. *Ibid.*, p. 44.
37. Bracey, Meier, and Rudwick, p. 173.

38. Redkey, pp. 213–224.
39. *Ibid.*, pp. 238–239.
40. Bracey, Meier, and Rudwick, p. 175.
41. *Ibid.*, p. 154.
42. Redkey, p. 275.

Chapter 3

1. John Hope Franklin, *From Slavery to Freedom*, New York: Knopf, 1948, p. 465; Gunnar Myrdal, *An American Dilemma*, New York: Harper & Row, 1944, pp. 191–197.
2. Alphonso Pinkney, *The American Way of Violence*, New York: Random House, 1972, pp. 79–93.
3. Harold M. Baron, *The Demand for Black Labor*, Cambridge, Mass.: Radical America, 1971, pp. 19–32.
4. For biographical sketches of Garvey's early years, see Edmund D. Cronon, *Black Moses*, Madison: University of Wisconsin Press, 1964, pp. 3–20; Amy Jacques Garvey, *Garvey and Garveyism*, New York: Collier Books, 1970, pp. 1–16; Elton C. Fax, *Garvey: The Story of a Pioneer Black Nationalist*, New York: Dodd, Mead, 1972; Theodore G. Vincent, *Black Power and the Garvey Movement*, Berkeley, Calif.: Ramparts Press, 1971, pp. 91–99.
5. Garvey, *Garvey and Garveyism*, pp. 3–4.
6. Vincent, p. 92.
7. Amy Jacques Garvey (ed.), *Philosophy and Opinions of Marcus Garvey*, New York: Arno Press, 1968, Vol. II, pp. 124–125.
8. Cronon, pp. 12–14.
9. Garvey, *Garvey and Garveyism*, p. 7.
10. Garvey, *Philosophy and Opinions*, (Vol. II), p. 126.
11. *Ibid.*
12. Garvey, *Garvey and Garveyism*, p. 11.
13. See Cronon, pp. 204–207; Arnold and Caroline Rose, *America Divided*, New York: Knopf, 1953, p. 187; Vincent, p. 3.
14. Garvey, *Garvey and Garveyism*, p. 32.
15. A complete listing of the officials of the UNIA is found in Vincent, pp. 267–270. See also, Garvey, *Philosophy and Opinions*, Vol. II, pp. 278–279.
16. Cronon, pp. 45–49.
17. Garvey, *Philosophy and Opinions*, Vol. II, pp. 135–143; Vincent, pp. 257–265.
18. Cronon, p. 61.
19. Garvey, *Philosophy and Opinions*, Vol. I, pp. 68–72.
20. *Ibid.*, p. 5.
21. *Ibid.*, Vol. II, pp. 23–24.
22. *Ibid.*, Vol. I, p. 52.
23. *Ibid.*, Vol. II, p. 122.
24. *Ibid.*, Vol. I, p. 6.

25. *Ibid.*, p. 97.
26. *Ibid.*, p. 37.
27. *Ibid.*, Vol. II, p. 62.
28. *Ibid.*, Vol. II, p. 134.
29. *Ibid.*, Vol. II, p. 37.
30. *Ibid.*, Vol. I, p. 13.
31. Cronon, pp. 189–190.
32. Quoted in *ibid.*, p. 190.
33. Garvey, *Philosophy and Opinions*, Vol. II, p. 71.
34. Roi Ottley, *New World A-Coming*, Cleveland: World, 1943, p. 81.
35. Cronon, pp. 50–60; Garvey, *Garvey and Garveyism*, pp. 84–92; Vincent, pp. 101–104.
36. Cronon, pp. 92–99.
37. Garvey, *Garvey and Garveyism*, p. 96.
38. Quoted in Cronon, p. 60.
39. Vincent, p. 166.
40. Garvey, *Philosophy and Opinions*, Vol. I, p. 44.
41. Vincent, p. 136.
42. Harold Cruse, *The Crisis of the Negro Intellectual*, New York: Morrow, 1967, p. 119.
43. Cronon, p. 115.
44. Garvey, *Philosophy and Opinions*, Vol. II, p. 69.
45. *Ibid.*, Vol. II, p. 70.
46. *Ibid.*, p. 72.
47. Quoted in Cronon, pp. 198–199.
48. Cruse, pp. 332–333.
49. Vincent, pp. 267–270.
50. Edwin S. Redkey, *Black Exodus*, New Haven, Conn.: Yale University Press, 1969, p. 293.
51. See George Padmore, *Pan-Africanism or Communism*, New York: Doubleday, 1971, pp. 79–82.
52. Cronon, p. 201.
53. Vincent, p. 245.

Chapter 4

1. W. E. B. DuBois, *The Souls of Black Folk*, Chicago: A.C. McClurg, 1904, p. 3.
2. Theodore Draper, *American Communism and Soviet Russia*, New York: Viking Press, 1960; Theodore Draper, *The Rediscovery of Black Nationalism*, New York: Viking Press, 1970.
3. Reported in John Gerassi, "Havana: A New International is Born," *Monthly Review*, October 1967, p. 27.
4. Stokely Carmichael and Charles Hamilton, *Black Power: The Politics of Liberation in America*, New York: Random House, 1967, p. 44.
5. George Breitman (ed.), *Malcolm X: The Man and His Ideas*, New York: Pioneer Publishers, 1965; George Breitman, *The Last Year of*

Malcolm X, New York: Shocken Books, 1968; George Breitman, (ed.), *Malcolm X Speaks*, New York: Grove Press, 1966; George Breitman (ed.), *By Any Means Necessary: Speeches, Interviews and a Letter by Malcolm X*, New York: Pathfinder, 1970; Kenneth Clark (ed.), *The Negro Protest: James Baldwin, Malcolm X, Martin Luther King Talk with Kenneth Clark*, Boston: Beacon Press, 1963; John H. Clarke (ed.), *Malcolm X: The Man and His Times*, New York: Collier Books, 1969; Archie Epps (ed.), *The Speeches of Malcolm X at Harvard*, New York: Morrow, 1969; E. U. Essien-Udom, *Black Nationalism: A Search for an Identity in America*, Chicago: University of Chicago Press, 1962; Peter Goldman, *The Death and Life of Malcolm X*, New York: Harper & Row, 1973; Benjamin Goodman (ed.), *The End of White World Supremacy: Four Speeches by Malcolm X*, New York: Merlin House, 1971; C. Eric Lincoln, *The Black Muslims in America*, Boston: Beacon Press, 1961; Louis Lomax, *When the Word is Given*, Cleveland: World, 1963; Louis Lomax, *To Kill a Black Man*, Los Angeles: Holloway House, 1968; Malcolm X, *The Autobiography of Malcolm X*, New York: Grove Press, 1965; Malcolm X, *Malcolm X on Afro-American History*, New York: Pathfinder, 1970; Dudley Randall and Margaret Burroughs (eds.), *For Malcolm*, Detroit: Broadside Press, 1966.

6. Breitman, *The Last Year of Malcolm X*, pp. 52–69.
7. Breitman, *Malcolm X Speaks*, pp. 195–196.
8. *Ibid.*, p. 198.
9. *Ibid.*, p. 71.
10. Malcolm X, *The Autobiography of Malcolm X*, p. 377.
11. Breitman, *Malcolm X Speaks*, pp. 21–22.
12. Malcolm X, *The Autobiography of Malcolm X*, p. 368.
13. *Ibid.*, p. 344.
14. *Ibid.*, pp. 446–447.
15. *Ibid.*, p. 372.
16. The complete text of this document is reprinted in John Bracey, August Meier, and Elliott Rudwick (eds.), *Black Nationalism in America*, Indianapolis and New York: Bobbs-Merrill, 1970, pp. 421–427; Breitman, *The Last Year of Malcolm X*, pp. 105–111; Clarke, pp. 335–342. The "Basic Unity Program" of the OAAU is reprinted in Breitman, *The Last Year of Malcolm X*, pp. 113–124.
17. Clarke, pp. 235–267; Goodman.
18. For the text of petition, see Clarke, pp. 343–351.
19. The complete text of the appeal to African heads of state is reprinted in Breitman, *Malcolm X Speaks*, pp. 72–77; and Clarke, pp. 288–293.
20. See Epps, p. 41.
21. Malcolm X, *The Autobiography of Malcolm X*, p. 430.
22. *Ibid.*, p. 344.
23. Breitman, *Malcolm X Speaks*, p. 199.
24. Breitman, *The Last Year of Malcolm X*, p. 39.

25. Breitman, *Malcolm X Speaks*, p. 211.
26. Robert Penn Warren, *Who Speaks For the Negro?* New York: Vintage Books, 1966, p. 264.
27. Clarke, p. xii.

Chapter 5

1. Amy Jacques Garvey (ed.), *Philosophy and Opinions of Marcus Garvey*, New York: Arno Press, 1969, Vol. I, p. 1.
2. See James Stewart, "The Development of the Black Revolutionary Artist," in LeRoi Jones and Larry Neal (eds.), *Black Fire: An Anthology of Afro-American Writing*, New York: Morrow, 1968, pp. 3–10.
3. John Killens, *The Cotillion*, New York: Trident Press, 1971.
4. *Time*, April 6, 1970, p. 98.
5. The *New York Times*, March 16, 1971, p. 44.
6. The *New York Times*, May 11, 1971, p. 44.
7. Peter Bailey, "The Black Theater," *Ebony*, August 1969, pp. 126–134.
8. The *New York Times*, November 22, 1969, p. 46.
9. George Dennison, "Demagogy of LeRoi Jones," *Commentary*, February 1965, p. 68.
10. See LeRoi Jones, *Blues People*, New York: Morrow, 1963; and his *Black Music*, New York: Morrow, 1968.
11. See A. B. Spellman, "Revolution in Sound, " *Ebony*, August 1969, pp. 84–89.
12. See Nicholas Alex, *Black in Blue: A Study of the Negro Policeman*, New York: Appleton, 1969.
13. Alex Poinsett, "The Dilemma of the Black Policeman," *Ebony*, May 1971, pp. 122–131.
14. *Report of the National Advisory Commission on Civil Disorders*, New York: Bantam Books, 1968, pp. 143–150.
15. *Time*, November 20, 1970, p. 13.
16. The *New York Times*, June 6, 1970, p. 52.
17. John Darnton, "Color Line a Key Police Problem," The *New York Times*, September 28, 1969, p. 69.
18. *Ibid.*, p. 1.
19. Alex Poinsett, p. 124.
20. The *New York Times*, November 29, 1970, sec. E, p. 3.
21. Charles Moskos, "Racial Relations in the Armed Forces," in Russell Endo and William Strawdridge (eds.), *Perspectives on Black America*, Englewood Cliffs, N.J.: Prentice-Hall, 1970, p. 165.
22. Wallace Terry, II, "Bringing the War Home," *The Black Scholar*, November 1970, pp. 6–18.
23. Thomas Johnson, "G.I.'s in Germany: Black is Bitter," The *New York Times*, November 23, 1970, pp. 1, 26.
24. The *New York Times*, September 28, 1971, p. 4.
25. The *New York Times*, November 23, 1970, p. 27.

26. Wallace Terry, II, p. 11.
27. The *New York Times*, January 25, 1970, p. 2.
28. The *Bond*, August 26, 1970, p. 8.
29. The *New York Times*, November 24, 1970, p. 2.
30. The *New York Times*, August 12, 1971, p. 8.
31. The *New York Times*, December 21, 1969, p. 37.
32. Milton White, "Malcolm X in the Military," *The Black Scholar*, May 1970, pp. 31–35.
33. The *New York Times*, December 21, 1969, p. 37.
34. The *New York Times*, December 1, 1972, pp. 1, 20; Henry P. Leifermann, "A Sort of Mutiny: The Constellation Incident," The *New York Times Magazine*, February 18, 1973, pp. 16 ff.
35. E. Franklin Frazier, *Black Bourgeoisie*, New York: Free Press, 1957, p. 235.
36. Paul E. Miller, "In Defense of the Rights of Angela Davis," The *Washington Sunday Star*, February 14, 1971.
37. The *New York Times*, August 8, 1971, p. 36.
38. Charles L. Sanders, "Detroit's Rebel Judge Crockett," *Ebony*, August 1969, pp. 114–124.
39. *Ibid.*, p. 118.
40. The *New York Times*, August 15, 1971, p. 22.
41. *The American Sociologist*, February 1970, p. 68.
42. *The American Sociologist*, February 1971, pp. 61–74.
43. Louie Robinson, "How Psychology Helped Free Angela Davis," *Ebony*, February 1973, pp. 44–52.
44. The *New York Times*, April 10, 1972, p. 27.
45. *Treatment of Prisoners at California Training Facility at Soledad Central*, Black Caucus Report, Sacramento, California, 1970.
46. The *New York Times*, February 1, 1973, p. 23.
47. *The National Black Political Agenda*, Washington, D.C.: Congressional Black Caucus, 1972, p. 3.

Chapter 6

1. The origins, ideology, program, and organization of the Black Panther party are reported in Philip S. Foner (ed.), *The Black Panthers Speak*, Philadelphia: Lippincott, 1970; Gene Marine, *The Black Panthers*, New York: New American Library, 1969; Huey P. Newton, *To Die for the People: The Writings of Huey P. Newton*, New York: Random House, 1972; Bobby Seale, *Seize The Time: The Story of the Black Panther Party and Huey P. Newton*, New York: Random House, 1970.
2. Foner, p. xx.
3. Seale, pp. 134–149.
4. Marine, pp. 62–66; Seale, pp. 153–166.
5. Newton, pp. 7–8; Seale, pp. 161–162.
6. Marine, pp. 77–105; Seale, pp. 187–207.

7. See Gilbert Moore, *A Special Rage*, New York: Harper & Row, 1971; Seale, pp. 240–244.
8. See Eldridge Cleaver, "Open Letter to Stokely Carmichael," *Ramparts*, September 1969, pp. 31–32.
9. Charles Garry, "The Old Rules Do Not Apply," in Foner, pp. 257–262.
10. Special Supplement, "Black Panthers: Behind the Myth," *Guardian*, February 1970, p. 1.
11. Newton, p. 20.
12. *Ibid.*, p. 31.
13. Eldridge Cleaver, *On the Ideology of the Black Panther Party*, San Francisco: The Black Panther Party, n.d., p. 1.
14. Garry, pp. 257–262; Alphonso Pinkney, *The American Way of Violence*, New York: Random House, 1972, pp. 118–126; *The Black Panther Party and the Case of the New York 21*, New York: Charter Group for a Pledge of Conscience, 1970; "The Panthers and the Law," *Newsweek*, February 23, 1970, pp. 26–30; The *New York Times*, December 21, 1969, p. 1.
15. The *New York Times*, December 21, 1969, p. 1.
16. Foner, appendix 2, p. 263.
17. Jerome Skolnick, *The Politics of Protest: Violent Aspects of Protest and Confrontation*, Washington, D.C.: Government Printing Office, 1969, p. 115.
18. *Newsweek*, February 23, 1970, p. 27.
19. William Jay Epstein, "The Panthers and the Police: A Pattern of Genocide?" *New Yorker*, February 13, 1971, pp. 45–77.
20. The *New York Times*, May 14, 1971, p. 20.
21. Sanche de Gramont, "Our Other Man in Algiers," The *New York Times Magazine*, November 1, 1970, pp. 30 ff.
22. *The Black Panther*, February 13, 1971, pp. 12–13; The *New York Times*, February 10, 1971, pp. 1, 46.
23. The *New York Times*, March 7, 1971, p. 26.
24. The *New York Times*, March 9, 1971, p. 22.
25. The *New York Times*, March 12, 1971, p. 43.
26. The *New York Times*, April 10, 1971, p. 24.
27. The *Black Panther*, June 10, 1972, p. 2.
28. The *Black Panther*, September 2, 1972, p. 12.
29. *Ibid.*, p. 8.
30. From an interview in *West Magazine*, The *Los Angeles Times*, August 6, 1972; reprinted in *Ibid.*, p. 13.
31. The *Wall Street Journal*, January 13, 1970, p. 1.
32. *Time*, March 30, 1970, p. 28.
33. Reported in Foner, p. xiv.
34. For a compilation of these editorials, see *Urban Crisis Monitor* (published by the Urban Research Corporation, Chicago, Illinois), January 2, 1970.
35. The *New York Times*, August 20, 1972, p. 59.
36. The *Black Panther*, July 1, 1972, special supplement.

37. Newton, p. 98.
38. Eldridge Cleaver, p. 32.
39. Newton, pp. 96–100.
40. For example, see Foner, pp. 246–248.
41. *Ibid.*, pp. 225–229.
42. The *Black Panther*, July 17, 1969; reprinted in Foner, pp. 223–225.
43. Newton, pp. 172–177.
44. The *Black Panther*, September 2, 1972, p. 3.
45. Newton, pp. 148–151.
46. *Ibid.*, pp. 152–155.
47. The *Black Panther*, September 12, 1970, p. 11.
48. See Harold Cruse, *Rebellion or Revolution?* New York: Morrow, 1968, pp. 111–118.
49. Seale, pp. 19–34.
50. Newton, p. 92.
51. *Ebony*, August 1969, p. 110.
52. Seale, pp. 269–273.
53. The *Black Panther*, February 2, 1969; reprinted in Foner, pp. 151–154.
54. *Guardian*, September 11, 1974, p. 9.
55. See *International Black Workers Congress*, published by the League of Revolutionary Black Workers, August 1971; and *The Inner City Voice*, the League's monthly newspaper, published at 253 East Warren Avenue, Detroit, Michigan.
56. See Robert Sherrill, "Birth of a (Black) Nation," *Esquire*, January 1969, pp. 70 ff.
57. The *New York Times*, May 7, 1972, p. 61.
58. H. Rap Brown, *Die Nigger Die!* New York: Dial Press, 1969, p. 128.

Chapter 7

1. See, for example, Edward Banfield, *The Unheavenly City*, Boston: Little, Brown, 1970; Nathan Glazer and Daniel P. Moynihan, *Beyond the Melting Pot*, Cambridge, Mass.: M.I.T. Press, 1963, p. 53; Gunnar Myrdal, *An American Dilemma*, New York: Harper & Row, 1944.
2. Melville Herskovits, *The Myth of the Negro Past*, New York: Harper & Row, 1942; see also August Meier and Elliott Rudwick, *From Plantation to Ghetto*, New York: Hill and Wang, 1966, pp. 16–22.
3. E. Franklin Frazier, *The Negro Family in the United States*, Chicago: University of Chicago Press, 1966; E. Franklin Frazier, *The Negro in the United States*, New York: Macmillan, 1957. The debate between Herskovits and Frazier is summarized in Hardy T. Frye, Charles Irby, and John C. Leggett, *Whither Black Studies*, Stockton, Calif.: Relevant Educational Materials, 1972, pp. 13–21.
4. Robert Blauner, *Racial Oppression in America*, New York: Harper & Row, 1972, pp. 155–156.
5. Norman E. Whitten, Jr., and John E. Szwed (eds.), *Afro-American*

Anthropology: Contemporary Perspectives, New York: Free Press, 1970; Blauner, pp. 124–161.

6. David Llorens, "Ameer (LeRoi Jones) Baraka," *Ebony*, August 1969, p. 80.

7. Imamu Amiri Baraka, "A Black Value System, " *The Black Scholar*, November 1969, pp. 54–60; see also (LeRoi Jones),'*Raise, Race, Rays, Raze*, New York: Random House, 1971, pp. 133–146.

8. Baraka, "A Black Value System," pp. 58–59.

9. Llorens, p. 82.

10. Fox Butterfield, "Experimental Class in Newark School is Indoctrinated in Black Subjects," The *New York Times*, April 10, 1971, p. 34.

11. *Ibid*.

12. Llorens, p. 82.

13. *An Evaluation Report: African Free School Classroom*, New York: AFRAM Associates, Inc., 1971.

14. Imamu Amiri Baraka, "The Pan-African Party and the Black Nation," *The Black Scholar*, March 1971, pp. 24–32.

15. For reports on the Congress, see Imamu Baraka (ed.) *African Congress*, New York: Morrow, 1972; Alex Poinsett, "It's Nation Time!" *Ebony*, December 1970, pp. 98–106.

16. Baraka, "The Pan-African Party and the Black Nation," pp. 24–32.

17. The *New York Times*, September 7, 1971, p. 32.

18. The *New York Times*, September 4, 1972, p. 5.

19. Baraka, *African Congress*, pp. 469–475.

20. *Ibid*., pp. 120–121.

21. *Ibid*., pp. 171–172.

22. *The National Black Political Agenda*, Washington, D.C.: Congressional Black Caucus, 1972.

23. Tom Hayden, *Rebellion in Newark*, New York: Random House, 1967; Alphonso Pinkney, *Black Americans*, Englewood Cliffs, N.J.: Prentice-Hall, 1969, pp. 205–206.

24. Fred J. Cook, "Wherever the Central Cities are Going, Newark is Going to Get there First, The *New York Times Magazine*, July 25, 1971, pp. 7 ff.

25. The *New York Times*, September 8, 1971, p. 50.

26. The *New York Times*, October 2, 1972, p. 58.

27. Cook, p. 37.

28. The *New York Times*, March 13, 1973, p. 30.

29. Maulana Ron Karenga, *The Quotable Karenga*, Los Angeles: The US Organization, 1967; Maulana Ron Karenga, "The Black Community and the University: A Community Organizer's Perspective," in Armstead L. Robinson *et al.* (eds.) *Black Studies in the University*, New York: Bantam Books, 1969, pp. 38–56; Maulana Ron Karenga, "Overturning Ourselves: From Mystification to Meaningful Struggle," *The Black Scholar*, October 1972, pp. 6–14. See also, "From the Quotable Karenga," in Floyd B. Barbour (ed.), *The Black Power Revolt*, Boston: Porter Sargent Publisher, 1968, pp. 162–170; Imamu Clyde

Halisi, "Maulana Ron Karenga: Black Leader in Captivity," *The Black Scholar*, May 1972, pp. 27–31.
30. Karenga, "Overturning Ourselves," p. 8.
31. Barbour, p. 165.
32. Karenga, "Overturning Ourselves," p. 9.
33. Robinson *et al.*, pp. 38–42.
34. Karenga, "Overturning Ourselves," p. 8.
35. Halisi, p. 29.
36. The *New York Times*, May 11, 1971, p. 44; see also Barbara Ann Teer, "Needed: A New Image," in Barbour, pp. 219–223.
37. Harold Cruse, *The Crisis of the Negro Intellectual*, New York: Morrow, 1967; Harold Cruse, *Rebellion or Revolution?* New York: Morrow, 1968; Harold Cruse, "The Integrationist Ethic as a Basis for Scholarly Endeavors," in Robinson *et al.*, pp. 4–12.
38. Cruse, *The Crisis of the Negro Intellectual*, pp. 12–14.
39. *Ibid.*, p. 565.
40. *Ibid.*, p. 497.
41. Robinson *et al.*, p. 9.
42. *Ibid.*, p. 27.
43. Cruse, *Rebellion or Revolution?* p. 112.
44. The *New York Times*, November 16, 1969, sec. 2, pp. 1, 7. See also Baraka, *Raise, Race, Rays, Raze*, pp. 125–132.
45. Karenga, *The Quotable Karenga*. See also Barbour, pp. 162–170.
46. Robinson *et al.*, pp. 38–56.
47. Baraka, *African Congress*, p. 99.
48. Barbour, pp. 168–169.
49. Baraka, *Raise, Race, Rays, Raze*, p. 130.

Chapter 8

1. Martin Luther King, Jr., "Letter from Birmingham Jail–April 16, 1963," in his *Why We Can't Wait*, New York: Harper & Row, 1964; also reprinted in Richard P. Young (ed.), *Roots of Rebellion: The Evolution of Black Politics and Protest Since World War II*, New York: Harper & Row, 1970, pp. 331–346.
2. For the complete text of the manifesto, see Robert Lecky and H. Elliott Wright (eds.), *Black Manifesto: Religion, Racism and Reparations*, New York: Sheed and Ward, 1969, pp. 114–126; Boris I. Bittker, *The Case for Black Reparations*, New York: Random House, 1973, pp. 161–175.
3. Lecky and Wright, pp. 127–132.
4. *Ibid.*, pp. 140–143.
5. *Ibid.*, pp. 144–147.
6. *Ibid.*, pp. 148–149.
7. E. U. Essien-Udom, *Black Nationalism*, Chicago: University of Chicago Press, 1962; C. Eric Lincoln, *The Black Muslims in America*, Boston: Beacon Press, 1961; Louis Lomax, *When the Word is Given:*

A Report on Elijah Muhammad, Malcolm X, and the Black Muslim World, Cleveland: World, 1963; Hans J. Massaquoi, "Elijah Mahammad: Prophet and Architect of the Separate Nation of Islam," *Ebony*, August 1970, pp. 78–89; Elijah Muhammad, *Message to the Blackman in America*, Chicago: Muhammad Mosque No. 2, 1965.

8. See Essien-Udom, pp. 33–36, 43–48.
9. *Ibid.*, pp. 128–135; Lincoln, pp. 76–80; Massaquoi, p. 84; Muhammad, pp. 9 ff, 110 ff.
10. Essien-Udom, pp. 122–142; Lincoln, pp. 67–97.
11. Lincoln, p. 222.
12. The *New York Times*, February 2, 1973, pp. 1, 5.
13. Lincoln, pp. 22–27.
14. Essien-Udom, pp. 211–230; Lincoln, pp. 80–83.
15. Elijah Muhammad, *How to Eat to Live* (Books One and Two), Chicago: Muhammad's Temple No. 2, 1970.
16. The *New York Times*, February 2, 1973, p. 5.
17. *Muhammad Speaks*, November 17, 1972, pp. S-7-8.
18. Massaquoi, pp. 80–82.
19. Essien-Udom, pp. 231–249; Lincoln, pp. 126–129.
20. Muhammad, *Message to the Blackman in America*, p. 39.
21. Gary Marx, *Protest and Prejudice*, New York: Harper & Row, 1967, pp. 94–105.
22. The *New York Times*, July 31, 1966, sec. 4, p. 8.
23. See "Black Theology," New York: National Committee of Black Churchmen, 1969, mimeographed.
24. "A Message to the Churches from Oakland," New York: National Committee of Black Churchmen, 1969, mimeographed.
25. The *New York Times*, July 3, 1970, p. 7.
26. Sister M. Martin de Porres Grey, "The Church, Revolution and Black Catholics," *The Black Scholar*, December 1970, pp. 20–26.
27. The *New York Times*, August 15, 1970, pp. 27 ff.
28. Sister M. Martin de Porres Grey, pp. 22–26.
29. The *New York Times*, October 9, 1971, p. 3.
30. James H. Cone, *A Black Theology of Liberation*, Philadelphia: Lippincott, 1970; see also his *Black Theology and Black Power*, New York: Seabury Press, 1969.
31. Cone, *A Black Theology of Liberation*, pp. 120–121.
32. *Ibid.*, pp. 34–45.
33. *Ibid.*, p. 125.
34. Albert Cleage, Jr., *The Black Messiah*, New York: Sheed and Ward, 1968, p. 3.
35. Alex Poinsett, "The Quest for a Black Christ," *Ebony*, March 1969, p. 174.
36. Albert Cleage, Jr., *Black Christian Nationalism*, New York: Morrow, 1972, p. 230.
37. Cleage, *The Black Messiah*, p. 272.
38. Cleage, *Black Christian Nationalism*, p. xiii.

39. *Ibid.*, pp. 44–66.
40. *Ibid.*, pp. 207–208.

Chapter 9

1. See *Black Studies in Schools* (Special Report), Washington, D.C.: The National School Public Relations Association, 1970.
2. See, for example, Allen B. Ballard, *The Education of Black Folk*, New York: Harper & Row, 1973; Harry Edwards, *Black Students*, New York: Free Press, 1970; Nick Aron Ford, *Black Studies: Threat or Challenge*, Port Washington, N.Y.: Kennikat Press, 1973; Martin Kilson, *et al.* (eds.), *Black Studies: Myths and Realities*, New York: A. Philip Randolph Educational Fund, 1969; James McEvoy and Abraham Miller (eds.), *Black Power and the Student Rebellion*, Belmont, Calif.: Wadsworth, 1969; Armstead Robinson *et al.* (eds.), *Black Studies in the University*, New York: Bantam Books, 1969; Thomas Sowell, *Black Education: Myths and Tragedies*, New York: McKay, 1972.
3. Sowell, pp. 157–159.
4. Kenneth Clark, "Letter of Resignation From Board of Directors of Antioch College," in Kilson *et al.*, pp. 32–34.
5. Edwards, pp. 158–183; Sowell, pp. 112–118.
6. Edwards, pp. 61–64.
7. Ballard, pp. 27–59.
8. Sowell, pp. 192–199.
9. Kilson *et al.*, p. 33.
10. Rhoda Goldstein *et al.*, "The Status of Black Studies Programs at American Colleges and Universities," mimeographed paper presented at the 67th Annual meeting of the American Sociological Association, 1972, p. 13.
11. Edwards, pp. 72–73.
12. Ballard, pp. 44 ff.
13. In addition to Ballard, extensive documentation in this area has been provided in several recent works. See, for example, Andrew Billingsley, *Black Families in White America*, Englewood Cliffs, N.J.: Prentice-Hall, 1968, especially the appendix; Edwards, pp. 120–144; Joyce Ladner (ed.), *The Death of White Sociology*, New York: Random House, 1973; Stanford Lyman, *The Black American in Sociological Thought*, New York: Capricorn Books, 1973.
14. See, for example, Wilson Record, "Black Studies and White Sociologists," *The American Sociologist*, May 1972, pp. 10–11.
15. Fred E. Crossland, *Graduate Education and Black Americans*, New York: The Ford Foundation, 1968.
16. Goldstein *et al.*, pp. 10–12.
17. Ballard, pp. 112–113; Vincent Harding, "The Future of Black Studies," in Kerry Smith (ed.), *The Troubled Campus*, San Francisco: Jossey Bass, 1970.

18. Kilson *et al.*; W. Arthur Lewis, "The Road to the Top Is Through Higher Education–Not Black Studies," The *New York Times Magazine*, May 11, 1969, pp. 34–53; Sowell, pp. 187–216.
19. *Report of the Faculty Committee on African and Afro-American Studies*, Harvard University, Cambridge, Mass.: Harvard University Press, 1969, p. 4.
20. Nathan Hare, "A Torch to Burn Down a Decadent World," *The Black Scholar*, September 1970, p. 5.
21. Information on Nairobi College was compiled from brochures issued by the college and from interviews.
22. The *New York Times*, June 13, 1971, p. 74.
23. James Wooten, "Malcolm X University to Open in Durham as Militants' School," The *New York Times*, October 28, 1969, p. 48.
24. *Ibid.*, p. 48.
25. Ballard, p. 116.
26. See Alex Poinsett, "Think Tank for Black Scholars," *Ebony*, February 1970, pp. 46–54; "Black World Without End. Amen," *Renewal*, October–November 1970, p. 3. The institute publishes a "Monthly Report" and a series of "Black Papers."
27. From "The First Year," first annual report, July 1969–August 1970, Atlanta: Institute of the Black World, 1970.
28. Ballard, p. 112.
29. Nathan Hare, "The Challenge of a Black Scholar," in Ladner, p. 69.
30. Alex Poinsett, "The Metamorphosis of Howard University," *Ebony*, December 1971, pp. 110–122.
31. *Ibid.*, p. 114.
32. Sowell, p. 40.
33. *Ibid.*, p. 65.
34. *Ibid.*, pp. 259–263.
35. The *New York Times*, June 2, 1969, p. 13.
36. William Delaney, "The Big Debate at Howard U.," The *Washington Evening Star and Daily News*, December 6, 1972, p. 1.

Chapter 10

1. W. E. B. DuBois, *The Souls of Black Folk*, Chicago: A. C. McClurg, 1904, pp. 250–264.
2. *Ibid.*, p. 3.
3. Richard B. Moore, "DuBois and Pan Africa," *Freedomways*, Winter 1965, p. 170. This entire issue of *Freedomways* was published as a memorial tribute to DuBois.
4. For a report on the congresses, see Moore, pp. 166–187; Colin Legum, *Pan-Africanism: A Short Political Guide*, New York: Praeger, 1965; George Padmore, *Pan-Africanism or Communism*, New York: Doubleday, 1971; "Pan-Africanism I," *The Black Scholar*, February 1971; "Pan-Africanism II," *The Black Scholar*, March 1971; "Pan-Africanism III," *The Black Scholar*, February 1973.
5. Legum, p. 155.

6. The *New York Times*, June 27, 1973, p. 4.
7. See Donald L. Noel (ed.), *The Origins of American Slavery and Racism*, Columbus, Ohio: Charles Merrill, 1972.
8. William Brink and Louis Harris, *The Negro Revolution in America*, New York: Simon and Schuster, 1964, pp. 119 ff.; William Brink and Louis Harris, *Black and White*, New York: Simon and Schuster, 1966, pp. 54 ff.; Angus Campbell and Howard Schuman, "Racial Attitudes in Fifteen American Cities," in *Supplemental Studies for the National Advisory Commission on Civil Disorders*, Washington, D.C.: Government Printing Office, 1968, chap. 3; Gary Marx, *Protest and Prejudice*, New York: Harper & Row, 1968, pp. 28–31, 123.
9. Gibson Winter, *Being Free: Reflections on America's Cultural Revolution*, New York: Macmillan, 1970, pp. 7–8.
10. U.S. Department of Commerce, Bureau of the Census, *The Social and Economic Status of Negroes in the United States, 1970*, Washington, D.C.: Government Printing Office, 1971, p. 82.
11. Stokely Carmichael and Charles Hamilton, *Black Power*, New York: Random House, 1967, pp. 58–84.
12. Boris I. Bittker, *The Case For Black Reparations*, New York: Random House, 1973, p. 31.
13. *Ibid.*, p. 24.
14. These data and those that follow are from publications and press releases issued by the Joint Center for Political Studies, Washington, D.C.
15. Kenneth Clark, *Prejudice and Your Child*, Boston: Beacon Press, 1963, pp. 37–65.
16. J. Hraba and J. Grant, "Black is Beautiful: A Reexamination of Racial Preference and Identification," *Journal of Personality and Social Psychology*, 1970, pp. 398–402; S. H. Ward and J. Braun, "Self-Esteem and Racial Preference in Black Children," *American Journal of Orthopsychiatry*, July 1972, pp. 644–647.
17. See Angus Campbell, *White Attitudes Toward Black People*, Ann Arbor, Mich.: Institute for Social Research, 1971; Andrew Greeley and Paul Sheatsley, "Attitudes Toward Racial Integration," *Scientific American*, December 1971, pp. 13–19; D. E. Muir, "The First Years of Desegregation: Patterns of Acceptance of Black Students on a Deep-South Campus, 1963–69," *Social Forces*, 1971, pp. 371–378.
18. The *New York Times*, November 6, 1972, p. 47.
19. Some of these ideologically free issues have been set forth by Charles Hamilton. See his "The Nationalist vs. the Integrationist," The *New York Times Magazine*, October 1, 1972, pp. 36 ff.
20. *Report of the National Advisory Commission on Civil Disorders*, New York: Bantam Books, 1968, pp. 143–145.
21. *The Police and Their Use of Fatal Force in Chicago*: Evanston, Ill.: Chicago Law Enforcement Study Group, 1972.
22. The text of this order was printed in *The Militant*, December 21, 1973, p. 7.

Epilogue

1. *Unity and Struggle*, November 1974, p. 12.
2. *Ibid.*
3. Haki R. Madhubuti, "The Latest Purge: The Attack on Black Nationalism and Pan-Afrikanism by the New Left, the Sons and Daughters of the Old Left," *The Black Scholar*, September 1974, pp. 43–56.
4. *Ibid.*, p. 43.
5. *Ibid.*, p. 54.
6. See articles and letters by S. E. Anderson, Alonzo 4X (Cannady), Ronald Walters, and Chancellor Williams, *The Black Scholar*, October 1974; Kalamu Ya Salaam and Mark Smith, *The Black Scholar*, January–February 1975; Preston Wilcox and Jomo Simba, *The Black Scholar*, March 1975; Gwendolyn M. Patton and Mark S. Johnson, *The Black Scholar*, April 1975.
7. Maulana Ron Karenga, "Which Road: Nationalism, Pan-Africanism, Socialism?" *The Black Scholar*, October 1974, pp. 21–30.
8. The *New York Times*, June 4, 1975, p. 49.
9. *The Militant*, December 21, 1973, p. 7.
10. The *New York Times*, June 30, 1975, p. 13.
11. *Muhammad Speaks*, August 1, 1975, p. 13.
12. *Ibid.*, p. 28.
13. Richard Quinney, *Critique of Legal Order; Crime Control in Capitalist Society*, Boston: Little, Brown, 1974, p. 108.

Index